A Practical Guide to Becoming

The Sexually Fulfilled Woman

Dr. Rachel Copelan

W

Published by
Melvin Powers
ILSHIRE BOOK COMPANY
12015 Sherman Road
No. Hollywood, California 91605
Telephone: (213) 875-1711

THE SEXUALLY FULFILLED WOMAN

COPYRIGHT © 1971 BY RACHEL COPELAN

Printed by

HAL LEIGHTON PRINTING COMPANY
P.O. Box 3952
North Hollywood, California 91605
Telephone: (213) 983-1105

LIBRARY OF CONGRESS CATALOG CARD NUMBER: 72-83290

MANUFACTURED IN THE UNITED STATES OF AMERICA

ISBN 0-87980-402-5

Preface
What This Book Is All About

*We are living in an era when old sexual mores are being set aside. Censorship policies concerning sexual matters have be-*come less austere, and the movie industry, the theatre, television, newspapers, and radio have all reacted to the pressing needs of uninformed people to learn more about sex. It is therefore not surprising to find a sudden deluge of books and newspaper articles appearing on that most fascinating of subjects—sex. Although most of this material is easily accessible and can be found on any newsstand, it is, in the main, pornographic trivia that proves tiresomely inconsequential to the real problems facing the average woman—because ninety-five percent of this material is written by men.

There are, of course, books written on a higher level, such as Masters' and Johnson's, *Human Sexual Responses,* and *Human Sexual Inadequacy,* but unfortunately, these books are difficult for the layman to understand as they are couched in the language of the medical profession. Every day, more and more books on sex techniques, marriage manuals, interviews, and sexual statistics of all kinds roll off the presses. Why, then, another book on sex? What makes this one different from all the others? While most books concern themselves with the general problems that exist between the male and female, this one offers specific exercises designed to help women overcome their special problems. Women—even more than men—need drastic reconditioning to help them get rid of their deep-rooted inhibitions about sex.

Most books suggest that it is the responsibility of the man to overcome a woman's sexual problems. He is assured that with patience and improved techniques he will bring her around. When this doesn't happen, he blames himself. This kind of faulty thinking does not help the woman to develop; on the contrary, depending entirely on the male causes a woman to remain nonresponsive. The inadequate woman clings to the hope that sooner or later the right man will come along and straighten out her problems.

As long as this kind of thinking persists, women will be unable to free themselves of outmoded Victorian concepts. Only when women take the initiative and assert their needs will they begin to function as nature originally intended, as fully *participating* members of the sexual act. Placing the entire burden of female sexual satisfaction onto the male not only doesn't help the woman, it has caused many a normal male to lose his own ability to perform. The prolonged stress of trying to please a resistant woman is one of the prime causes of emotional disturbance in men. Out of the 44,000 people who committed suicide last year, seventy-five per cent were men. Most of the estimated six million alcoholics in this country are also men. Psychiatric investigation shows that lack of virility is a fundamental cause of mental depression among men.

The inability to cope with normal male-female relationships is the most poignant problem that exists between men and women, and it is the fault of neither. THEY ARE BOTH VICTIMS OF AND SUBJECT TO THE SAME EVIL: SEXUAL IGNORANCE.

Sexual ignorance, more than any other factor, is responsible for the fact that one out of three marriages ends in the divorce courts. Research indicates that of the enduring marriages, perhaps half can truly be considered happy. We all are aware of the many marriages that are merely tolerated because of religious restraints or lack of funds required for divorce.

Beneath the surface of most incompatible marriages lies the inability of the wife to function as a mature sex partner. Unfortunately, most women are reluctant to discuss their problems even with their closest friends. They shy away from the biological facts about their bodies, as if knowing too much would somehow prove them inferior. To continue this ignorance is to confine themselves to a level of neurotic existence.

Women who want to live fully must get to the deeper truth about themselves. They must be more aggressive about learning how their genitals work and how to release the dynamic power of the orgasm. It is up to the woman to assume the major share of this responsibility to herself. Of course a man can help, by being unselfish and by providing effective preliminary stimulation, but the woman herself must eliminate the basic cause of her resistance.

Ultimately, a woman must free herself, because it is her own *inside thinking which shuts off the instinctual peak of feeling necessary for orgasm to occur*. She must be aware of how her mind and body affect each other. She must then bring them back into harmonious concert, as nature intended, before negative conditioning set in.

Unfortunately, this is not taught in schools. It is something a woman must learn for herself. *This book has been written to help her do just that*. It has been written not just for women who are considered "frigid" (by men) but for all women who would like to improve their sexual responsiveness.

THIS BOOK HAS BEEN WRITTEN FOR

1. The nine out of ten women who are not able to reach orgasm every time they have sexual intercourse.
2. The many women who fake orgasm *sometimes,* and the others who fake it *all the time.*
3. The vast majority who are limited to clitoral sensation and believe that sex offers nothing more.

UNLESS YOU ARE THAT RARE 1 IN 10 WHO HAS NEVER HAD ANY SEXUAL DIFFICULTY, THIS BOOK HAS BEEN WRITTEN FOR YOU.

Contents

Introduction

*For many years a veil of hypocrisy has surrounded everything associated with sex. The mere mention of the word was suffi-*cient to arouse consternation. In spite of the fact that we are now living in a more permissive era, some of us still have many qualms, inherited from our ancestors. These antiquated notions stick like leeches. Until the present, hypocrisy has even hindered scientific investigation of this vast subject.

Sex is the foundation of our being, yet it is the thing most folks know least about. The misunderstanding of normal sexual function is responsible for vast mental and physical suffering and emotional unhappiness. Fortunately, members of the rising generation are refusing to accept dogmas just because their forebears did so for centuries. The flowering youth not only *wants* to know, but *insists* on knowing all about sex and its ramifications. Thus the clouds of ignorance and superstition are fading away before the radiant sun of knowledge, and books like this one are helping to bring this about.

Youngsters approaching adolescence become aware of changes taking place in their anatomy or body functions and instinctively run to their parents to have their fears allayed.

Too often they are met by some silly rebuff, with the result that the condition is not discussed at all. This is not always the fault of the parents, for they may be even more ignorant than their offspring. There are few who realize the extent of mental imbalance caused by this gulf between parents and children.

In dealing with sex problems we must first be honest. Human anatomy and physiology must be accepted as a creative force. Currier Bell once said, "Such annoyances as society cannot cure, it usually forbids utterances, on pain of its scorn; said scorn being only a tinselled cloak to its deformed weakness."

A fact that we must not overlook is that the sex instinct is possessed regardless of gender. Byron said, "Man's love is of a man's life a thing apart; 'tis woman's whole existence." Yet in spite of women's emotional feelings, they are not always physically satisfied. A well-regulated sexual life is essential to the well-being of every individual, both male and female.

Sexual function is not an instrument of the devil, designed to drag men and women down to sin, but is one of nature's physiological functions. Sex has existed from the beginning of time and will continue till the end or there will be no world.

RACHEL COPELAN has written a fascinating and informative book which emphasizes woman's role in improving her sex life. She imparts step-by-step guidance on how to attain greater heights of sexual happiness. Her scope of knowledge is vast, and she covers the sociological and psychological aspects of female sex to an amazing degree. She not only sheds light on female sex problems, but most important of all, shows how to overcome them.

HERMAN H. RUBIN, M.D.

ONE

Causes of
Female Sexual Inadequacy

*The sexual problems which plague modern women have their origins in the dark days of female slavery. Female slavery pre-*dates black slavery, and the viciousness of its claws is evident in the many scars that are still visible in the female sexual personality. The result of this early crushing of the female spirit manifests its destructiveness in both the psychic and physical being of every woman.

The resistances to female slavery remain etched in the deeper crevices of the female mind. Just as with the blacks, the ruling white male has invented myths of inferiority about women to justify his oppressive position. Strangely enough, women have in many cases accepted this image of themselves as the less valuable half of the population, and in so doing have fallen into the trap of believing themselves to be inadequate.

We keep hearing about a "sexual revolution," which supposedly has freed women to enjoy equal rights with men in real-life situations. Outwardly, women may appear to be participating to the same degree, but they are by no means getting the same satisfaction out of the sex act as their partners.

Admittedly, many doors once closed are now wide open and women are freely pursuing careers in industry, politics, and higher learning, but somehow this does not really make them happy. Even though some of the old slave concepts (such as that a girl must remain a virgin until marriage) have been discarded by the more enlightened, the inequality is still very evident.

Women's Struggle For Equality

The gains which women have succeeded in achieving have occurred only on the surface. Underneath, more significant stirrings are beginning. Women are recognizing that something is deeply wrong, that they are a long way from being the joyful, sensually satisfied people that nature intended them to be.

They are still handicapped by the burden of moral guilt and physical fears which they unconsciously associate with sexual freedom. They find themselves, in the actual practice of the sex relationship, unable to shake off the hang-ups inherited from antiquated customs and past parental restrictions. After years of being taught that the sexual act is wrong and bad for them, women cannot make a sudden, complete switch to an affirmative attitude based on the simple fact that they have grown a little older. The effect of the establishment's rules about what is right or wrong manifests itself even among the freest of the "Now" generation. They pride themselves on being non-conformists, and "self-liberated," yet their early training invariably asserts itself and interferes with their ability to surrender to the force of sexual feeling. Even though they may have a burning desire to enjoy sex as much as their partner, they are often disappointed to discover that they are unable to do so. We are born into a society that, rather than being built on the basis of equal division of responsibility and social function, is one in which men inherit the ruling power and manipulate the status system.

There are, perhaps, very few women who would openly agree with the notion of "male supremacy," yet all women are aware that men play the dominant role in all major areas of our modern society. In spite of talk about women having greater dollar wealth than men, it is really men who control and manipulate both the economy and the major political policies of our country.

Although there have been a few breakthroughs—Golda Meir in Israel and Premier Ghandi in India, they are the exception rather than the rule. After all is said and done, it is still a man's world. I point this out to underline the fact that every woman's life is affected in a very personal way by relationships in the world around us. It would be foolish to ignore the fact that woman's position over the centuries still influences her sexual function.

Women's Contribution to Early Civilization

Up until the present century, the life that women lived was determined almost solely by their biological role of sex-mate and mother. In primitive times women stayed home in the cave tending the fire and the children while the males moved about the plains and forests hunting for food for their families. Civilization owes its beginnings to the women who made the dwellings so comfortable that they enticed the hunters to stay closer to home instead of wandering far away to look for food.

The need for food in this newly settled society led to the tilling of the soil and the beginning of agriculture. In early civilizations it was often women, rather than men, who were the dominant force for progress. They were the mainstay of society and gave stability to the building of community life and later to the growth of cities. It was their biological need for security in raising families that kept males from wandering off into the forests, to be killed by animals (and just as often to kill each other).

Historians estimate that primitive man seldom lived beyond the age of twenty because of the hardships of his life. Women made the continuation of life possible. In primitive history women were often revered. They shared equally in communal living. They helped build the homes, made the pottery and clothing, reared the young, cooked, and helped in the labor of the fields.

As communal life developed to a higher level, it was discovered that some women possessed talents for doing certain necessary tasks better than others in the group. Perhaps one woman excelled at making clothing and produced more than was needed by her immediate family, another became the best pottery maker, another the best weaver for the commune. By means of bartering they raised their living standards, each servicing the other's family with the task she was best qualified to do. It is the female of the species who insured the perpetuation of the human race by settling the male down to a communal life instead of a nomadic existence where the mortality rate was very high because of animal dangers and hazards of climate.

Men devoted themselves to agriculture, and the tilling of the soil eventually brought about the advent of slavery. When men stopped wandering and hunting and attempted to get their sustenance from the soil, they discovered that their own labor was insufficient to get enough food for themselves and their growing families. So once more, men became hunters, but this time they began to hunt other men. Instead of killing animals, they captured other human beings and put them to work in the fields. This was the birth of slavery of man by man; this was also the time when women first became enslaved. When early man became master over the slaves in the field, he carried over his masterful attitude into his relationships with the women of his own tribe or family. Personality was affected by the ownership of the means of production.

The Problem Is Worldwide

To this day, there are still many countries where women are bought and sold as chattel, and countless more where they are treated as inferiors. In many Arab countries a husband still buys a wife from the girl's father. The wife is then kept veiled and isolated for her entire lifetime. She is expected to work for him as a servant, to bear his children without complaint and, when he so chooses, he may take two or three younger and fairer wives. She has no access to any means of self-support and must accept servitude or go hungry. This has become the accepted norm in much of the Arab world.

Orthodox Jewish laws are little better than the Arab's where women are concerned. Religious Jews say, as part of their morning prayer, "Blessed be God, that He did not make me a woman." And in the orthodox Jewish wedding ceremony, only the husband is asked if he agrees to the marriage, while the wife is not consulted at all. She says not one word in the entire ceremony. It is assumed that she is a possession and is "taken," whether she likes it or not. These customs are hangovers from the days of female slavery, and they are not unusual.

Outdated and antiquated customs are still all around us. They are at the core of the female sexual problem. Present-day women are victims of great social confusion about what is right or wrong for them sexually. They are caught in the current of change from old customs to modern attitudes. For example, in homes where women are completely dependent upon their husbands for the necessities of life, they continue to behave in a more subservient way. Where the husband is the sole provider, he expects and gets a special kind of deference. The economic position woman finds herself in usually determines her relation to men.

Economic Independence

If a wife works and earns as much as her husband, she is inclined to assert her independence and demand equal treatment, *both in and out of bed.* However, if she happens to earn more than her husband, almost invariably trouble ensues because this is a difficult relationship for the average husband (*and* wife) to cope with, since both were raised in a culture which looks down on men who earn less money than women. Friction often develops in this kind of situation, and few marriages survive this affront to a man's inbred need for economic superiority.

On the other hand, women who are unable to work and are totally dependent upon their husbands, often suffer from a lack of self-esteem, and have secret or open resentments. This straining for dominance on the part of the male (and its feminine counteraction) reflects itself not only in their lives together in general, but very specifically in the kind of sexual intercourse that exists between them. *Sex is not something apart* which exists in a vacuum, separate from all other relationships. Not only does the past affect our present-day responses, but every phase of life from morning until night colors our sexual personality.

The Story of Rhama Khan

I would like to cite an interesting example of how the social status of women affects their most intimate relationships with men. A short time ago I had the good fortune to meet a fascinating woman from India, who was introduced to me by a mutual friend, Sandra. Sandra had discovered the Indian woman while strolling through Central Park one sunny Sunday afternoon. Sandra asked permission to share the park bench and, in the course of their casual conversation, the Indian woman began to ask her many questions about the life of women in the United States. Sandra suggested to her that they visit me, explaining that I was writing a book about women and that it might be a pleasant way to have her many questions answered, as well as, perhaps, some of mine.

Her name was Rhama Khan, and she was an extremely intelligent and beautiful woman. Her fine silk sari was gracefully draped around her rather tall figure, which she carried in a regal manner. Her softly modulated voice communicated the fact that she had been reared in an atmosphere of culture and refinement. She had flawless coffee-colored skin, and her delicately defined features were in perfect symmetry. The expression on her face was aloof and suggested great emotional restraint.

Between her eyebrows was the traditional red dot, signaling the fact that she was a married woman. She informed us that she was married to a leading Indian industrialist. As far as worldly goods were concerned, there was no doubt that this gracious woman had the very best of material possessions.

Yet there was an aura of sadness surrounding her, especially in the expression of her exceptionally large black eyes. I was frankly interested in knowing more about her personal life as a wife and mother. I told Rhama that I would honestly answer any questions she wished to put to me if she would do the same in answer to my own. With a bit of reluctance, she finally agreed when she learned that the purpose of my book is to help women overcome their problems of sexual inadequacy.

I started off the questioning by asking her what brought her to the United States. She answered, "I am here on a mission to find a suitable school for my daughter who is sixteen years old. You see, most girls of this age are already married or promised in marriage, as I myself was at her age. I am hoping to postpone this for awhile so that she perhaps may have a chance some day to make her own free choice of a husband." I expressed surprise that family-arranged marriages still existed in India. Rhama explained, "Yes, they still do exist, especially among the higher classes and wealthier Indian families. There is more freedom of choice among the poorer people. Non-segregated but upper-caste families wish their daughters to marry on the same level, otherwise they consider that the daughter will bring shame on the family." I said to myself, "Here again is another classic example of the economic factor deciding the fate of women." Rhama expressed shy curiosity about the sexual behavior of women in the United States, and commented that she had the impression that American women control the men and get from them whatever they want.

I decided to be very direct and asked, "Rhama, do you get from your husband what you want out of life, or is something lacking?" At first, she stood up as if to leave. She had obviously never discussed her intimate life with anyone and was visibly embarrassed. Finally, she sat down again, adjusted her sari around her shoulders and, for a few moments, just shifted her dark gaze around the room. Suddenly she looked straight ahead and said, "You would like me to tell you the story of my sex life, but there is nothing to tell of interest, either in my marriage with my husband or otherwise." She went on to try to assure me that her husband was not a bad person. "He is a very kind man and I do the best I can for him. In my country, that is considered a wife's duty."

I asked her if she was aware that there are many women in the world who don't think of sex merely as a duty, but thoroughly enjoy the experience. As I spoke, I noticed that her enormous eyes were shining, moist with tears. I quickly said,

"Let's talk about something else. I see that I have been getting too personal. Please forgive me." So we talked about other subjects for awhile, about her daughter, about her tremendous eighteen-room house in Bombay with nine servants in residence. I remarked that she seemed to have everything many women dream of. Gradually, she herself brought the conversation back to her sex life. She obviously needed to learn something from the conversation, or perhaps she wanted to relieve her pent-up emotions.

In any case, as if speaking to herself, she said softly, "You asked me before if I enjoy sexual relations with my husband or if something is lacking. I have to explain to you that, although my husband is a very fine man, he would not consider it proper for me to be too interested in sex. Only the low-class women behave in this way. They are looked down upon, as if they were animals." Sandra asked, "Are you suggesting that the upper-class women are frigid, and poor working-class women are not? How can that be? After all, their bodies are obviously the same biologically." Rhama smiled for the first time, and answered, "Ah, yes, their bodies are the same, but *they do not think the same.*"

Women Who Work

Rhama went on to explain, "I will tell you a story about one of my servants and you will understand that a servant-woman has more chance to live as a free person than does a woman like myself, who is born to wealth." She explained that the difference in their class positions placed a burden on her to behave in a "proper" manner, and to be obedient to her husband under all conditions. As in the days of old, he is her lord and master and absolute ruler over his entire family. She is not permitted to pursue a career, she complained, because it would be considered a poor reflection on her husband's ability to provide.

Rhama went on to say that the relationship between men and women differs in India on the lower economic levels. "Among my servants there is a married couple. The wife is a housemaid and the husband looks after the cars in the garage adjacent to the house. They constantly try to see each other as they are not given a place to sleep together, which is according to custom. It is expected that she sleep on the floor in the hallway, near the entrance-door. Her husband sleeps in a cubicle in the garage basement."

Apparently she noticed that I was shocked at the idea of people living in this way and she tried to reassure me that this was standard practice in her country. "Poor people are delighted to get such a good job, an opportunity to sleep in such a fine house; they do not mind sleeping on the floor. It is, after all, much better than sleeping on the streets."

I expressed surprise that such a sensitive person as she seemed to be would accept such conditions of inequity. Rhama looked at me helplessly. "But there is nothing that I can do about it personally. I have no power to make important changes in the way my servants are treated. I live in an isolated way, coming in contact only with my family and a few friends of my own caste. Besides, you need not feel so sorry for my maid for you can be sure she is happier than I am." I asked, "Why? —when you have everything and she has nothing?" She answered slowly, "Listen and I will tell you why. One night, when I saw that she was not sleeping in her usual place, I went down to the garage and discovered her in the small cubicle with her husband. They were wrapped in each other's arms, so intensely entwined that they didn't even hear me approach. I was transfixed by the sight. There was no doubt that she was enjoying him as much as he was enjoying her. I did not disturb them, just slipped away quietly. Later, when I went to bed, I cried into my pillow because I knew that in my whole lifetime this kind of closeness would never happen to me."

"Why not?" I asked, "if it happened to her, why not you?" Rhama's answer was very revealing. Perhaps, in a more profound way, it is the crux of the problem that affects all women who feel sexually incapable, because of their lack of self-esteem: "She, the housemaid, feels equal to her husband because she is able to work and earn her own keep. This, I think, makes it possible for her to let him know her desires. She can make demands on him. When she is angry, she lets him know. I could not do that with my husband. I would be afraid of the consequences of his anger." She continued, "You see, women of my caste are not permitted to work and because of this are doomed, I'm afraid, to remain forever a chattel or possession of their husbands. It seems to me that in order *to enjoy sex equally* with a man, *one must feel equal to him as a person.*"

I was interested in learning whether her attitude was also evident among the younger generation and she brightened up. "I hope that my daughter will study so that she can become the kind of woman who is able to support herself. Her father is naturally opposed to this, as all of the good families keep their women in the background. But I hope to bring him around to a more liberal point of view, at least about her if not for myself. He is really a good man and would like for me to be happy, but this way of life is the only way that he knows."

Women's Problems Are Universal

Compared with India, our own country is supposed to be on a much higher level of female evolution. Yet, American women are far from being the emancipated people that they should be. They are still not free of the problems of inferior status, resulting from hundreds of years of enforced slavery. In spite of the fact that many women hold jobs and are capable of earning more money, in some cases, than men, they still lag behind men in their psycho-sexual development. Having a successful career doesn't add up to a successful sex life. Indeed, it often works the other way, because some men feel threatened by the image of the too-independent woman.

Unfortunately, too many men equate manliness with two things:

The amount of control they have over money.

The amount of control they have over women.

Both are remnants of master/slave ideology. When a husband and wife jockey for positions of power, it does not make for a mutually satisfying sex relationship. Women must be aware that a career may prove to be less of a boon and more of a handicap if she lets it take away from her her basic femaleness.

On the other hand, it would help men to adjust to the changing woman if they understood that when she seems to be too aggressive, she is really trying to pull away from her inhibiting hang-ups. And that when she does assert her true self-image, she will be a better woman for him to live with and with whom to share the joys of full sexual maturity. Women really yearn for their men to be strong and affirmatively masculine, but *not at the expense of being treated as inferiors*. A woman, like any other oppressed person, tends to react to the oppression by *over-reacting* against it—like the pendulum on the clock swinging sharply from one extreme to the other.

If men will just be patient and understanding about *why* this is happening, the pendulum will eventually settle down. Women want to be neither inferior nor superior to men, they merely want to be recognized as having the same right to enjoy a fully rewarding life. An overly assertive woman can become self-destructive in her drive to challenge all things masculine.

The answer is not in one sex having power over the other, but in both men and women having a deeper understanding of the needs of the other so that together they can set about correcting any problems which might interfere with their mutual gratification. Present-day research shows that the vast majority of women in the world have difficulties in responding sexually to the point of orgasm during penile-vaginal coitus. Although responsiveness seems to increase with freedom of expression, women still are inclined to place a limit on their own ability to enjoy sex purely for pleasure.

Freedom to experience is not enough when you consider that females have been taught for centuries that sex is a *man's* pleasure. The ancient rule that females are bought and sold for sexual use still clings deep in the female mind. It is in those dark caverns of the unconscious that resentment and resistance have their silent twin-births and grow into giant obstacles; for *no slave can really love a master*. This accumulation, since the days of slavery, of attitudes of sexual inequality is the reservoir from which parents have absorbed the ideas which they hand down to their children. For example, the idea that a girl must remain pure and virginal until she is taken in marriage stems from the premise of slavery that a female is an object, a commodity, and that used merchandise is worth less at the time of sale.

The Problem With Parents

Parents may not be consciously aware of what they are doing, yet many of them persist in perpetuating this attitude. If, in fact, there has been some sort of sexual revolution for women, its gains are hard to find. In interviews with hundreds of young women in their late teens and early twenties, it was found that they suffer from the same sexual difficulties that their mothers and grandmothers had before them. Although researchers differ on many points, there is general agreement on this one:

> There is no organic reason why a healthy woman should not reach the same high peak of sexual sensation as her male partner.

The instinctual reflexive action of orgasm is triggered by the thinking mind and, in the case of the female mind, much has been done to her as a child to stifle this instinctual reflex. She has been imbued by her parents with the idea that sex is improper unless she is married, and, in the case of the more restrictive religious taboos, even then, only when pregnancy is desired.

This mental image of female functionality is formed during a girl's most impressionable years and is difficult to shake. These deeply engraved cerebral messages of "right" and "wrong" cause women to react negatively to stimulation.

Within their computer-programmed mind's eye, a red light flashes "Stop," when they should get a "Go Ahead" signal.

After this kind of continuing repetitive repulsion of instinctual sensation, the female sexual organs set up a pattern of immunity and become further desensitized to feelings of pleasure. In order to insure that the young girl remains "chaste until wedlock," many parents teach her to fear the consequences if she strays onto the path of sexual permissiveness. A young girl is almost always taught to mistrust and resist the advances of the male. She is told that his interest in her is purely animalistic and that she must avoid becoming involved. She is further indoctrinated with the fear that he will use her and leave her when he becomes tired of her.

Ignorant parents even implant the idea that the first experience will be painful and bloody. As if that were not enough, she is dutifully warned about the horrors of venereal diseases and—worst of all—she is deterred by the overshadowing fear of PREGNANCY.

Parents are confused themselves by the conflicting attitudes around them and tend to transmit their own confusion to their offspring. They plant the seeds of fear and from these seeds sprout all the many problems of future sexual inadequacy.

Pregnancy As Punishment

With the emergence of "the Pill" and its wide acceptance, many young women who were perhaps timid about sex before began engaging actively in sexual affairs. Though many are using the Pill, they are still worrying about pregnancy. Whether they use the Pill or other methods of contraception, they still anxiously count the days from one menstrual period to another. Fear overshadows their sexual pleasure as they worry about whether or not the Pill will work. They realize that as the result of a few moments of love-making they may face the possibility of a lifetime of responsibility. Young men are content to let the problem rest with the female.

Many unwanted pregnancies take place because young lovers are reluctant to discuss contraceptives at all. Their thinking becomes clouded with the pressure of passion and each assumes, or hopes, that the other one has taken the necessary precautions. Very often neither of them has and an unwanted pregnancy results. Not only does the young girl find that she is pregnant, but what is even sadder, she is often pregnant without having even enjoyed the sexual experience which caused it.

It seems inconceivable that in an age when science has put men on the moon, modern technology has not come up with a proper solution to such a comparatively simple problem—that of family planning.

It isn't just a problem which affects the females of our race, but is more important than ever in the light of the world's ever-growing over-population problem. The urgency of the world situation in this regard has stimulated much discussion among leaders of every country. Let us hope that women will, at last, receive proper help in this area.

The many advances in all phases of biological research should facilitate the invention of a formula or device to insure a woman's peace of mind about pregnancy so that she can really let go of her inhibitions to sexual feelings. Perhaps men have some sort of innate fear of women realizing their full potential. They may subconsciously consider a fully sexed woman as posing a threat to their masculinity and therefore resist the emergence of a real woman.

In truth, they have nothing to fear on that score because

the opposite is nearer to reality: a functioning female is easily satisfied and a satisfied woman makes a more contented wife. A sexually satisfied woman also makes a happier mother or a more cheerful, understanding schoolteacher. From a purely masculine point of view, men should eagerly welcome the idea of women being fully gratified, if only for selfish reasons.

Boys spend a great deal of their youth under the supervision of females who can make or break their masculinity. They are directly affected, not only by their mothers, but by nurses, aunts, teachers, grandmothers, all of whom can either build or take away something of their maleness.

The average boy spends three-quarters of his formative years under the direct control of women. Sexually frustrated women cannot do a good job of molding future men. For this reason alone it is in the best interests of intelligent men to help women in their struggle to overcome the obstacles to happier living.

Basic improvements in the sexual reflexes of females can only take place with the help of enlightened parents. Parents are the "time-binders" who tie children to past conventions. Without even knowing that it is happening, girls grow into women with a built-in chastity belt, a caution system which keeps them from relaxing and enjoying their bodies. One must feel a certain amount of sympathy for the confused parents. The fact that they themselves never had proper sex education causes them to transfer their own ignorance, rather than knowledge, to their offspring. Having been taught that way themselves, they consider it their parental duty to teach their daughters to stifle any emerging signs of sexual desire.

Just as their parents did to them, they use fear as a weapon. "Don't let yourself go," they warn, "or you'll get into terrible trouble—even PREGNANT." The threat of pregnancy is constantly used by parents as a punishment for making love. Instead of the budding young woman welcoming the onset of her sexual feelings with joy, she becomes anxious and restrained. The fear that has been nurtured over the years grows into an automatic reflex which, like a switch, shuts off her responsiveness. What parents fail to realize is that by nipping in the bud the early signs of growth, they are also prohibiting its full flowering later. This lays the groundwork for future problems of incompatibility in the girl's married life.

The problem can become deeply enmeshed not only in her relationship with her husband, but in the relationship between her mind and the functions of her body. A woman can become alienated from her own biological needs.

Mothers Mold Daughters

Girls are even more directly influenced by their mothers' manner of living and loving. If the mother silently endures an unhappy marriage, it can hardly have a happy effect on her daughter. Does her mother wake up in the morning irritable and depressed, or does she awaken cheerful and revitalized? "The morning scene" in a home teaches a girl more about what to expect from sleeping with a man than any study-course could give her. The emerging young woman needs to see an example of how a woman reacts to sexual satisfaction.

She needs to learn that love-making can be warm and spontaneous and to become aware that it increases happier living. She needs to be aware of her mother as a person who can give and receive love freely. She needs to see her mother's sexual image as a positive one, because it is her mother with whom she most closely identifies. This is the kind of demonstrational lesson that teaches a young girl what she needs to know. It prepares her, by positive example, to look forward to sex with happy expectations rather than with the more common attitudes of trepidation and anxiety.

When sexual happiness is nonexistent in the home parents usually try to hide it from the children, but children are somehow always aware of it. They become part of the unresolved tensions that develop between their parents. They cannot be fooled by superficial attempts at covering up. They see through it and they know what is happening.

When sex is hidden, lied about, children learn their lessons from this also, but not necessarily to their advantage. The fact is, *all* children learn about sex from infancy on, and girls learn that the problems are mostly female.

"No-No's" and "Don'ts"

Fear of letting go begins with the first parental "no-no," or "don't touch." An invisible shield appears later on at any sign of sexual interest from the opposite sex. Even at the getting-to-know-you stage of romancing, a young girl who has been conditioned to hold back will not only withhold any verbal assurances to the young man, but will often reject the slightest demonstration of natural affection.

This kind of repeated rejection deflates his budding masculine ego and forces many a young man to become overly aggressive, hunting and pursuing in order to prove his manliness. If he happens to be insufficiently aggressive and cannot fit himself into this lopsided situation, he is doomed to become a loser, left out in the cold where girls are concerned. And there are countless men of all ages who prove this point.

When a young girl accepts the rules of "don't" and "no-no," holding back any signs of sexual interest, and instead making repeated statements of *disinterest,* she is actually preconditioning herself not to enjoy physical contact in the future. When she keeps saying no and repulses her boyfriend with disgust or abhorrence, she not only is saying no to him, she is also saying no to herself. She not only crushes his developing manliness, she also shuts off her own womanliness. What started out as a rejection of his sexuality becomes instead rejection of her own. It is a simple law of nature that the body follows the mind. Rejection in thought becomes rejection by the body's autonomic sexual nervous system.

All modern literature on this subject stresses the fact that the most casual idea has bodily repercussions. Each and every thought has its automatic physical followthrough. This dynamic power is called "psychosomatic preconditioning," which simply means that, if you think negatively, your body may suffer from such thoughts.

On the other hand, the reverse is also true. Psychosomatic preconditioning can also set the stage for good things to happen biologically. If women understood the basic law of cause and effect it would help them to honestly and joyfully accept and satisfy the demands of their bodies. They would then discover that sex can be a spontaneous, exhilarating, freeing experience. Unless a frigid woman makes up her mind that she wants to learn how to do this, she may remain enchained to a destructive set of conditioned reflexes for the rest of her lifetime.

It is time to shed antiquated habits that have

turned women into victims of male-controlled conventions. It is time that women got off their backs and got into the act as full participants; to do otherwise is to continue to allow themselves to be used as receptacles and nothing more. All women, universally, cannot help but resent the role of sexual servitude. Old-fashioned parents should realize that when they crush the sexual spirit of their growing daughters, they are often condemning them to living the life of a sexual servant. They should think twice before implanting "no-no's" and "don'ts" into the receptive, vulnerable minds of their children, both male and female.

Sexual Honesty Helps

Just imagine, for a happy moment, that this attitude were reversed and that parents, especially mothers, freely admitted that they enjoy sexual intercourse. This kind of "telling it like it is" would go a long way to bridging the gap of misunderstanding between the two generations. Parents are too often dishonest about sex. They avoid an honest confrontation because they themselves are somehow ashamed of what they are doing. Open discussion would give the child the security of knowing that lovemaking does take place between the mother and father. This would help compensate for the quarrels which children are too often subjected to hearing.

Sooner or later little children learn about their parents' sex life and when they do, they begin to distrust their parents about other things as well. When little girls learn that their mothers engage in sexual intercourse they are almost always shocked and find it difficult to accept. The idea that someone so pure, so virtuous, would participate in something they have been taught is unclean and improper makes many girls become hostile to their mothers.

"Nice girls don't do that" and other clichés take root in their minds, and many of them reach the age of puberty feeling not only repugnance toward their sexual function, but also with a decidedly scornful attitude toward their mothers. This reaction is understandable when you consider the effect of the accumulation of all the mother's warnings against her daughter's doing what she herself has obviously done. Many girls become permanently estranged at this stage of their development.

The great parental fear of pre-marital pregnancy should be handled in an intelligent, non-emotional way. Instead of panicking when they find out that she is going with a boy, they should help her by communicating even more than before. If an honest relationship exists between mother and daughter, mother should be able to discuss contraception and any other phase of sexual life that the daughter may need to know about. Mothers should drop their prudishness and be forthright about conception so that their daughters will know how to protect themselves. The daughter should hear directly from the mother that sex is a pleasant, satisfying experience and how to avoid negative consequences. She is the most logical one to implant in her daughter's mind the proper expectation of sensory pleasure as well as the basic facts of self protection. But how many mothers can honestly do this?

More and more young women are realizing that the image they have of themselves, sexually, is a direct "hand-me-down" from their mother's (or grandmother's) own mixed-up sexual problems. A mother's sexuality either strengthens or weakens her daughter's female identity. If a mother expresses feelings of sexual inferiority, how can her daughter be otherwise? Mothers often unwittingly undermine a growing girl's trust in men by picturing them as users, exploiters of women. They often describe their own sex as "too weak to resist." Other kinds of mothers train their daughters to use men as objects for obtaining economic security.

Many girls are presented with stereotyped concepts of what a man should be and are deprived of the privilege of making up their own minds based on the reality of the situation in which they may find themselves. The reaction to this pressure causes many girls to select boyfriends in direct opposition to their parents' desires. Dishonest parents cause much of the sexual rebellion of youth.

Unfortunately, most of the information about sex that children receive in the home and from their peers is the wrong kind of sex education. It is the kind of knowledge that emphasizes the problems, but does not teach how to enjoy a good relationship with the opposite sex. A mother is the logical one to teach the daughter how to accept her body joyfully as a beautiful instrument of love. She should unashamedly teach her to give sexual pleasure and to receive it as well. Simply avoiding the whole problem, as most mothers do, gives the impression to the young girl that her mother does not sanction sexual activity where the daughter is concerned.

Improvement Is Possible

Most women reach adulthood while still remaining children in their thinking about sex. In spite of the fact that they may cling to an adolescent, or even younger, stage, the possibility always exists that they can help themselves reach a higher level of maturity. It is never too late. *Feeling that has been diminished by wrong suggestion can be restored by proper suggestion.* The accumulated blocks of "pleasure resistance" have to be removed in order to clear the way for the natural flow of sensation to the genitals.

Fortunately, nature always strives to assert itself and, in spite of the fact that a woman may be sexually incapacitated by her early conditioning, her drive can be restored and brought to life if she sincerely applies herself. *THE CENTER OF ALL LEARNING IS THE CONDITIONED REFLEX, WHICH IS OUR AUTOMATIC REACTION TO OUT-SIDE STIMULUS.* If our reflexes have been conditioned to reject sexual pleasure, they can be *DE-CONDITIONED AND THEN RE-CONDITIONED TO ENJOY IT!*

Any woman can bring about remarkable changes in herself. She can use positive auto-suggestion at any time and at any age to improve her self-image and to strengthen her sexual identity. This can be accomplished through verbal and non-verbal techniques which will be described in detail in the second half of this book. Very bad early training makes some women feel that they must accept a lesser role in the man-woman relationship. They assume that men have a stronger sex drive and that theirs is the job of servicing that drive. They heave a mournful sigh, lie on their backs and complain: "After all, sex is really a man's pleasure . . . After all, it's a man's world, etc., etc."

It's time to roll over, get off your back and get into the act because sex was never intended to be a one-sided affair. The mating instinct is the strongest of all the forces of life. This is equally true for both sexes. Proof of woman's intense sex

drive is illustrated by the enormous amount of time that she
consumes in trying to attract the opposite sex. It has been estimated that the average woman devotes four to six hours each
day shopping, grooming, and planning her conquests. The
amount of money can only be guessed at, but the figures must
be astronomical.

What happens once she gets her man? The sad fact is that,
once having attracted him, she often doesn't know what to do
with him. She is inclined to be physically reticent and belie
the ardent enthusiasm with which she applied herself to en-
snaring him. Men are confused by this duality. First she at-
tracts and then she repulses him.

This kind of ambivalent sexual behavior is found only in the
human species and is contrary to the best interests of both the
male and the female. While men react to the attraction of the
female in a physical way, women react first on an emotional
level. Very often the attraction remains at an emotional level,
as many women are not geared to respond physically.

As we have stressed before, there is no biological reason for
this failure to respond with the same measure of desire and
enthusiasm as the male. The female sex organs are just as
well supplied with sensory feeling as the male's, and a woman
is equally able to reach orgasm when she has been properly
conditioned to do so. The fact that much of her sensation has
been diffused to other areas of her body increases the disparity
between the male and female ability to centralize feeling to the
point of orgasm.

In addition, there is another important difference: that difference is in the way that a man thinks about sex in contrast
to the way a woman thinks about it. The most powerful
stimulant to a man's libido are his own thoughts which arouse

him well in advance of the actual physical contact. On the contrary, a woman's thoughts are inclined to shut off her entire arousal apparatus. Her inbred resistance turns down the dials of her sensory reactors while his eagerness turns his dials upward. He uses his senses—his sight, hearing, smell, touch and taste—to further excite himself, while a woman holds back these built-in stimulators which could assist her greatly in her quest for sexual gratification.

Being Positive Helps

When a woman allows herself to think freely about sex she will inevitably increase her desire. When she allows herself to openly manifest interest in being satisfied, the manifestation itself will trigger her mind to send the right vibrations to help her reach a higher peak of orgastic pleasure. Because of centuries of interference with the automatic mechanics of female orgasm, this seldom happens to woman instinctively anymore.

Although the female sensory responsive system is constructed basically the same as the male's, hers has a different set of repressive reflexes. His instincts propel him to let go sexually, to dispose of his sperm and thereby relieve himself, while her instincts ward off the intromission of that sperm in fear of the consequences. This is the great conflict of interest between the two.

The general attitude toward sex that is implanted in a girl's mind differs radically from that which a boy develops. The differences are based on a double standard regarding what is right and wrong for the boy, and what is right and wrong for the girl. This is the kind of double standard which admires and looks up to the boy who has early sex experiences and condemns the girl who does likewise. Too often young girls become confused and grow into sexually detached women, alienated from the normal function of their sexual apparatus. There are untold numbers of women so separated from sensory contact with their sexual nervous system that their genitals fall into disuse, numb and lifeless. There are cases where the tissue becomes entirely atrophied.

Frigid Women Affect Others

Although actual figures are unavailable, due to the paucity of research on this subject, it is obvious that the vast majority of women live through their entire lives not even suspecting that there is an answer to their problem of frigidity. Hopelessly, they just accept their lifelessness. They drift into the kind of self-pitying, self-defeating personalities that we observe all around us, caught in the trap of their early negative conditioning about sexual matters. The problem affects not just a woman's own life. A lifeless woman, struggling with her sexual inadequacy, can make life miserable for her entire family, and she usually does.

On the surface the frigid woman may seem controlled, she doesn't necessarily show open anger (perhaps it would be better if she did). Perhaps she doesn't get angry, but she does "get even" in many subtle, unconscious ways. This is the kind of frustrated woman who, without realizing the impact of her behavior, aborts the dynamic life-force of her children. While she may openly speak of loving them, she very often hates them unconsciously, having begot them, not through pleasure, but through subservience. These, then, are the "incomplete" women and we see them all around us.

It is only reasonable to expect that sexually frustrated women adversely affect every area of our lives from infancy on. The man who leaves his wife in a tense state of repressed anger, leaves a woman who carries this tension with her in everything she does. The husband is also affected in a negative, hostile way, for every man deeply desires to satisfy his woman. His own tension is reflected in whatever work he does for the rest of the day. The factory boss who barks at his workers, or the politician who votes down beneficial legislation, are both indirectly influenced by the relationship they have with their women. The man who has the gratification of not only pleasing himself, but thoroughly fulfilling his woman, is a milder, more relaxed person in every area of his life.

I'm sure a great deal more could be discovered about the far-reaching repercussions of sexual inadequacy throughout the world. Suffice it here to point out that it is the responsibility, not only of individual men and women, but of society at large to find sensible solutions to this universal problem.

Is Modern Woman Sexually Liberated?

Since the beginning of the human race, women have been taught that their main role in life is procreation. Today, many women who pride themselves on being modern in every sense of the word, still cling to the image of coitus as a "duty." Even the more sophisticated ones are unwittingly bonded to this outmoded, self-defeating concept—this image of passivity. The idea that sex is something women must do to oblige men has been handed down from one generation to another since slavery. Its destructive influence is still evident even among the new "NOW" generation, who are trying to free themselves of old taboos and restrictive behavior.

According to personal interviews, today's women have not risen above the mores and customs of antiquity. They are still guilty and disturbed by their own sexual needs, and the most advanced intellectual girl is still ignorant of her basic body needs.

The suicide rate among young adults has been rising at alarming speed. Eighty percent of all teenage suicides, and this includes both boys and girls, are traceable to:

Feelings of sexual inadequacies.

Unwanted pregnancy.

Guilt and fear of social ostracism.

Girls raised with strong religious taboos have the greatest difficulty of all in accepting pleasure. They tend to associate sex pleasure with sin and punishment and therefore have to cope with the deepest inbred resistance to sensory feeling.

Yet very often they will be propelled by strong romantic feelings and allow a boy to satisfy himself rather than risk losing him to another less inhibited girl. They "give" themselves to him in spite of the fact that they are unable to relax themselves sufficiently to enjoy the experience. This kind of "unselfish giving" is harmful rather than helpful because it reinforces a pattern of frigidity. Each subsequent "giving in and not feeling" experience worsens the frigidity by reinforcing it. The girl's mind and body become acclimated to *not* feeling. This conditioned phenomenon is rare among men, the majority of whom do enjoy sensation, once they are aroused. However, a complete lack of any sexual feeling at all is not uncommon with many women.

The inhibiting reflex against sexual feeling becomes a self-inflicted habit syndrome which seeps into the involuntary nervous system. This shut-off feeling becomes strengthened by each negative encounter. Repetition reinforces the problem.

Vaginal Tension

As the inability to respond becomes deeply imbedded over the years, it results in *internalized vaginal tension*. This tension, though mental in origin, becomes physical in fact. It eventually prohibits the flow of sensory awakening to the nerve endings imbedded in the tissues of the genitals. By so doing, it also puts a stop to the possibility of orgasm taking place. In extreme cases, so much excess tension has accumulated internally that there is extreme difficulty in even permitting the entry of the penis into the vagina, and this can only be accomplished with considerable pain. What happens is that the sphincter muscles go into spastic contraction at the mention of sex, ruling out the possibility of a pleasant experience for the woman.

There are other women who have the opposite problem, which is equally disturbing. They are loose and limp internally. Neither the man nor the woman feels sufficient contact for proper friction to take place between their genital parts. Most women suffering from this problem are completely unaware that they have internal sexual muscles and that they can develop mastery over them to cure this condition. Too often they accept themselves as being permanently over-sized, assuming that they were born that way, or were stretched from childbirth. They give up and live with the imaginary problem of being an unsatisfactory sex partner.

If either of the two problems, excess tension or flaccidity, troubles you, you may take heart because both conditions are easily remediable. They are, in fact, two sides of the same coin: *lack of muscle control*. Every woman is able, with self-training, to tighten and loosen these vaginal muscles. The exercises described in detail in the second part of this book will enable you to contract and expand this muscle structure at will. Just as you can learn to exercise and strengthen any other part of your musculature, you can also strengthen your sexual muscles. This will not only make it possible for you to increase your own sensation, but will intensify your lover's pleasure.

A woman who has trouble reaching an orgasm must face the fact that her problem existed long before she met her mate. It will help her improve if she stops putting the onus on the male. The average normal man wants to be a good lover. But whether he is good, bad, or indifferent, a woman must assess her very own behavioral pattern in order to reach her own full sexual potential. She cannot "copout" and leave her problem to the man. If she is to bridge the gap between her present reactions and full maturity, she must assume the major responsibility of her own sexuality—RIGHT NOW. This is the only kind of assertive feeling that can successfully eradicate the repressive habits of the past.

One wonders why more women don't make some active attempt to do something about their sexual unhappiness. The sad truth is that most of them are not even consciously aware of having a problem. They assume that the way they are is the normal way to be; that the condition of their genitals is the same as everyone else's. They rationalize that women are just less sexually capable than their masculine counterparts. Frigid women resist facing the obvious fact of any kind of genital malfunction. They evade reality and delude themselves by thinking that the way they are is the way that they are supposed to be. Some of them secretly hope that someday, somehow, they will meet a special kind of lover who will "turn them on." They dream that he will possess some kind of magic power that no other man had before him. They expect that somehow he will make sure that they respond and that they then will, because of him, reach fantastic heights of ecstasy. Time passes and recurring sexual disappointments leave them physically tense and emotionally depressed. Still, they hopefully try again and again, searching for the "magic lover." They become trapped in a web of their own invention, unable to avoid repeating the same silly syndrome.

Without their dreams of adolescent romantic fantasy, many women, both married and single, could not sustain themselves emotionally. Like a teenager who wistfully dreams of true love solving all, they too cling to their fairy tales of a knight in shining armor.

If women were truly mature and faced reality, they would realize that there is little that the best lover can do for a woman who is shut off sexually. To lift herself out of this bind, a woman must first learn how to use her mind instead of being carried away by her emotions.

Rational Thinking Helps Sexuality

Human beings, female as well as male, possess a highly evolved thinking mind capable of logical deductions. This is the basic factor that differentiates human beings from other forms of animal life. Women must use logic in approaching a solution

to their problems. They must be rational, rather than senti-
mental, where sexual function is concerned.

Emotions can be powerful levers for self-improvement, but
they must be directed by the proper thoughts. It is never too
late to change one's thinking, and when one's thinking
changes, the body changes its way of functioning. The mind
has powerful control over sensory reactions. It is this basic
fact which makes it possible to correct the bad effect of previous negative conditioning.

The mind not only acts as an inhibitor and controller, it
also can act as a releaser. You can train your mind to send
messages of increased pleasure and thereby counteract the old
syndrome of negative sexual reflexes. You can exert a positive influence on the development and enlargement of sensation
in any area of the body. The proper use of auto-suggestion can
cause the sensation in the sexual organs to become keener and
keener. The proper use of auto-suggestion can also spur you on
to the point of orgasm. If once you accept the simple concept
that sex is *supposed to be pleasurable, that it is natural and
proper,* you will be taking the first giant step in the direction
of eventual fulfillment—and complete womanhood.

If a woman is not hampered by early sexual crippling, she
will gracefully glide from one stage of her development into
the next. To reach her potential, she should be permitted to
pass through all of *the vital stages of sexual development,* from
infancy to maturity.

TWO

Vital Stages of
Female Development

The simplest way to understand why most women tend to be immature is to examine how, when, and where, their normal maturation was intercepted and suppressed. Just as with the male, there are coinciding levels of sexual growth through which every female must also pass if she is to reach her emotional and physical potential. We have all witnessed examples of feminine immaturity on an emotional level. Upon examination, we find that the emotionalism is merely a surface manifestation of the underlying physical problem.

There has been a great deal written about the emergence of the masculine personality and abundant reference to the drives and activities which take place at the various stages.

These recognized steps are progressive links in a chain which should lead to the final culmination of adult sexuality. Like that old adage, "A chain is as strong as its weakest link," an individual's sexual identity can only be as strong as his or her weakest link of development. When a person grows into adulthood with an unsettled sexual hang-up, chances are that this is a link to past problems which were left unresolved. This becomes even more evident when you consider the female sex drive, as it exists (or does not exist) in the average woman.

A clearer picture of why most women are sexually retarded can be garnered by examining the chain of links through which every female should pass. Unfortunately, the stepping stones from infancy to womanhood are fraught with many slip-ups resulting from implanted fears, and when fear makes feet falter, stepping stones become stumbling blocks. Most women have not passed through all of them without some memory of serious growing pains. It sometimes takes years of therapy to undo the harmful results of parental misdirection.

In answer to a recent survey, college students said that the greatest problem that troubled them in their adolescence was the lack of freedom to meet members of the opposite sex without stirring up antagonisms within their family circle. Parents were inclined to be suspicious of boyfriends, which led girls to meet them away from home with the resulting guilt and anxiety that such behavior brings.

This lack of freedom to explore the possibilities of sexual encounter and to grow with such exploration was blamed for the confused and damaged female sexual image. Lack of sexual freedom in the attitudes of parents and society in general was blamed for much of the ensuing female sexual ills. This feeling has been expressed not only by American students, but by female college students in many countries throughout the world. Many girls stressed the unfairness of the way that college men are treated in comparison with the girl students. Whereas the young men get away with "loose" sex morals, the girls are looked down upon and in many cases are socially ostracized for doing exactly the same thing.

What Is Feminine?

What constitutes a truly feminine woman? For centuries women have been stereotyped as being either "good" or "bad," idealized for being virginal, or scorned for being sexual. The good woman has been traditionally described as being above animal instincts, the bad one as being loose and free for pleasure and profit. The second category has always been presented as the kind men don't marry. Even many progressive, open-minded men, some of whom even accept the women's liberation movement, prefer to think that their own women are naive and inexperienced. Perhaps they fear comparison with other men, because the male ego has also suffered in the backlash of female frustration.

In a survey taken among young bachelors twenty-five to thirty-five years old, they described a truly ideal, feminine woman as one who lets the man make the decisions sexually. In answer to other questions, they preferred her to be passive, modest, and shy. And most of all, "not too experienced with other men." It would be laughable, if it were not so tragic, because the results of this kind of thinking cause unhappiness for both the male and the female.

A great many men who have had good relations before marriage, find that once married, their sexual interest in their wives diminishes. These are the men who married the "good" women; good and proper in the sense that their mothers were good and proper. While they often hang on to the "good" women, they seek their real sexual satisfaction outside the marriage. Their wives plod along spending their lives trying to answer their husbands needs, but never feeling a real part of the sexual union. They go along with this one-sided, unfair kind of relationship, giving more than they receive. This habit of selfless over-giving fast becomes an unconscious habit and keeps such a woman from seeking a solution to her own sexual frustration. Because of this idealized "angel of perfection" label, women often become reluctant to express sexual desires. They fear that an aggressive demonstration of sexual feeling might spoil their image of demure feminine modesty.

Too often women react like puppets or robots manipulated by the phoney ideas their husbands have of what a woman should be. Men could do the women they love a great service if they applied the following advice from the philosopher, Goethe: "Treat people as if they were what they ought to be and you help them to become what they are capable of." An understanding, sensitive lover who brings a woman's desires to the fore and directs them openly with her, can help greatly because women are often reluctant to express their true feelings.

Incomplete Women

Incomplete women, those who have not been permitted to emerge from their stages of sexual growth, are inclined to be neurotic and difficult to live with. Men who are asked to describe thē personality of a typical woman use words like unpredictable, moody, changeable, emotional, irrational, a riddle, an unfathomable enigma.

Recently a man who lived with his wife for fifty years was quoted as saying, "You know, after all this time I still can't figure her out!" This husband was at a loss to understand what made his wife tick, what made her irritable "without reason." He described her as "super-sensitive about trifles." He wondered why she resorted to tears at the slightest provocation. She was paradoxically described as both demanding and all-giving, childishly immature and completely domineering. When questioned about her sexual response he answered, "She doesn't object to sex, but she has a struggle to reach orgasm and sometimes I know she doesn't make it."

Some men when asked to describe their conception of an ideal woman said, she is "ephemeral, her feminine mystique keeps her shrouded in a veil of mystery."

All of these divergent points of view may be true for some facet of a particular woman's personality, but could hardly apply to the general mass of disturbed women. One thing that they do have in common, however, is that their thinking is often clouded by an undeveloped sexual identity. Investigation and research points up the fact that when a woman cannot reach orgasm, she behaves like what she really is, a childish person, acting out a childish stage of her unresolved development.

One of the greatest handicaps to a woman's reaching sexual maturity is her tendency to cling to adolescent romantic notions about male-female sexuality. Unless a girl emerges from puberty-adolescence with an awareness of her physical self and an acceptance of how her genitals function, she can be hooked to romanticism for the rest of her life. A romantic outlook is fine and has its place in the developing of close feeling, but when it becomes the overpowering factor in a relationship, something is wrong.

"Romantic" stems from the word, "*roman*," which means fiction or novel. In other words, romantic is that which is based not on reality but on fantasy or imagined wishes. Female immature notions are nurtured by romantic movies and magazines where everything always ends happily. Somehow, the perfect man shows up at the perfect time, handsome, clever and conveniently rich. The stories always end with the implication that he will be "true 'til death do us part." It fits our childlike dreams of what a man-woman relationship should be.

When a woman is fully grown and yet fails to function sexually, she tends to regress nostalgically to a previous sentimental-romantic era. She will idealize love and set her mind on impossible goals of perfection in the man that she meets. When things don't work out "à la Hollywood," she reacts by becoming irrationally despondent and increasingly withdrawn sexually. This kind of childish over-exaggeration of romantic emotions brings out the worst in her feminine personality. She feels rejected, jealous, and more and more insecure about her sexuality.

Many women do not marry because they cannot find a man who fits into their preconceived expectations of omnipotence. When this kind of immature woman does happen to get married, she usually turns out to be a chronic complainer, the classic, stereotyped nagging wife. She cannot understand why her husband doesn't fit the mold of her own fabrication.

While romance and sentimentality have their place in the

feminine personality, in most cases they are magnified beyond their usefulness. A limited amount can cast a rosy glow and add to the warmth of sexual love, but when it is exaggerated out of proportion to the reality of the adult situation, it can be an indication of adolescent immaturity. Most sexually immature people are completely unaware that a gap exists between what they should be and what they are.

Is Compulsory Sex Education the Answer?

It depends. It could be if it were the right kind of sex education. Unfortunately, public schools cannot be as effective as they should be. The limitations imposed by society, church, and parental ignorance make freedom to educate extremely difficult.

Many parents are even now bitterly fighting the inclusion of any kind of sex education in the public school system. They go so far as to resist the addition to the curriculum of biology courses which would teach the simple facts of how one's body functions. They object to something as basic as children knowing how their sex organs work for reproduction. Without the fullest cooperation of the family, any attempt at honest sex education is doomed to failure. Only confusion and guilt can result for the child.

Parents must play an assertive role in this program, if it is to succeed. They cannot shift the problem to someone else and then hide their heads in the sand. Public schools can help, of course, in answering factually the many questions in the mind of every growing child. They can give general education but sexual self-identity can best be learned by the example of one's parents in the home environment.

The Home Is the Teacher

It is the natural atmosphere of every-day living that teaches a child the deeper truths. For example, making sex a hush-hush subject at home, while relegating its discussion to the teacher, who is, after all, a stranger, can only impress the child further with the shameful attitude of his parents. Having this to contend with, a child is apt to wonder about his or her own conception. A child thinks, "Was I conceived in shame and fear? Is there something wrong, therefore, with life itself?" If being conceived is sinful, then love itself must also be sinful.

A proper sense of values, from which springs a future standard of behavior, can only be learned at home. Confusion of what is right and wrong leaves women with hangovers which restrict their sexual behavior. Many of them are eager to leave the past behind them, but in spite of their eagerness, they find themselves unable to function freely.

Even though society has given them the right to seek fulfillment, they are still groping in the dark, unable to find answers to their profoundly inbred problems. There is a time-binding to the past, from grandmother to mother to daughter. Each family has its own set of rules. In many cases what would seem liberal to one family would be considered shocking to another.

At the present time more and more of the younger generation of women are facing the needs of their bodies and trying to do something about it. In spite of the great sexual rebellion in the thinking of the younger generation, they are not necessarily fulfilled. Not all of them recognize that to be truly feminine, one must feel like a female, inside as well as outside.

Women who are determined to attain real sexual freedom to function as nature designed them, must toss aside old regressive body reflexes. This is not as easy as changing outward attitudes. A self-determined young woman must approach the problem of her frigidity as no longer suited to her present desires and emotional needs. Only when she is able to grow away from the old pattern of sensory withdrawal will she attain her goal. A woman's sexual self has been formed by the way she has been taught to think and behave.

By the time she grows into adulthood she no longer can react spontaneously to instinctual stimuli. Her mind has been programmed, like an IBM machine, to act as controller and inhibitor, squelching sensation. This inhibition becomes a shut-off valve in her sensory machinery. It restricts circulation and stops the flow of feeling to the genital area.

The answer to this universal problem is for girls (as well as boys) to be educated about sex from early childhood on. However, debate continues about whether it is the responsibility of the home or society to provide this vital service to the growing child. As the issue is shunted back and forth, the confusion is magnified. Opponents to providing public school sex education argue that the impersonal presentation of this information might scar the child's mind, while the people on the other side stress the opinion that most parents are incapable of answering questions on sex, because they themselves lack proper knowledge.

The Forces Against Sex Education

The forces aligned against sex education have released many shock-provoking stories, most of them unfounded, about so-called mishandling of the school sex programs. Dr. Ronald J. Pion, Seattle obstetrician and director of the University of Washington's family planning and sex education department, spoke at a recent symposium of the American Medical Association where he said, "If I were a parent, I'd be very upset to read in my mail that a kindergarten child was being shown stag movies. I'd be very upset to learn that my ten year old's teachers turned out the lights and told the kids to go feeling around in the dark and then describe the experience, but I can't find out where any kindergarten classes have been shown any stag movies. And I can't find out where any school kids have had the lights turned out and have been told to go feeling around in the dark. These things just *never have happened*!"

On a national level, within the policy councils of the American Medical Association, there has been continuing debate between the right and the left wing factions of the organization, with the right wing taking a hostile attitude toward the inclusion of sex education in the school curriculum and the liberal faction arguing for the dissemination of more scientific information at each succeeding level of public education.

The controversy has not been confined to the United States alone. The London BBC has recently been telecasting regular sex lessons for ten-year-old children. This progressive step has met with general audience approval. However, as is to be expected, there has been a conflict among the more conservative leaders of the British nation. This prompted a showing of the disputed program to thirty government functionaries, including Mrs. Shirley Williams, Minister of State of the Home Office.

They saw a screening of two particular sex programs which were designed for primary school children. One was a show illustrated by a film clip showing nude paintings of men and women and a couple having sexual intercourse. The Ministers of Parliament were also shown a television program which shows a woman giving birth to a baby.

One of the ministers explained that there had been letters from her constituents asking for a halt to the sex programs. Most of the objections came from people who are religiously opposed to children learning the facts of reproduction as perhaps in some way challenging the concept of the Bible's Adam and Eve story of the beginning of life. The consensus after viewing the sex programs was that, "If I had daughters who were about eight or ten, I would have no hesitation in allowing them to see either of these programs." They went on further to explain that if children received the proper factual information at this early age, they would be bulwarked against the infection of harmful misinformation later on in their lives.

The battle for and against sex education continues to rage all over the world and is especially apparent in our own country where it has come to a boiling head. On one side of the conflict is the SEX INFORMATION AND EDUCATIONAL COUNCIL OF THE UNITED STATES, a composite organization which includes psychologists, teachers, churchmen, parents and their many conglomerate organizations such as the National Education Association, the country's largest teacher group, in addition to numerous parent-teacher organizations.

On the opposing side are arranged many vocal groups with names as, MOTHERS OF MORAL STABILITY, (MOMS), SANITY ON SEX, (SOS), PARENTS OPPOSED TO SEX AND SENSITIVITY EDUCATION, (POSSE). They include the extremes of Victorian-minded parents, religious zealots, and those who stress the possible psychological damage that might

occur due to the exposure of the child's mind too soon to too
much information.

Parents With Problems

All of these groups agree on the main issue. They insist that
parents should be the ones to make the decision on how much
and how soon children should learn about the subject, and if
they should be taught at all.

The problem with this kind of attitude is that the type of
parent who joins such organizations usually has problems of
his own. This kind of parent would be inclined to shy away
from any discussion at all with his children and thereby doom
the children to either remain ignorant or to pick up their information from gutter sources. If this kind of parent does
make an effort to inform his children, he does it with embarrassment, and often inaccurately, and at a time when it is already too late to do any good. Their opposition is propelled by
emotional feeling and they seize on the little sex education that
does exist to distort and explode it into a national political
issue.

In spite of all the controversy and adverse publicity, the New
York City school system has had comparatively good results
with its program. It has not been disturbed by any massive opposition from parents. On the contrary, parents have been inclined to cooperate with the newly launched program. Out of
the approximately one million students in this large metropo-
lis, 70,000 have been involved in the sex education and they
have reported satisfactory results. The head of the New York
City program pointed out that it is precisely because they

worked closely with the community that they have fared so well. They have had cooperation from neighborhood organizations, religious groups, and from the parents themselves from the very beginning of the program's inclusion in the classroom curriculum.

Before a film on sex is shown to the children, the parents are invited to a preview screening. This action has a two-fold purpose. It not only educates the child, it also helps to educate the parents. After the parents see the movie, there is a spirited question and answer period at which time the parents can voice their opinions on the subject and clear up any unanswered questions of their own.

It is generally agreed among modern educators that some sort of educational system must eventually be installed in the public schools to counteract the absorption of violent, dirty, threatening images of sex which are thrust at children from all sides of their environment. Even a casual observer cannot miss the fact that no matter where a child turns there is a panorama of commercialized sex. It may be beyond their intellectual comprehension in some cases, but it still has its negative emotional effect upon them and their future life as functioning sexual beings. Also, an educational job needs to be done because venereal disease among teenagers has reached epidemic proportions.

In every candy store wherever newspapers appear, children also see an increasing array of erotica, most of it on a very low level. Sex is sensationalized all around us and its misuse is gaining in momentum. Pornography is nurtured and supported by people in their forties and fifties, according to surveys conducted by government "Commissions for Standards of Decency". The reason for its over-exaggeration at the present time is the lack of education in earlier years. Most adults are ignorant of the very basic facts of sexuality. The average person has accumulated his bits of misinformation from equally ignorant individuals. People feel this lack and there is a constant search among adults of both sexes and all ages for the answers to the very questions denied them at the growing-up stages of their physical and emotional development. This explains the massive array of pornographic literature with its sexual half-truths. Trash is easily accessible to children as well as adults, yet the truth is hidden.

The only sane answer to this confusion is in the public school systems where sex can be taught in an impersonal manner, where necessary, and with the active assistance of the parents to make the program even more effective. Whether it takes place at home or at school, proper sex education should provide every growing girl with the following:

1. It should free her to grow into womanhood without guilt or fear of punishment.
2. It should give her an understanding of how her own sexual organs work.
3. It should inform her of how the organs of the male sex function.
4. It should assure her of the fact that her awakening feelings are normal and natural.
5. It should teach proper contraceptive methods to prevent unwanted pregnancy.
6. It should answer all questions about lovemaking and techniques for reaching orgasm.
7. It should provide assurance of a future, healthy heterosexual life.

It is not suggested that this information be given to a child regardless of her age. Information should be fed depending on the immediate need of the child for that information. It should not wait until the child reaches the junior high-school level, as is most often the case at present. Proper sex education should answer the natural curiosity of a child at each vital stage of its development. Advanced information should not be pushed too soon, but neither should it wait until the child has been confused by incorrect facts received from questionable sources.

There should be enough flexibility in the carefully prepared program so that it can be adapted to the differences in age, maturity, and any other factor that might influence the child's ability to absorb the knowledge. Needless to say, the teacher must be sensitive, understanding, and able to handle these intimate questions in a relaxed, easy manner. It would be necessary to set up a special orientation program for these teachers who, in many cases, need to be taught the basics themselves.

The greatest conflict exists over whether or not to teach adolescent girls methods of contraception. Not to do so would be foolish because they find out what they want to know from their friends anyway. This kind of vital information travels very fast. Not to teach the meaning of planned parenthood, in its most practical sense, negates any other knowledge that she may receive. Without removing fear of pregnancy, a girl cannot open up emotionally and mentally to the oncoming physical changes. Even a pubescent girl has undercover fears of pregnancy and childbirth. These fears feed the resistance to maturity. The shutting off of sexual feeling starts at a very young age.

From the time a child is born until he or she leaves the family circle, the home is, of necessity, the major source of sex information. It helps if parents answer questions, simply, straight away, and without embarrassment. It is in the home that children receive the emotional attitudes and confidence which is such an important part of sexual happiness.

In the school environment, education increases in complexity as the child advances into the higher grades. We can see that both the home and the school play their equally important roles in preparing the girl for future maturity. The family gives her the emotional security and the school the factual knowledge on a non-emotional level. For example, menstruation is best learned about in a school atmosphere among a group of girls who share in the wonder of the discovery about what is happening to their bodies. This should take place in about the fourth or fifth grade. Waiting until a girl is older often defeats the purpose. They must be prewarned and preassured that what is soon to happen to their bodies is good and natural. They should welcome its oncoming as a sign of future fulfillment as complete women.

When girls reach the eighth grade they are ready to study about their glandular system and how it brings about each individual's body changes. They should learn at this age about the unfolding and flowering of their female identity. They should learn how the glandular system causes the transition from child to adult.

From the eighth grade on upward through the teens, both the home and the school should provide as much personal information as the young girl needs. She should have her questions answered without hesitation or traumatic tension.

Most teenage girls want to know everything that can be learned about contraception (because, let's face it, many of them are sexually active). They should be taught that every act of human intercourse must be preceded by a conscious act of contraception (unless the couple desires a pregnancy). Teenage girls should also learn all of the facts about venereal disease, its prevention and cure. They should learn about prostitution, its social implications and the dangers involved. They should learn about homosexuality, its causes and how to avoid it.

Above all, girls must be taught to gracefully accept the many changes which take place within themselves at each level of growth. It is interesting to note that men generally fare a lot better in passing through their own vital stages of sexual development. The pressure of sexual mores are easier on him and, in the main, he emerges a lot less scarred.

These are the vital stages of sexual development in the male:
1. Childhood
2. Adolescence
3. Masturbation
4. Homosexuality
5. Sexual Affairs
6. Married Sex

Psychiatrists generally agree that where this natural growth is impeded there is a definite imbalance in the sexual personality of the man, as well as in his physical function. Improper handling of early signs of homosexuality, for example, can cause this state of behavior to become a fixed, rather than a transitionary stage. Men who marry early, before they have had sufficient freedom to develop their masculine image, will tend to be more promiscuous after marriage than those who have had the reassurance of successful premarital affairs.

What are the vital stages of female development? It may surprise some women to learn that *they are exactly the same as for the male*.

1. Childhood
2. Adolescence
3. Masturbation
4. Homosexuality
5. Sexual Affairs
6. Married Sex

Although the list *reads* the same, it is seldom that a girl is encouraged or even permitted to pass through these stages without parental restrictions. It is as if little girls were fitted with an invisible chastity belt designed to keep away all contact with their genitals. Parents transplant their own fears which fall into two main categories. The fear that the young girl will be "deflowered," (that her hymen will be ruptured) and that forever after she will be considered less than perfect—somehow damaged or "second hand" for marriage. Even the most contemporary parents secretly hope that their daughters will remain virgins until marriage. The second vaginal fear is that someone will cause the daughter to become pregnant before this all-important marriage takes place and by so doing bring shame down upon the family.

Let us examine in how many open and subtle ways a young girl is prevented from exercising her natural instincts to mature. Let's find the "mental/emotional" blocks that have been constructed along the way to interfere with this evolution process. When once you are able to uncover your own blocks, you will then be better able to remove them so that you can replace them with proper thinking.

Sexual retardation starts in infancy and continues step by step. As you read through these pages, I am sure you will recall some personal experiences which influenced your present sexual behavior. Analyze your own repressions. Become aware, evaluate past events in the light of your present sexual needs.

THREE

Childhood Exploration

The search for sexual identity starts at a very early age. The little girl who first notices the difference between the sexes and reacts with wide-eyed wonder is merely carrying on the puzzlement that little girls have experienced through the ages. She sees that boys have something valuable which she does not possess, a penis, and she wonders why she has not been so endowed. She is made to feel that it is a very special valuable possession because of the very special treatment that goes with it.

Recent studies comparing male and female behaviorism indicate that there is a marked difference in the way that society and parents treat their children depending on whether the child is a boy or a girl. Based on ancient religious customs in all parts of the world, males are most often preferred. In many cultures, such as the Hebrew and the Moslem, elaborate special celebrations mark the birth of a son. The celebrations are even more extreme when the firstborn is a son. When a wife does not bring forth a son, her husband is permitted to leave her and take another wife. This reverence toward the male sex is sensed by every female, whether she grows up in a modern society like our own or in the most remote corner of the globe.

From early infancy on, a boy is given more attention and affection than a baby girl is given. This becomes more and more apparent as time goes by. When the infant reaches its first year the difference is firmly established. Research shows that boys are spoken to more frequently, and more .often praised for deeds that they accomplish.

Female children, on the contrary, receive relatively less attention. A study conducted among preschool children produced the following rather remarkable results. A group of little girls ranging in age from three years to five years were asked if they would rather be a girl or a boy. Almost 80 percent of the girls said that they would prefer to be boys. When the boys were asked the same question, only about 5 percent said that they would rather be girls. This seemingly strange response becomes understandable when you consider that parents have inadvertently molded this ego imbalance. This parental error in handling children stems from another era when girls were not permitted to work outside of the home and were consequently a burden to their families until marriage.

Without necessarily being consciously aware of it, parents definitely put more into their sons than they do their daughters. This applies not only to the amount of time and thought, but also to the amount of money spent on each child. The rationale is that males have a greater potential for returning the investment, financially as well as emotionally. Fathers, who are normally the ones who control the larger expenditures in the family, favor sons in a more profound, unexpressed way because sons carry on the family name. They hope that their larger investment in their sons will reflect greater honor to themselves. A man who is not "blessed" with a son and has a succession of daughters instead, is made to feel by other men that he failed somehow in his maleness.

This preferential treatment is demonstrated toward a child even in the purchase and selection of the kinds of toys that are presented to each sex. A great deal more money is spent on educational toys for boys. The motivation for this is the idea that boys have a larger stake in learning and developing skills for future career selection. Much of this kind of unfair treatment takes place on an unconscious level, but in spite of the lack of intent, its malicious effect seeps into the personality of the female child. Many parents who think of themselves as being very aware and as having raised their children on equal standards as to sex, will be amazed at the imbalances if they examine the situation honestly.

Other research on this subject shows us that as children grow older and reach high school and college levels, there is even more of a difference in how they are treated, not only at home, but in school. Teachers, both male and female, have very frankly admitted in detailed questionnaires that they decidedly prefer to teach boy students. The essence of their reasoning falls into the following categories:

Girls are inclined not to follow through on careers.

Girls drop out and get married at a younger age.

Boys take higher education more seriously than girls.

The above reasons do not hold true when examined. More and more girls are preparing themselves for careers, not only to support themselves, but to assist in the economic situation of family life.

All of these manifestations of a double standard have the tendency to make girls become increasingly insecure about their femaleness and, in many cases, to secretly accept that they are the "lesser" sex. Without knowing where or how it all started they become victims of sexual "brainwashing" and begin believing in the myth of male supremacy. Instead of her true sexual identity, the girl assumes an image of worthlessness. As a result, she finds herself unable to function sexually with the same degree of naturalness that men do.

People professionally trained in the large-scale observation of young children have noted that both boys and girls, from early infancy on, show many signs of sexual interest and excitation. Sigmund Freud had much to say about this and his thinking was decidedly contrary to the popular opinion of his time. It was generally believed that sexual interest starts at puberty with the oncoming of body changes. He disputed this contention and declared that sex interest does not wait for puberty, but starts much earlier, in infancy itself.

One can easily imagine how shocking Freud's ideas were considered at that time. How could anyone in their right mind accuse an innocent babe of such sinful activity? His theories were ridiculed, not only by the ordinary person on the street, but by some of the leading psychologists of that period. Many sincere people thought that he was completely insane and campaigned to have him committed to an asylum for even suggesting such an unpopular, far-fetched idea.

Time has proven him to be correct and this is no longer a controversial issue. In spite of the fact that many leading psychologists and psychiatrists of today dispute a great many of Freud's early theories, they generally are in agreement on this basic point. That there are outward signs of sexuality in the very young child has been proven by extensive research throughout the years.

Sexuality is not something which can be superimposed, it is always there. Only the lack of sexuality can be affected by forces outside of one's body. Sexuality is first learned by the tiny infant through the feel of its mother's flesh. The infant's joy in the feeling of flesh against flesh starts in the security of the womb itself. The floundering infant at its mother's breast feels the magnetic attraction of her warm body and the gentle touch of her hand. The infant absorbs the emotional vibrations of its mother through this early contact. Where children are raised in an impersonal manner by servants, (and often when they are bottle fed), they show the lack of sensory warmth throughout their entire lifetime.

Not only the mother is important in forming the sensitivities of the child. The father also affects the budding sexual image of the infant girl. No matter how young she may be, the infant girl absorbs the radiance of affection that emanates from the maleness that is her father. The way he handles her, the sound of his voice, and his nuzzling embrace all help form a picture of what a man is like.

The baby learns very early the delight of being physically fondled. She also begins to store memories of the pleasure that she brings to others, most especially the responsiveness of her father. This is the normal sexual beginning that lays the foundation for a female's *ability to respond to another male later on in her life.*

Unless parents are emotionally ill, they instinctively enjoy the touch of a soft, warm baby. They will fondle it, carry it about, sing to it, hug it, squeeze it, tickle it and even kiss its bottom. However, when the infant begins to show signs of sexual interest in its own body, their attitude abruptly changes from parental playmate to parental disciplinarian.

Sexual self-interest is first expressed in the infant's curiosity in exploring and discovering its body parts. Just as with the boy, the infant girl finds that touching her genitals produces a vague sensation of pleasure. This is something which forward-thinking parents should welcome and feel happy about. It is a natural manifestation of the normalcy of their child, without which future sexual happiness would be impossible. Instead of welcoming these signals of health, many parents become anxious and overly concerned. They worry that the child will develop unwanted masturbatory habits, and so they put a halt to this very *necessary period of self-discovery.*

It is now an accepted fact that small children not only have great curiosity about their own sexual organs, but require some amount of sex play with other youngsters. If left to themselves, they will invent all sorts of games to satisfy this need. Some sort of "playing doctor" is a universal pastime. The real purpose of these play situations is to explore the sex organs of their playmates and thereby give sanction to their own. Youngsters are adversely affected when deprived of this essential interaction with other children. Parents must realize that this is neither abnormal nor unnatural, that its purpose is self-education rather than sexual gratification.

When children are not scolded or hampered in any way, but left to freely explore and experiment, they have even been observed to experience some degree of sexual sensation. In some cases the sensation appeared to culminate in a sort of climax. This has been noted in children as young as two to four years of age. It may come as a shock to the frigid woman who cannot remember ever having had feeling, that she herself may originally have reacted with strong feeling as a small child. It is entirely possible. In fact, if left to her own devices, the female child shows as much evidence of sexual excitation as does the male. Sexual literature often describes the rocking action of infants masturbating against their cribs, and this is more common to the girl than to the boy child.

What happens to the awakened feeling in the female child? How is it thwarted and where has it gone? Another question may provide the answer to the first two. How many parents who come upon a child in sex play have had the good sense to back away without disclosing their presence? Any enlightened parent knows that a child will turn its interest to other things as soon as its curiosity is satisfied. If parents would accept the fact that no body damage results from this exploration, they would handle this growing stage lightly and with good humor. They would avoid creating the massive load of guilt and anxiety that many children grow up with.

Most women can remember that as a child touching certain parts of the body was frowned upon. In many families it is still a common practice to tie young children's hands to the sides of the bed to make it impossible for them to touch their genitals. If they should break loose from their bindings and disobey, severe punishment may be inflicted. Among backward parents many cases of child abuse are based upon this problem. Even in the more educated, modern family, it is a common practice for mothers to remove a child's hands from beneath the covers when they tuck them in for the night. The origin of this gesture is so that parents can see what a child's hands are doing. Many women who are now burdened by problems of sexual self-acceptance can still remember being slapped on the hands and the scolding which followed, "Don't you dare touch that again! *Nice* girls don't do that!"

The idea is systematically implanted that contact with one's genitals is unclean, unhealthy, and very sinful. The long series of "don'ts" culminates in a woman who is psychologically finished before she has had a chance to get started. The fertile mind stores the memories of repeated warnings one receives throughout childhood. Sexual warnings serve as negative training. They motivate a girl to react with distrust and wariness of the opposite sex. Growing older or even getting married doesn't make a mature woman out of her. She can remain childishly immature where sex is concerned throughout her adulthood. Fear of masculine contact can only be erased from her thinking by deliberately relearning proper, healthy sex attitudes and responses.

Almost all parents say to their small daughters, "Watch out for strange men. Don't accept candy from strangers." It is understandable that parents are troubled by incidents of child molestation and abuse and find it necessary to protect their children from possible harm. However, it should be explained in its proper context, so that the little girl does not associate all men with this fearful warning. If small girls are not made to fear the sexual drives of adults, they will also be more inclined to accept the signs of sexual development in themselves. If they get through childhood unscarred, puberty comes easier.

FOUR

Puberty and Adolescence

Puberty is often called the threshold of maturity. It is a time when a child stands upon this awesome threshold and looks with apprehension upon the vision before her. Sometimes what she sees facing her has the effect of tearing her in two directions; one the desire to remain a child free of adult responsibilities, and the other the biological need to fulfill herself. Puberty marks the farewell to childhood and its dependency and the onset of sexuality and self-reliance. It is because of the stress of this duality that puberty is almost always an emotionally disruptive phase.

It is a period when the body of the child undergoes many changes, the first signs of body hair, the swelling of the breasts, bring with them the fears of what the future may portend. If she hasn't been stifled and made anxious, she should welcome these early signs of approaching womanhood, but it is seldom in our society that small girls are sufficiently aware of what to expect. Most people are not informed and do not educate a child in advance of puberty. Puberty begins with girls as young as nine and in tropical climates even younger. It lasts until the onset of the menstrual period, when a girl is technically and biologically considered a woman and able to conceive and bear children.

It is considered that the adolescent period commences with the first menstrual period and continues on through the teen years. Puberty-adolescence is a time in the life of every girl when she needs the utmost patience and understanding. It is often a troubled time of her life when she suffers from great confusion as to what and who she is.

If her future personality is to develop properly, she must have the calm assurance that everything is right and natural, that there is nothing to fear in growing up. It is a strange new body that she has to cope with now, and rather than the joyful occasion that it should be, the onset of the menses often comes as a traumatic shock. Its occurrence carries with it the responsibilities of living up to a long list of new restrictions, with "stay away from boys" heading the list.

The further one gets from civilization the better women fare in their biological function. In many primitive tribes there are elaborate festivities to celebrate the oncoming womanhood. When a girl gets her first period she also receives many presents, there is tribal singing and rejoicing. Contrast this with what happens in our society. The difference stems from the fact that our culture frowns on early marriage and childbirth, whereas primitive cultures let nature take its own course. The denial of sex to females when they are physically ready makes it necessary to morally justify the waiting. The time span between biological readiness and sexual consummation averages ten years. Parents are faced with the problem of warding off the natural urges of the female for copulation and its resultant pregnancy. So this becomes a time of severe warnings from parents, who themselves are inwardly frightened of the great physical changes taking place in their little daughters. They instill their own anxiety and caution in them and lay the groundwork for the mistrust of masculine signs of attention.

It is a common occurrence to hear parents say, "Don't believe boys if they say they like you, they only want one thing, SEX." Parents also tell girls, "If you give in and lose your self-control, you'll get pregnant." In order to postpone its happening until marriage, they often implant the idea that the first sexual experience is a painful, unpleasant encounter. The following are a few examples of the kind of negative suggestions that parents inadvertently implant in the fertile minds of young girls. This causes the accumulation of resistance which acts as a block to sexual pleasure in later years.

DO ANY OF THESE "NO-NO'S" APPLY TO YOU? CHECK THE LIST.

1. Don't let a boy get you alone.
2. Don't let anyone touch your breasts.
3. Don't let anyone touch the other place either.
4. Don't lose control—you might get pregnant.
5. Don't trust men—they are all alike.
6. Men want only sex, not love.
7. Watch out for venereal disease.

8. A boy's penis hurts—you might bleed.

I'm sure you could add many other "no-no's" to the above list. The threats and warnings are endless and come at a time when the young budding woman is extremely vulnerable to fear. Right now the important thing to consider is not just what was said to you, but the effect that it had upon you in your ability to feel sexual pleasure.

It is rare that one comes upon a woman whose parents had the courage to tell her, "Sex is a wonderful experience. You will surely enjoy it as we do. Don't worry about pregnancy. Use the best possible contraception and then just relax and enjoy it." It may seem absurd to imagine a mother and father telling a daughter to let herself go sexually for pleasure, because we know that what actually happens between parents and child is quite the contrary.

If parents were able to have this natural approach to a girl's growing up, there would be a far better chance of bridging the generation gap born from the alienation which ignorance breeds.

A properly prepared young woman should eagerly welcome her first sexual union. It should be the culmination of her emotional love for the young man and should bring her some real depth of physical pleasure. In spite of the fact that most sexually active adolescents participate with abandon, they generally have little sensory feeling. They are simply searching for sexual identity which was trampled earlier in their life by the sexual "don'ts."

If parents freely discussed sex and all its ramifications, their daughters would be more inclined to wait until the right man comes along, rather than run from boy to boy hunting for the answers. The fact that she seldom finds the answers is attested to by the large percentage of dissatisfied women. It is inevitable that parental pressure causes the young girl to become negatively conditioned to sexual stimulation particularly in the most vulnerable area, the vagina.

If she accepts parental rules, she often becomes repulsed by the masculine sexual drive. What is even more destructive, she can become repelled by the natural needs of her own body. This breaking down of the female libido often happens without conscious awareness on anyone's part. They do not always know when and how it happens. It just does. When the conditioning is successful, they fall into step with the conformity which obstructs any advancing signs of sexual maturity. In extreme cases, repulsion to everything sexual seeps into their involuntary thinking and starts its debilitating affect on their nervous system. This is the time when the impulse to reject masculine attention and repress instinctual feeling becomes a structured pattern of behavior, having a permanent effect on many women.

There are girls who, in their eagerness to reject the rules laid down by their parents, go to extremes in the other direction. More and more teenage girls give their bodies freely and without regard to self-pleasure. It is a common practice among girls as young as thirteen or fourteen to offer themselves to the young men they admire. It is a time for distortion of romantic feelings and the adoration of singing and rock-and-roll celebrities. It is a time for great disappointments in love and repeated "heartbreak." Emotional feeling and sensitivity to rejection are stronger during the teenage period than at any other time. Girls worry about their looks, if they are too short or too tall, too fat or too thin and about their breasts. They want to conform to the current ideal and when they don't they suffer very deeply.

Teenage Suicides Increasing

It is not generally known, but ten to fifteen per cent of all teenagers attempt suicide, and this alarming figure does not include the many cases that are hushed up and not reported. It also does not indicate the many who just brood about it within themselves. Based on the confirmed research of a leading sociologist, more than eighty per cent of the teenage girls who attempted suicide were involved in a sexual relationship that caused them unhappiness. Others were depressed over unrequited love, and some of these were even more depressed due to unwanted pregnancies.

It is interesting to note that since the sex barriers have been lowered, suicide has *increased* rather than decreased. The sexual revolution has forced girls to follow the trend and to participate in the free flow of sexual intercourse. It has not succeeded, however, in freeing the young woman to the point of sexual gratification, without which "freedom to act" means very little. Many girls are driven into sexual relationships in their quest for companionship and affection. They find it is often fleeting as companionship and affection cannot long endure without mutual sexual satisfaction.

From the masculine point of view, a boy's activity is shaped to a great extent by the crowd he travels with. It is expected of him to engage in sex relationships with girls, otherwise he is considered by his peers to be less than a man.

While boys are inclined toward sex for the sake of sex, girls need to rationalize their participation. From the very first question that a girl asks about sex, she is fed the idea that "true love" can be the only valid reason for such action. Girls cling to the alibi of "Love and Romance" for the rest of their lives. They tell themselves that they must be "In Love" in order to respond and then the rude awakening comes when they do fall in love and find that they still cannot function. Men are less inclined to be romantic in their affairs with young women because their growing up has been handled with a great deal more honesty. The forces that repress the female drive deliberately protect the male drive. Perhaps this is because the repressors are themselves men. In any case, the results prove the fact that there is a marked set of double standards.

Women are not always what they seem. They may appear physically mature on the outside and yet have built-in problems of immaturity. These are the women whose emotional-mental attitudes have become anatomical ones. Grown-ups must be made aware of the delicate susceptibility of the adolescent girl to the implantation of psychic fears that affect the physical structure. Young people are constantly made the target of psychological arrows which deflate their budding sexual egos. Critical attitudes of parents make young girls very conscious of their appearance and the slightest problem can throw them into deep despair.

Girls as young as ten or eleven study their appearance for flaws which they become extremely sensitive about. They try make-up, stuff their bras, and do anything else they can think of to make themselves look older and sexier. As they grow into their teens they strive for the "natural look," and many throw away the brassiere and the lipstick and attempt an individual attractiveness within the realm of whatever happens to be the "In" thing of the time. Whatever she does, it always adds up to the same thing—trying to attract the opposite sex. The girl who tries too hard to be sexy in her appearance and outward attitudes, usually runs from sex when the situation presents itself. The super-sexy looking girl is usually a disappointment to the boy who finds that the sexy shell houses an inner fear of physical contact.

Magazines tell them how to look more sexy. To quote a recent add for brassieres—"If you've got it, flaunt it. If you haven't got it—fake it!" Both puberty and adolescence are times of great turmoil. A girl is torn between two fears: fear that she may not develop soon enough, and fear on the other hand that if she develops too soon she might not be able to cope with it. She feels that men are too aggressive and want only her body instead of loving her for what she is.

Unfortunately, parents react to the changes in their daughters by retreating. Rather than increasing affection, fathers stand back, perhaps fearful that their signs of concern might be improper now that the little girl is on the verge of being a full-fledged woman.

There is also a decided separation from the mother at this stage and a tendency to cling to friends outside the home environment.

There is an increasing national problem of young girls who leave home in their search for some sort of emotional security. Many of them wander around from one group to another seeking some sort of love and understanding. These are not necessarily girls from homes where love was non-existent. Very often these are girls from very permissive homes, where they were given ample opportunity to pursue their individual talents and where money was not a problem. The economic situation does not seem to be a deciding factor in why girls leave home. We have all read about the many cases of teenagers from prominent families who toss it all aside and disappear into a run-down hippie neighborhood in search of a deeper meaning to life. There are others, however, that we seldom read about in the newspapers; these are the young people who are in the majority. They are the ones who make their adjustments and are able to cope with the changes in their relationships to family and environment. These are the young people who, very early in their life, developed a closeness and trust of their parents and can easily discuss their innermost fears and anxieties with them.

Throughout the entire learning program there must be ample time for children to ventilate their thoughts and to ask as many questions as they wish in order that every misconception and fallacy can be cleared up.

We must, above all, stop frightening girls with the old four cornered sex bugaboo.

INFECTION
CONCEPTION
DETECTION
REJECTION

Does knowing the real facts about sex encourage girls to be promiscuous? On the contrary, the tendency is definitely in the other direction. This is exemplified by what is happening in a "teen clinic" run by the planned parenthood group in San Francisco. It's purpose is to help the sexually active teenage girls prevent the first out-of-wedlock pregnancy.

During a two-year period, 600 girls under the age of eighteen participated in the group discussions on sex and birth control. Out of all of those sexually active girls, only ten had an unplanned pregnancy. Of the 600, 476 were given physical examinations and taught how to use specific contraceptive devices. The ages of the girls varied: 216 were 17 years old; 156

were 16 years old, 76 were 15 years old; 23 were 14 years old; 4 were 13 years old; and *one was* 12 *years old.*

The attitude of the clinic toward the girls is one of openness and complete acceptance of their sexual activity. The director of the school, a woman, explained that the clinic does not pass judgement on the girls, but instead stresses the use of contraception. It has been proven that the more ignorant the girl, the more vulnerable she is to sexual misuse by the opposite sex. Ignorance about how the body functions breeds unnecessary anxiety about personal normalcy.

It is the home itself which spurs young people to experiment before they are physically or emotionally ready. By leaving the important questions unanswered, parents push their children to find out through experience. The standard for sexual conduct is inadvertently set by parents who nullify sexual curiosity. When a married couple avoids questions and behaves in an embarrassed way in front of children, children wonder not only about the normalcy of their parents, but also about their own normalcy.

When parents hide any outward signs of lovemaking, when they act sneaky about sex, children sense that something is wrong. These are the home conditions that prompt most teenage girls to investigate sex and to discover how their bodies will react to lovemaking. They are not propelled by sexual drive, but rather to assure themselves that nothing is amiss in their sexual self. A girl who reaches her teens doubting whether sex pleasure ever existed between her mother and father, will be more inclined to try sexual intercourse in order to discover some of the answers to the mysteries created by her misguided parents.

Not all girls get involved in sexual affairs. Most of them succumb to the environmental pressures and sublimate their instinctual drives into school work or other interests. There are those who find solace among friends of the same sex. Some homosexual affairs spring up as a result of society's disallowance of heterosexuality for the young. Many girls become increasingly introverted and moody. They display fits of emotional hostility toward their parents with the slightest provocation, it would seem. Actually the provocation has been building since early childhood and is merely triggered by the parent at this time. When children reach their teens and have no sexual outlet, they often begin to satisfy themselves through *masturbation*. This is true of both girls and boys, although women will seldom admit to this.

FIVE

Masterbation

There are few women who will honestly admit to ever having masturbated. Surveys on female sexuality reveal that there is a wide difference in self-acceptance between men and women. While men freely admit masturbation and joke about it among friends, women become shocked at the mere mention that they might have taken this kind of liberty with their bodies.

Prudishness makes women lie about it. Thus, surveys are false, and do not really indicate the extent of the problem. Women have been so strongly structured to believe that touching oneself is "not nice," that they often go through their entire lives avoiding contact with their genitals. It is no wonder that they remain ignorant of their sexual anatomy.

From infancy on, the vagina is declared untouchable, with a built-in "no trespassing" sign. Those women, who when young, ignored the admonitions of parents and masturbated anyway, have been found to be less frigid when they reach adult womanhood.

The term masturbation comes from the Latin word, *masturbo*, which when divided in half means, *manu* for hand and *sturbo* which stands for rubbing. The term is deceptive because masturbation does not necessarily involve using the hand. In early childhood, for example, girls have been noticed rubbing the front of their bodies against the bed or pillow and rocking back and forth to give themselves pleasurable feeling.

Girls also have been noticed crossing their thighs and in this way exerting pressure against their clitoris and labia to bring about orgastic sensation. As women grow into maturity without the sexual love of a male partner, they resort to all sorts of methods of self-gratification. Modern social attitudes have become more accepting of women's independent role in sexual self-discovery and almost any large drugstore features assorted devices for sexual stimulation and satisfaction.

The terms auto-erotism and onanism are also used to denote masturbation. Auto-erotism means self-loving and is applicable to either gender, while onanism generally refers to a grown man who masturbates habitually beyond his youth, a man who prefers his own company sexually. The term is derived from the Bible story on Onan, the son of Judah. It is said of Onan, in this ancient tale, that he preferred to "spill his seed upon the ground," rather than give something of himself to a woman.

Since that early time, all religious sects have looked down upon masturbation as shameful and contrary to the dictates of nature and God. This attitude of disapproval is even more marked in regard to women, who have traditionally been expected to be above self-indulgence.

Most religious denominations list masturbation as a serious sin and warn that its punishment will not only be meted out in the here and now, but that dire consequences await the perpetrator in the hereafter. As punishment, all sorts of illnesses have been attributed to it, from insanity to sterility. In spite of all the warnings and threats of damnation, it has continued to flourish since the early ages of mankind.

The fact is that masturbation actually exceeds normal heterosexual practice in the frequency of its indulgence. This is not surprising when you realize at what an early age it begins and that it continues on throughout a lifetime into senility. At least it does for men. Women are less inclined to accept it due to the emotional stigma of rejection which they attach to it.

When you consider the amount of masturbation that takes place during the teenage years, plus the increasing number of divorced people, widows and widowers, it is conceivable that masturbation can be a far more common practice than coition. Being alone encourages its practice.

As people become more and more alienated, one from the other, in our pressurized society, the more likely they are to become habitually addicted to auto-erotism. It relieves them from the responsibility of communicating with another person, of giving to that person, and perhaps becoming emotionally attached. Auto-erotism is actually a more meaningful word than masturbation. It was coined by the famous writer on sex subjects, Havelock Ellis. He used it to depict a person involved with sexual self-gratification. In his writings he used the term to suggest not only stimulation of the genitals, but also any other erogenous areas of the body, such as the breasts, nipples, anus, etc.

Masturbation is not peculiar to our present-day society. It has also been an accepted practice in many ancient and primitive cultures. It is even encouraged in many tribes as a means of physically developing the sex organs to insure better functioning in adulthood. Not only boys, but very often girls are taught to massage their genitals in order that they may mature earlier and bear children sooner. It has been recorded that this practice not only makes the female more responsive to stimulation, but helps them to have easier childbirth.

If left to themselves without interference, people, regardless of gender, will tend to masturbate at various periods throughout life. For the young this is a means of self-exploration and a prelude to self-acceptance. It is an aid in the emergence of the individual's sexual identity. For an adult, it should, at best, be only a temporary substitute for male-female intercourse.

Its prolongation and fixation is contrary to the emotional-physical best interests of both men and women. When auto-erotism becomes the sole sexual behavior of adults to the exclusion of loving and being loved, it acts as an affirmation of loneliness and rejection. A person who has fallen into this self-defeating trap should recognize it for what it is, *a neurotic act,* no longer suited to the needs of maturity.

Masturbation would be less of a problem in adulthood if it were handled properly in childhood. If they allowed the process of growth to happen gracefully without embarrassing children, it would probably be just a transient phase.

In the male, masturbation starts with the onset of puberty.

Young men continue to masturbate even when they are dating girls and experiencing normal intercourse. The man who has reached maturity without ever having masturbated is a bit unusual, to say the least. Psychiatrists would describe such a young man as one with decided problems, and many doctors believe that masturbation answers an important need for the release of pent-up tensions. There would no doubt be many more sex crimes and violence, were it not for this safety valve.

But what is society's attitude toward women who masturbate? In the main, society tends to discount masturbation as a normal activity for women. Books written on the subject give the impression to the reader that this is not a serious female problem. They suggest that women who masturbate are either oversexed or abnormal in some way. It is as if the men who write about it are somehow ashamed to face the facts of female sexual needs.

Surveys point out that 90 percent of all men admit to masturbation, compared with only 50 percent of the women interviewed. The other half of the women questioned were to one degree or another shocked at the implication that they might have indulged even in childhood. When you consider that women as well as men do not often tell the whole truth about their intimate sex life, one may assume that the percentage is probably much higher.

Double Standard Affects Behavior

There would be no difference in the percentages were it not for double standards of sexual behavior. The very fact that there is such a wide disparity in the responses of males and females indicates how real the problem is, in relation to women's acceptance of their sexual needs.

The problem grows out of the first seeds planted in infancy and some women never are able to overcome it. I spoke to a woman in her fifties who stated emphatically that the only time she ever touched her "privates" was when she took her daily bath. Although she had been married for almost thirty years and given birth to three children, she still carried with her the feeling that it was not proper for her to touch her genitals.

Most psychiatrists tend to agree that almost all women do masturbate at some time in their lives. When they have been forced to abstain in childhood, they are more inclined to try it, even to the point of overindulgence when they are on their own away from the restrictions of their families. Even when they do it regularly, they will deny it because they have been led (by men) to believe that it is an unfeminine thing to do. Another reason for their resistance is that they believe it takes away from their romantic image. They feel that making love to oneself is an admittance of being unwanted and that they will therefore be unworthy of a masculine lover.

In spite of all of this rationalization, there is a new attitude growing among the new generation of women, spurred by the many liberation groups. Young women are demanding equal rights not only at the ballot booths, but in the bedroom.

Many young women claim that the use of devices, as well as manual manipulation, helps them to respond better when they are with a man. A woman must feel free to try anything that encourages her sensory development. *Masturbation that leads to improved heterosexual intercourse can only be considered as a positive conditioning force.*

One contra-indication is in the cases where women masturbate by clitoral manipulation exclusively. When they deliberately avoid contact with the vaginal opening they are perpetuating the "no trespassing" reflex. Having been trained and successfully conditioned to the idea that the vagina is not to be tampered with, they constrict and restrict themselves only to clitoral sensation.

I do not intend to imply that vaginal masturbation is a must and absolutely necessary for every growing girl. It very well may be, but there is no conclusive evidence to support either point of view. Masturbation as well as clitoral-versus-vaginal orgasm has been such a "hush-hush" subject that too little inquiry has taken place. What I am saying very definitely is, however, that the anxiety which parents project onto their children is especially apparent where *girls* are concerned; that most of the stress is centered on and associated with the vaginal opening, that this, therefore, causes increased difficulty for women to respond with *internal* vaginal feeling.

When a child is left on his own, he will shamelessly explore his sexual parts. This is a simple direct way of assuring himself of normalcy. Once having seen what there is to be seen and having felt what there is to feel, children will generally leave this activity behind and move on in their progressive growth toward maturity.

When any stage of development is abruptly arrested by parents, that particular activity may become a future stumbling block to sexual happiness. When people become hooked on masturbation, it is usually because their parents focused too much attention on it in previous years. If a girl (as well as a boy) is not permitted to explore and experiment with the erogenous areas of her body when she is young, she will be inclined to resort to this adolescent form of sex play later on; she will use auto-erotism at a time when masturbation is only a poor substitute for the real thing.

Exploration even by the very young girl leads to the discovery of some sensation in the clitoral area. As girls reach puberty they are ominously warned that the vagina is covered with a skin called the hymen which is supposed to remain intact until marriage. They are told that they must be careful and protect it until their future husband breaks it open, like some sort of festive prize. The young girl is warned that if she should accidentally break this protective cover, she may experience pain, bleeding, and the exposure of a strange unfamiliar opening in her body. She is also impressed with the idea that she will be less desirable to her future "true love." She is cautioned even more rigorously against letting any boy get near this precious opening. The debilitating fear of pregnancy and disease is pounded into her relentlessly. It has been discovered by researchers that when a girl is left on her own she will masturbate and often reach orgasm, even as young as 12 or 13 years of age.

Habitual masturbation is a symptom of alienation of a person who is living through fantasy. The physically mature woman should also be psychologically mature and involved with the real world of the present, peopled with real men who make her feel like a real woman. *Auto-erotism in the grown woman is the sexual life of the solitary, lonely personality.*

If a woman has not completed her evolutionary process in its chronological order, it is still possible to pass through each stage and on to a more meaningful sexual life. She must first be aware that exclusive masturbatory habits make relations with men more difficult. Habitual masturbation can set up a response pattern only to her own methods of touch, pressures and rhythm and thereby make the role of a lover less satisfying.

Some women become so accustomed to solitary sex that they exclude men from their life entirely. Such a woman visited me. Her name was Marge. She was trying desperately to convince me (and herself) that she did not need men. She was small, vivacious, in her mid-thirties, and very feminine in her mode of dress and manners. She had never been married and stated that she intended to stay that way.

Contented Without Men?

During the daytime hours she was employed as a secretary to a prominent surgeon. Her work was very interesting and financially rewarding. There was a note of disdain as she said, "I make more money than most of the fellows around." She was even more emphatic when she stated, "There's nothing a man can do for me that I can't do for myself, BETTER!" I asked her how she spent her evenings and she assured me she had a good social life, went to shows, night clubs, and parties with other women friends. She said the only thing she missed was perhaps, children. She avoided her married friends because "They keep taking out pictures of their kids." Other than that, she insisted that she preferred the freedom of coming and going as she chose, without having to answer to a husband.

Marge disliked the entire role of womanhood, felt it was subservient. She especially rebelled against the idea of catering to a man's needs. "I don't want to be used. There's only two kinds of men. The kind who use you and the kind who abuse you." She said, "I refuse to submit to their sexual whims." Marge resented bitterly male supremacy. Her attitude was typical of the views expressed by lesbians. But, she was quick to assure me, "Don't get the wrong idea. It's not that I prefer women sexually. I think that sex between women is even more disgusting than sex with a man. I just never have enjoyed it. I would rather just be left out of all this sexual stuff. Personally, I think it has been grossly overrated."

Why then had she come to my office? How could I help her? She explained that she was taking some study courses to advance herself in her job and found that she had a great deal of trouble concentrating. Her memory was also growing increasingly undependable and she wanted to learn autosuggestion to help herself get ahead financially.

I asked her how well she slept and at first she answered, "Fine," then she became strangely uneasy, shifting around in her chair until she was no longer facing me. Suddenly she began pacing the room, picking up objects and examining them. She did not answer my simple question so I repeated it, "How do you sleep?" She looked around the room and selected a chair in a darkened corner and sat down with her shoulder turned toward me so that I could not see her face. "I sleep okay," she whispered very softly. "I put myself to sleep by masturbating." When she saw that I was not particularly shocked by her disclosure, she hastened to add, "I only do it because sleeping pills don't agree with me. They leave me so groggy the next morning I can't concentrate on my work." She got up from her chair and walked over and faced me directly, "Listen, everybody knows that masturbation is not harmful, so why shouldn't I? It's a lot healthier than getting into the pill habit again."

Her attitude was challenging, almost to the point of being

belligerent. "Well," I said softly, "If you are happy as you are, there is nothing to be said." She said nothing for a while and then, "No, I guess I really can't say I am really happy this way. To tell you the truth, I wasn't always down on men. Once I had a boyfriend. It lasted for several years, but it turned out to be a very disappointing affair. Every time we slept together I would wind up masturbating after he went home. I've had enough of catering to men."

She bitterly listed all of the masculine traits that she found objectionable. "They are selfish, inconsiderate, egotistical, bossy, and promiscuous."

I pointed out that many women also have these personality problems. After some thought, her mood shifted to introspection and she said thoughtfully, "You know, he really wasn't that bad. In fact, in some ways he was a rather nice person. I remember one night when he tried everything in the books to get me to reach an orgasm, but nothing helped. He really wanted me to respond to him, but the most that ever happened was a slight sensation in the clitoris. I don't understand it because on my own I have no trouble at all in reaching a strong orgasm. Sometimes I have as many as eight or ten clitoral orgasms a night by masturbating."

She explained how she would fall asleep in a state of exhaustion and awaken in the morning just as tense and irritable as when she went to bed. It has been my observation that too much clitoral stimulation, even when it culminates in orgasm, has the adverse effect of increasing tension and frustration.

Marge's deeper, inner, inside female self was left unsatisfied and *this is the crux of the female problem*. She explained that since her early childhood she had never touched her vagina, had no idea what it looked like and certainly had no internal sensation. The idea of even looking at a picture of the female sex organs was repulsive to her. She said that as a young child of about six she had sneaked into the attic where her father kept some medical books from the days when he was a student. She had found a book which had a profound traumatic effect upon her. It was a photograph of a baby being delivered out of its mother. This picture had caused her a great deal of concern and she had developed a strong mental image of associating the vagina only with the act of motherhood or birth.

One day she told me of a strange dream that she had had the night before. "It's a dream I have been having all my life. I guess since the time I saw the picture of the baby being delivered. I dream that I am pregnant and very worried about whether my child will be normal or deformed in some way. My mother stands over my bed and keeps repeating, 'Oh, what did you do to yourself?' I know what the dream means because of something that happened when I was about four years old, even before I saw the picture. I must have been fingering my vagina without even being aware that I was doing it. My mother tied the blanket up under my arms so that my hands could not touch my body. She frequently told me that I must not put my fingers near that place because it is where babies come out of and I might get it dirty."

Her story speaks for itself. It is not an unusual one, but rather typical of the misguidance that most mothers continue to give their daughters about sex. Marge was an intelligent person and eager to overcome this burden from her past. With the use of autosuggestion, she developed a great new awareness of the effects of her parental/environmental influences.

Several months later I received a long letter from her telling me how well she was doing with the training she had received in autosuggestion and that she was once again dating men. She wrote, "It's amazing that after twenty years of masturbating clitorally, I am now able to transfer the major sensation to my vagina by using the mental exercises you taught me." The difference between masturbation and true sexual satisfaction is the difference between being outside of life or being the inside part of it.

SIX

Homosexuality

*A girl's struggle for female identity usually gets stymied before she is even old enough to understand the differences be-*tween the sexes. She usually winds up with an impression that the female is less perfect than the male.

The confusion of "male-female identity" has existed since the beginning of the human race. In spite of all the advances mankind has made, it is far from being resolved. How widespread this problem is among girls can only be conjectured. Back in the days of Sigmund Freud the same reluctance to face the facts of female sexuality existed. He said at that time, "Homosexuality in women has been neglected by psychoanalytic researchers." The situation has not changed since Freud made that statement, back at the turn of the century. One can only surmise that the problem must exist to the same degree as with men (based on the premise that all of the vital stages of female development have been interfered with in childhood).

When little girls first notice the special privileges afforded the male members of the family, they often wish that they were boys. Then the girl discovers that not only is he treated better, but that he has something extra on his body which she does not possess. Somewhere in her mind the two ideas connect and she begins to wish that she too had not only the penis, but the many special privileges that go with it.

How much of a role penis-envy has played in women's inability to respond *internally* can only be guessed at, but the results point to the common identification with the *outside* sex feeling of the male. Constant reference to the clitoris as a small, dwarfed vestige of the penis adds to the picture of a female being a less perfect version of the male. Most literature on sex assumes that women can only reach an orgasm through manipulation and friction with this "small deformed penis." Perhaps the fact that men have written most of the books might explain the lack of accuracy about how a female's genitals were designed to function.

Let's consider the role parents play in guiding a daughter through the normal period of homosexual attachment. Unless parents are wise enough to handle this delicate phase with empathy and sympathy, it can and often does extend into adulthood. When nervous parents set up taboos about boys, it is to be expected that the girl will draw closer to friends of the same sex. As the body matures and she has no counterpart to her female drives, she may find her friendship toward a girlfriend converted into physical love.

Lesbians are made, not born. They are home-grown, usually by their own families. When parents harp on the dangers of heterosexual love, they misdirect the fearful young woman toward the "safety" of her own sex. There are strong indications that this happens quite frequently in such an atmosphere. Parents reflect their own sexual anxiety by keeping a nervous eye on their children.

When a girl's friendships are *exclusively female and persist beyond her early teens,* such behavior must be regarded as a possible indication of future regressive problems.

People involved in studying this growing problem agree that a girl will not become a fixed homosexual unless she undergoes emotionally disturbing experiences during the course of her youth. A child who is made to feel ill at ease with the opposite sex, will react by feeling more at ease with its own. Anything that parents do to discourage heterosexuality, encourages homosexuality. These are the simple facts. Confused gender identity would be greatly diminished if it were handled in advance of it's appearance at the "prehomosexual" stage of a child's development.

Early recognition should lead to professional help which could, in most cases, clear up the disparity between what a child thinks he or she is, and what he really is physically. Research in gender identity stresses the fact that sex confusion does not begin during adolescence, but, rather, shows itself in early childhood. Parents can do a great deal to instill gender awareness in young children. This can only be accomplished with a general overhauling of our national attitude toward sex education, both in the home and in the schools.

A clue to a great deal of the existing sex confusion can be discovered in examining the roles that parents play in the home. Where they have reversed their roles, with the father a passive, milk-toast type, the mother too strong and decisive, there are bound to be resulting problems. A girl will be predisposed to mixed-up sexual identity as a result of this early conditioning. In trying to identify with the parent of the same sex, she is at the same time copying the characteristics of the opposite one.

Girls are not only adversely affected by having a weak father-image, they are also equally disturbed by the father who is too domineering and feels the need to constantly assert his masculine power over the family. Both extremes of personality reflect the deeper problem of the parent, his or her own confused sexual image. When parents are themselves confused, they can only pass on further confusion. This is why sexual education in the impersonal atmosphere of the school is of such great importance.

Homosexuality is a term used in describing overt behavior of either of the sexes, whereas lesbianism refers specifically to the female. Both terms are derived from the Greek. The word "lesbian" derives from the Greek story of Sappho, the poetess who lived in 500 B.C. on the Greek island of Lesbos. There she conducted a campaign (using her poetry) to convince the women of the island to make love to each other, rather than to submit to the slavery of their male captors.

Lesbianism connotes relationships between physically normal women who have difficulty accepting the sex that nature has given them. Paradoxically, they resent men on the one hand and try to emulate them on the other. One common trait is their fascination with the phallus which is perhaps a continuation of their early "penis envy." (It is interesting to note that the word, "fascination" itself, is derived from the fertility god, Fascinus. This is the god represented in ancient fertility rites as a huge penis, carried about in festivals by worshipping men and women alike.) In many primitive societies, young maidens publicly deflower themselves with a small replica of the god, Fascinus, as a manifestation of their readiness for mating. Girls who refused to worship the phallic god were ostracized and in some tribes, even put to death. Although present-day lesbians might object to being classed with worshipers of the male phallus, all of their behavior points in that direction. They are torn between the reality of what their bodies tell them they are, and the fantasy of what their minds have created.

Most lesbians are deeply unhappy people, even more miserable than homosexual men, because underneath the superficiality of their masculine affectations, there is a normal yearning to fulfill their biological role of motherhood. Men, whether homo or heterosexual are generally quite content not to be rooted to the home. For many young women who practice homosexual love it is a transition to a normal male-female way of living and loving. Unfortunately, labeling a young woman lesbian makes it difficult for this transition to take place. Labels are destructive devices. Very often a girl goes through one or two fleeting experiences which can be left behind as she moves on to a more meaningful maturity. It is important to distinguish between temporary homosexuality, such as occurs during the adolescence, and the fixed lesbian way of life. As we described previously, there is a normal urge for young adolescent girls to draw very close in affectionate friendship during those trying years of sexual adjustment. Even when the relationship slips into a physical bond, this is usually temporary when it is not traumatized by parents. The closeness is more often on an emotional rather than biological level and in many cases brings a greater understanding of femininity.

The crush on an older member of the same sex is also a common experience, and a necessary one, in the quest for complete womanhood. The love for a schoolteacher, aunt, or other female adult can be the forerunner of a girl's increased femaleness as she aligns herself with a more mature image of her own future development. The need to identify with the same sex is understandable when you consider the great changes that are taking place, both physically and emotionally. The internal turbulence frightens girls and they become increasingly sensitive, unsure of who they really are. One moment she feels like a woman, the next moment like a child. Very often they express great feelings of tenderness for their closest friend. There is embracing, kissing, holding hands, whispering secrets, and lots of giggling together over little things that would not be funny to anyone else. In most cases normal homosexual friendship during adolescence does not go beyond these overt demonstrations of affection. At most, the average girl who is not restricted, will engage in mutual examination of body development, breasts and pubic growth of hair.

Actually, the purpose is a healthy one. It enables the rapidly changing girl to compare and evaluate her own changes with someone who is going through the same metamorphosis. It must be accepted by parents as a necessary period of self-discovery. If it is not inflated out of proportion, a young girl will glide through it gracefully. Homosexuality in both the male and female is a temporary, transitory period of self-education through comparison. It will wear itself out if parents do not attach too much importance to it by over-reacting.

In addition to serving the purpose of self-discovery and self-acceptance, adolescent homosexuality among girls serves as a safety valve for their exaggerated sense of the romantic. The abundance of emotionalism that young girls feel is in direct ratio to the amount of suppressed sexual feeling that they have experienced. Not being permitted by parents and society to engage in sexual love with the opposite sex, the power of their feeling is converted into emotional tension. Girlfriends help release this tension in their emotional relationship with each other. They share their most intimate thoughts, their fears and apprehensions. They worry together about their sexual attractiveness, and confide their great concern over their breast development and menstrual problems. Perhaps the greatest empathy a woman experiences in her lifetime is at this stage of closeness and sameness.

Close friends also share and compare their experiences with boys about petting and necking, and in this way give each other the kind of assurance that they cannot get from their families. They not only are confidants to each other, they also inform each other of what is new in the field of birth control devices. They often encourage each other to try sex because in spite of all the implanted fears, they are drawn to it irresistably.

What causes a woman to feel like a real woman? Is it how she looks or how she feels? What is the key that determines femininity? Is it the mind or is it the equipment above and below the navel? Is it influenced by whether a girl is dainty and female looking or the "tomboy" type? Lesbianism is not always discernible by outward appearance. The "butch" or blatant masculine type, who wears her hair clipped short and walks with a swagger, is in the minority. Most of the 1,400,000 women who are considered homosexual look as feminine as any other women. This figure represents just two per cent of the entire female population. These figures are from the 1953 Kinsey report, but most experts believe that an investigation right now would double the figures.

There are many girls, even larger numbers than outright lesbians, who practice bisexual love. That is, they share their sexual activity with men as well as with women. They consider themselves normal, and protest that they are merely filling in with women until the right man comes along. This seldom happens because they become so adjusted to the lesbian way of making love that they are conditioned to it biologically and emotionally. Many women of this type have used the exercises in this book to affect the transference from female to male, but it is very difficult without some sort of systematic discipline. They have difficulty in getting back to a male-female relationship since the company of other females who are anti-male makes them intellectually critical of men. These women get together and malign men in every area of being. They enjoy verbally castrating them and from this destructive atmosphere it is almost impossible for a girl to emerge with a healthy, trusting attitude towards the opposite sex. As the years pass by, many of the relationships take on a permanent nature. Even the so-called bisexual women find they are caught in the bag of habitual homosexuality. Even getting married and having children doesn't always break the bond they have established over the years. They often cling to the close girl-friend all through their marriage. Sometimes it is not even a physical relationship, but the deep need manifests itself in other ways.

There is nothing more pathetic than an aging lesbian. It is even sadder if she doesn't know she is so inclined and reaches middle age without having fulfilled herself, either with a man or a woman. Latent, unresolved homosexuality is very prevalent not only among men, but perhaps even more among women. It often goes undetected throughout a woman's entire lifetime.

This condition of confusion is more destructive in a woman because of the inbred guilt associated with the denial of the biological drive of motherhood. A classic example of this problem was brought to my attention by a woman who was attending one of my discussion groups on methods of relaxation.

Dorothy gave as her reason for being especially tense the fact that for over forty years she had been harassed by a woman friend who kept, "hanging around, always popping into my life and causing me heartache." She said the other woman's name was Margaret and that they had known each other since they were about fourteen years old. Dorothy was in her late fifties, a widow and grandmother of four. She seemed on the outside to be a typical suburban middle-class youngish grandmother. Dorothy often spoke of her lamented husband in glowing terms and described him as the ideal husband. One day she surprised me by adding that during the thirty years of their marriage, they had never had a normal sex relationship. She blamed it on her husband's unusual sex habits. She was shy about disclosing what these were in front of the group, but later confided, "You know, he could only reach an orgasm if I humiliated him, insulted and degraded him." "In what way?" I asked. She continued. "He would demand that I urinate on his genitals. That was the only way he enjoyed sex."

In spite of this bizarre sexual relationship, she felt that they had had a good marriage and she cried as she described how much she missed his companionship. She said that re-

gardless of his erotic practices, he had been a good husband and
father to their three children. "What about Margaret?" I
asked, "How does your woman friend fit into this picture?"
"Well, Margaret always wanted to keep in touch with me since
we were close friends in school. Whenever I was sick, she came
to see if she could help. When my children were born, she
played with them. Sometimes she hung around so much my
husband would chase her out. She got on his nerves because
she always catered so much to me. Sometimes I think he was
actually jealous.".

I wondered silently if he had any reason to be as she continued her story. "Since we were teenagers she has been telling me how much she loves me, that she would do anything in
the world for me. Sometimes she would get very emotional and
I would feel sorry for her because she was all alone. She used
to make a lot of trouble between me and my husband. You see
she never married and had no family of her own. I actually
think she was happy when my husband passed away." I asked,
"Do you think her feelings for you were homosexual?"

She considered her answer for a moment and then said, "I
want to be perfectly honest about it. We never actually slept
together, but I think too much affection went on between us.
When we were in our teens we used to write love notes to each
other and swear our ever-lasting devotion. I think she would
have died for me."

I suggested she bring Margaret to the next group and that
perhaps they could both talk it out and get some better understanding of the situation. When Dorothy walked in with Margaret, they were arm in arm, giggling like adolescents, (which
they actually were in the emotional sense). A moment later
they were quarreling about some small trifle and I heard Doro-

thy say, "I wish you would stop calling me on the phone and annoying me. Just because you don't have a normal life and never married, don't think I have to make up for it!"

Margaret shouted back at her that she was ungrateful for all she had done, and then suddenly in the twinkling of an eye they were again laughing and teasing each other like children. During the general discussion in the group their eyes were fixed on each other constantly. They were aware of nothing except their own empathetic, immature closeness.

After the others left, Margaret said she was eager to tell me the story of her life and explain her feelings for Dorothy, which she insisted were not homosexual, but the love for a longtime friend. Margaret did not look like the stereotyped version of a lesbian. Neither her attire nor her attitude were masculine. Her gestures were soft and feminine and there were still some slight signs that she might have been very pretty when she was much younger. Now she was slovenly, her clothes dirty and disheveled, her hair unkempt. This was in sharp contrast to Dorothy who looked like the type of upper-middle-class woman who spends most of her time in the beauty parlor and shopping for the latest fashions.

Dorothy must have been reading my thoughts as she said, "Look at her. A real slob. How can you expect anybody to want to been seen with you?"

Margaret's puffy white face trembled as she tried to hold back her tears. In fact her entire body heaved and swayed as she rocked with the blow to her self-esteem. It was evident that their relationship over the years had been one of sado-masochism with Margaret the obvious victim. She looked up at Dorothy from wet, bloodshot eyes that told the story of

having already cried oceans of tears. Gathering the last ves-
tiges of long forgotten self-respect she said, "I come from a
very fine family. My father was a famous lawyer. I always
had the best of everything."

"Everything?" I asked. "Well, everything except kindness
and love. No one ever took time with me. They were always
so busy. I felt like an outsider." In addition to the words she
was speaking, she was also explaining, without realizing it
that she was continuing with Dorothy the same relationship
she had suffered in her own childhood: constant rejection.

She continued, "The first person I ever felt close to was
Dorothy. I loved her from the moment I met her and I still
do, even though she treats me terribly." She leaned toward
Dorothy and kissed her on the cheek. Dorothy pushed her away
and said, "Slob! Don't touch me!"

I asked Margaret, "Didn't you ever find a man you felt like
being close to? How come you never married?" "I never believed that anyone really loved me. Even though I was very
beautiful . . . Wasn't I beautiful, Dorothy?" Dorothy didn't
answer. She laughed cynically and looked up at the ceiling.
Margaret was obviously used to her cruelty and kept talking.

"Once I almost got married. He was a paraplegic from the
war. He loved me, but he had a terrible temper. I was so
afraid of that man. Could he holler!"

"How in the world could you feel threatened by a crippled
man in a wheel chair?" She ignored my question, so intent was
she in telling her story.

"I used to love wheeling him around the neighborhood. I
think he really loved me, but I backed out at the last minute. I
should have married him. He had a good government pension.

It would have been a good marriage for me. I wouldn't have had to bother with sex. He couldn't do anything because of his injury."

We talked about her sexual problems and she revealed the fact that she had a spastic condition of the vagina. The few times she had attempted normal coital union, it had been extremely painful and the man had been unable to enter her vagina. She resorted to oral intercourse and this had been the only sexual satisfaction she had ever known. Even this was rare because of her unattractive appearance. Her story revealed a great deal and concealed even more. It revealed her many problems, but concealed the greatest one of all, the fact that she was suffering unresolved homosexual desires.

She became very maudlin and sobbed, "It is too late for me now. I wasted my whole life. I am nothing. I have never been a sweetheart or a wife or a mother. No one ever loved me or wanted me." She was gushing tears and now Dorothy became tender, put her arms around her to comfort her. She rocked her in her arms like a mother with a small infant. Like a small infant, Margaret quieted down and then I noticed that Dorothy was also crying and they sat, huddled together in each other's arms, sobbing together. It was evident that a very profound kind of love existed between these two women on an emotional level. They supplied something missing in each others lives. Even though they insisted there had never been a sexual relationship between them in the past, I had a premonition that it still might happen in their future. As they left arm in arm, Dorothy was telling Margaret that she was now living all alone in a large house. She spoke of her loneliness since her children had married and her husband was dead. Margaret offered to move in with her to clean and keep house, and the last I heard from them, that was the conclusion to the story.

Whether they finally got into bed together and practiced lesbian techniques of lovemaking, I will never know. It is possible that they did. Who is to say that it is wrong for these two particular women at this late stage of their lives?

The time to make sure that they would lead normal heterosexual lives was at the stage of formation when both sets of parents made their original mistakes of judgment. Especially in the case of Margaret, who wasted her life in guilt and fear, the parents were directly at fault, if not consciously, then certainly by their own ignorance. If they had treated her budding femininity properly, she would have been confident enough to pass through the transitionary stage of homosexuality during her early teens and then happily transferred to love affairs with the opposite sex.

SEVEN

Premarital Sex Affairs

*All forms of sexual activity need to be better understood for their contribution to the growth of confidence in the non-*married woman. The sexual love affair is important as further preparation toward the ultimate goal of a happy marriage. The term "affair" is used here to describe a relationship that is not purely physical, but has some element of emotional closeness. To be considered helpful, an affair must be mutually satisfying. It should serve the needs of the woman as well as the man. She should participate not merely to please him, but to free herself of pent-up sexual tension.

For the majority of women it takes knowing a man for some time in order for her to relax sufficiently to make the sex act a joyful experience. Brief encounters sometimes have an adverse effect on her shaky sexual confidence. The average woman only begins to respond when she has had time to learn to trust her partner. In most cases where women have sex on short acquaintance they fake orgasm to please the man and are themselves left high and dry and unfulfilled.

Sexual love affairs are important to the maturity of a woman and are not to be equated with promiscuity. An affair is often an enduring association which prepares a woman for the more demanding role in marriage. Making love before marriage teaches her about her biological capabilities and can save her from many sexual mistakes later on. Sex among the unwed is no longer considered the greatest evil. Neither is marriage considered the solution to all a woman's sex problems. Marriage is not magic. A woman who enters marriage with her sexual problems unresolved, brings to the marriage burdens that could have been worked out prior to marriage. It has been observed that if people have some sex experience before marriage, they are more inclined to settle down and be faithful when married. Marital fidelity is becoming more and more of a rarity. If there were more pre-marital affairs, perhaps there would be less extramarital affairs.

Is Romance Necessary

A fallacy about unmarried sex is that romantic love must always be an essential part of it. This myth must be exploded like the empty balloon that it is, if women are to become truly emancipated. The inflated sentiment that only "true love" is able to turn a woman on has kept women in the Puritanical refrigerator.

When a woman is obsessed with a "right and wrong" standard of rules, she places crushing limits on the ability of her
body to function. Having been indoctrinated with the idea that
her body was designed primarily to preserve the species, she
may turn down copulation with disgust unless she is legally
married. After marriage this sort of woman merely tolerates
sex anyway, doing her wifely duties within the confines of the
marital straitjacket, which she has bought for herself at the
price of her freedom to explore. If a woman can train herself
to enjoy the pleasures of guiltless, joyful coitus before marriage just for the fun of it, as men do, she will certainly make a
better wife when she does get married. For one thing, she will
not be troubled about her normalcy or her desirability. So many
married women suffer from these feelings if they have not had
the assurance that premarital love-making brings to a woman.

I think that it is about time to de-bunk, kick out of the hay,
all the old-style Calvinistic barriers set up to keep women
from enjoying equal status with men in the sex act. It's time
for them to participate in sex simply for the enjoyment of it.
No excuses should be necessary to justify pure pleasure.
Women must not let obsolete taboos about marriage rob them
of the right to satisfy the natural demands of their bodies.

Because sex is more easily available to everyone than it ever
was before, many affairs lack the kind of stability that women
find so comforting in a close man-woman relationship. Being
caught in a circle of constantly changing bed companions can
have a devastating effect on a sensitive woman. She strives for
a sustained, meaningful love affair with the hope that it will
eventually lead to marriage. In most affairs, the man wants
sex and the woman wants marriage. She doesn't always get
it, but she stands a better chance if she is a warm, sexually
responsive person.

Joyful Anticipation of Sex

If a young woman has not been too badly inhibited by her early upbringing, she may approach her first affair anticipating a joyful experience. That exceptional girl who has been permitted to glide easily through all her earlier stages without traumatic shake-ups has a good chance of shaping up as an adequate female, adequate both for her own needs and her lover's. A normal young woman should look forward to sex as the high point in a continuing chain of life's discoveries.

In the past few years a great many of the traditional barriers have crumbled and the new generation of young women are eager to be treated as first class citizens both in and out of marriage. They seek, through sexual equality, a more meaningful, larger life-scale. Encouraged by the more permissive climate, many younger women have become assertive, reaching out to claim their birthright. There is a definite lessening of parental control over teenagers. Where parents resist, and insist on Victorian standards of behavior, girls retaliate by simply leaving home. The attempt to restrain has the opposite effect. Rather than acting as a deterrent, it serves as a propellant, pushing them into the mainstream of sexual experimentation, sometimes before they are really ready.

Compared with just one short generation ago, it seems that girls these days are living an extraordinarily free and sexually liberated life. That is the way it appears on the surface, but deeper probings reveal all is not well. Direct discussions with these girls makes it clear that they may be exploring and experimenting, but that they seldom are discovering the answers to the problems of sexual inadequacy. This is especially true of the numerous sexually active teenage girls who leave home seeking love and adventure. Very young girls engage in sex primarily because of their infantile need to belong to another person. There is a wide gap between the sexual readiness of teenage boys and teenage girls.

The First Experience

In the large majority of cases, young girls do not respond during their first sexual encounter. They are usually disappointed, yet they try again and again. They change partners hoping that will help. It doesn't, because their problem cannot be solved by outside stimulation. With each new disappointment they sink deeper and deeper into sexual "vegetablism," caught in the trap of being used as an object, a non-functioning receptacle.

These days girls are usually not seduced by their boyfriends. Very often it is the other way around. The "now" generation of teenagers initiates and encourages their own seduction by making themselves readily available.

Some of them resort to drugs of all kinds in their search for a sexual "high." While some young girls report that smoking marijuana makes them more responsive, others claim the opposite effect. It parallels the use of alcohol in many ways, in that the mood that a person is in when partaking of the stimulant is the mood which is intensified by its use. Neither drugs nor alcohol hold the answer to sexual health. There is no instant panacea. The solution lies dormant in the mind of every female with sexual problems.

Although most young girls are shocked and repulsed by the

growing trend toward group sex parties, they often go along with their young man in the fear that if they seem less than eager they will be considered cold and sexless. They fear losing the boy to someone who may be warmer and more willing.

Just as with a boy, a girl's first sexual experience is tremendously important to her and can set the mood for future sexual behavior. Unfortunately, it usually turns out to be a disappointment. Not just young girls, but women of all ages go through all sorts of emotional games with their lovers before rationalizing themselves into participating in coitus. They most often use the excuse of "being in love" to sanction the act. If she cannot muster any romantic feeling herself, a woman may tell herself that the man is so sincerely in love with her, wants her so badly, that somehow it is all right.

It is rare that a young girl engages in sexual intercourse because of her own physical desires. When she is a virgin, it is even rarer for her to feel strong sensual pleasure. She is so mentally and emotionally involved with the experience that her body reflexes take a back seat. A girl in love uses a veil of romanticism to cover over her imbedded guilt and tells herself that she is doing it to make her boyfriend happy.

Anti-Sexual Blocks

Many young girls, though sexually frigid, are at the same time warm and demonstrative. When you consider that her sexuality has been lying dormant since infancy, it is not surprising that she finds it difficult to freely enjoy her body. She begins to wonder why her genitals remain unaroused and unsatisfied in spite of the fact that her emotional feelings are so strong.

The anti-sexual blocks erected all through her childhood have become a rigid wall, standing in the way of her fulfillment. Pity the frustrated young man who tries to make love to her; for no amount of petting or foreplay can arouse her. Neither variation of technique nor lover moves her. Outside cures do not solve her inside-of-herself problem. The idea that something is physically wrong seeps into the unconscious thinking of many girls as time after time they are left sexually ungratified. Often a girl will discuss it with her physician and find that there is nothing organically wrong. Sometimes she blames her lover or, worse still, gets the notion that it is congenital, that she inherited a frigid type of body. She worries that perhaps her mother was genetically deficient and, therefore, she must be that way too. She becomes anxious, wonders if she is capable of improving. Sometimes she tries too hard and that doesn't work either, or she just gives up and sublimates her sex drive into other channels such as work or raising her family.

The purpose of this book is to assure every woman that *sexual problems that have become physical were first implanted psychologically*. The second half of this book will show you that anything which has been learned can be unlearned and supplanted with correct information. Negative reactions to sexual stimuli give way to the positive force of a good sex experience. Good experiences soon begin to happen when a woman learns how to assume some of the responsibility for her behavior and then set about to alter that behavior. She can have a powerful effect on her own progress by removing her invisible wall of frigidity, brick by brick, just the way that it was constructed.

Is Sex Sinful?

The most common obstacle, among single women, to good sex is a deep-rooted sense of wrong-doing. The unmarried woman still carries in the back alleys of her mind the idea that sex is supposed to be for married women only, to be performed only with the legally wedded spouse. This obsolete hangover from another era should be treated like an old battered hat, tossed out to make room for something more appropriate to the time we live in. Men no longer expect to marry virgins. Most of them prefer a girl with some sex knowledge and experience. These days it is customary to expect that when a couple marries, not only will the groom have had some previous sexual experience, but the bride will also have shopped around a bit so that she knows what she wants.

However, pre-marital affairs do not always serve the purpose for which they are intended. Because sexual affairs are often beclouded with sentimentality and super-romanticism, a woman holds back instinctual animal feelings rather than detract from her "virginal princess" image. As we have stressed before, she suffers great apprehension about the possibility of pregnancy. This is true whether she takes "the Pill" or not. Somehow the message of being punished for sex pleasure by an unwanted pregnancy has a powerful impact on her libido. A single fearful thought about conception can throw cold water on emerging genital warmth and cause her to be wary, watchful and self-protective rather than freely passionate. Fear makes it impossible to be carried away by instinctual desire, fear of pregnancy and fear that in the process of losing her control during orgasm, her partner will also lose his and ejaculate prematurely.

Pregnancy-Punishment

The female has been programmed to expect to suffer as a result of sexual liberty. She is apt to worry that in giving in to the pleasurable feeling she will also be surrendering her restraint. She brings with her into the sexual act a dread of the consequences of an unwanted pregnancy. She has been indoctrinated with the expectation that she will be punished for her sexual wrong-doing.

I spoke to a girl recently who had just had an abortion. She was very bitter about the pain and anxiety associated with it, and she had had to spend more than one thousand dollars for it, without any financial assistance from the man, who disclaimed paternity. She could not take him to court for legal redress because she feared exposure. It was necessary for her to travel to another state, where abortions are legally performed, in order to have the proper environs of a hospital room.

In many states of the United States the abortion laws are still antiquated and cause a great deal of unnecessary heartache to the girl who unwittingly becomes pregnant. In the face of these cruel, unnatural laws against their very lives, millions of women throughout the world struggle to find some way to abort what should not have been conceived originally.

Feeling desperately that a particular pregnancy is detrimental to them, they drive themselves in search of relief and each year between 5,000 and 10,000 women die needlessly from lack of the proper kind of abortion. In affluent America, which leads the world in all sorts of technical skills, young girls die at the clumsy hands of midwives and self-proclaimed abortion doctors. This huge underground of illegal surgery is supported by some of the most respectable families, whose wives and daughters are not immune to unwanted pregnancies any more than the poorest woman.

In the latest report of the President's Commission on Crime, it is cited that the enforcement of these obsolete, slave-society abortion laws cost the United States taxpayers $120,000,000 yearly. To how much better use could this money be put than in forcing women to abide by sexual servitude laws passed and enacted a century ago? $120,000,000 could go far in providing the proper sex education for young women so that their lives would not be placed in jeopardy every time they accidentally conceive. These death-dealing laws, which make abortion a criminal offense punishable by jail and imprisonment, *were put into the law before women had the right to vote*!

These laws made by men force women into endless pregnancy and child care. In many states it is illegal for a woman to have an abortion even if she has been raped, or made pregnant by a member of her own family. Abortion laws treat a woman's body with less humane consideration than the laws of the American Society for the Prevention of Cruelty to Animals. As things stand now in most of the United States and in most of the rest of the world, a woman has to face the chance of bearing an unwanted child or give up having sex.

In spite of the fact that we have made some progress in the

last ten years toward solving the problem of prevention of pregnancy, the real solution has not yet been forthcoming. Any sensible woman who thinks, will arrive at the conclusion that contraception should take place at the original site of sperm manufacture, with the male himself.

Contraception

The much heralded "Pill," which promised to be a boon to all womankind has been a disappointment. It has produced some hazardous side effects, the full impact of which is still unknown. Its effect on unborn, future generations remains a mystery and more and more girls are avoiding it and resorting once again to older and not so dependable methods.

A solution to this problem lies in scientific research. The magic key to its discovery is the same magic key which brings other great discoveries to light—the magic of the dollar sign. Money in sufficient quantity must be allotted to this all-important lifesaving research. The vast majority of American women of childbearing age have been grist in the abortion mills at least once in their lives. This is the monstrous shadow that hangs over every single woman when she agrees to sexual union. Men must become conscious of the cruel inequity and help in changing the laws of our nation, which not only burden the woman, but the man also who is made to suffer in this ridiculous mockery of lovemaking. Because of the absence of health laws to protect the unmarried pregnant woman and the equally backward level of their own understanding of contraception, each year the rate of illegitimate births increases.

Still, sexual love does go on and no amount of fear of pregnancy stops it. Until such time as proper contraception is provided to all who desire it, young women will be forced to try to function without all of their cylinders in action.

Sexual affairs affect each other in sequential order. Each is linked to the next by a conditioned habit pattern. The woman must avoid repeating sexual activities which lead to dead ends. She must also avoid selecting the kind of male partners who inevitably lead her to sexual failure because of their own ineptness and lack of positive experiences.

Is Frigidity Caused by Men?

When a girl keeps going back to the sort of male who is inconsiderate of her needs she is telling herself, "It's his fault. It's not because I don't respond. He is the bad lover, not me." She must be alert to the "copout" on her part in failing to face up to the reality of her own sexual hang-ups. What happens to the male lover when he fails to satisfy his partner? Very often he is left equally frustrated, in addition to having feelings of guilt and inadequacy. There are many men who spend their entire lives straining to help their women have orgasms. Many of them become physically and emotionally ill from the struggle. They have been impressed with the idea that to be a real man, one must make sure that the female has her orgasm before he can relax and enjoy his. Although this book is primarily written to give council to women, in fairness to men, it should be pointed out *in most cases a woman's sexual failure is not the man's fault.* Even though some men are clumsy and inadequate lovers, they can be taught to be better if a woman is adequate herself and doesn't expect him to provide all the stimulus in the sexual act. Many men lose patience with the slow rate of arousal that most women have, and fall into the unhappy trap of merely using women for their own sexual relief.

It is the biological nature of man that once he is aroused to the point of orgasm, he must follow through. Women must recognize that it is most often their own inability to make use of their sexual apparatus, that it is their own anti-natural climatic resistance that keeps them from orgasm. Only when a woman has developed the inherent skill of sensory control can she free herself and her partner to reach the high potential of ecstasy that is lying dormant within her.

It is up to the liberated, fully functioning, feminine females to take the onus off the suffering, much maligned male lover. She should be able to take herself over the peak of orgastic feeling once he has done his job of effective preliminary stimulation. It is unfair to expect a man to bring about two orgasms, his own and his female partner's. Most men suppose, judging by the mass of books which stress this concept, that a woman's sexual success depends on him. Most men have accepted the idea that it is their skill as a lover which determines whether or not the woman they are making love to will be frustrated or satisfied. Many men have suffered an unwarranted assault on their manliness by the frigid resistance that they have encountered. IT IS TIME MEN WERE RELIEVED OF THIS GUILT.

The greatest lover in the world could not warm up a woman whose mind has been rigidly computerized to send messages to her genitals to stay cool. Negative conditioning over a period of years causes the mind to transfer automatic signals of resistance to her sexual organs. The straining and striving of a man cannot by itself overcome this long conditioning that sex is wrong.

A man is naive if he believes that a woman's ability to reach orgasm depends entirely on what he says or does. If this were true, women would come off a lot better than they do because, by and large, *men are a lot better lovers than women are responders*. All that a woman should expect of a man is that he function normally and be tender and thoughtful to her needs.

The Normal Man

Stripping aside all the variables for the moment, what are the normal requirements of a man? What are his physical and emotional responsibilities as a lover?

A. A Man Must Be Considered Normal If:

1. He can take as much time as the woman needs in order for her to become fully aroused. This could range anywhere from ten minutes to an hour. During this stage it is not important to the woman whether he sustains an erection or not. In fact, many women feel less pressured if he does not make his own needs apparent, but instead focuses his attention on her own stimulation.

2. He should be able to maintain his erection long enough so that it is there at the right time for insertion into the vagina. (It has been found that over-indulgence in alcohol acts as a deterrent, rather than a stimulant to good sexual performance.) Every man knows his limits and should abide by them if he wishes to function as a normal lover. Drunkenness turns most women off.

3. He must be able to sustain his erection, after insertion into the vagina, long enough to allow his partner to reach her orgasm first, if she so desires. Many women can reach orgasm after about five minutes of penile penetration. Others may need as long as a half hour. Still others cannot reach orgasm at all with the penis inside the vagina. They may need outside manipulation of the clitoris. This is not the male's problem, though he may wish to help his woman with her problem.

4. He must be uninhibited enough to try various techniques of arousal and methods of intensifying orgastic sensation. He must be free of squeamishness about the female body. These days it is considered normal for males to practice cunnilingism and many women have become conditioned to it in order to reach orgasm. Although it is often expected, it is not a prerequisite to male normalcy.

5. A man is considered to have a normal-sized penis if it measures from three to seven inches when erect. The size of the flaccid resting penis is not an indication of its size when aroused. Men who appear to have a very small penis before arousal can double and in some cases even triple its size when sexually excited.

Effect of Age on a Man's Virility

In a survey recently conducted among men aged 18 to 50 years, it was found that the length of time they could maintain an erection varied from five minutes to an hour. One of the startling facts revealed is that while there is a tendency for the length of endurance to diminish with age, this is only in relation to the individual man's original capacity for virility. For example, a man who as a teenager was able to maintain an erection for an hour might still be able to sustain the erection at age 65 for fifteen minutes or more.

On the other hand, another man whose erection lasted for fifteen minutes as a youth, might be reduced to perhaps three to five minutes. A great deal depends on the general health and vitality of the individual man. How he eats, how he sleeps, and the stress and tensions of his work are all contributing factors in his sexual well-being. There are many men who even as newly-weds desire sex as infrequently as once a month. There are otherwise robust young men who can only keep an erection for a few moments.

Normalcy Varies With:

Physical structure (general health and vitality)

Environment (country, locality, climate, etc.)

Genetic inheritance (what the parents and grandparents handed down)

If a man is able to satisfy the woman of his choice in any way that they mutually decide, for all intents and purposes, he can consider himself *normal*. If he wants to be a super kind of lover above and beyond what is expected, he can cultivate his timing and improve his self-control, and be especially thoughtful of her wishes.

Sexual intercourse is the human function which cannot lie. It exposes both men and women to the glare of their own personal reality. It reveals all of the secrets that we conceal by clothing. It strips bare our mannerisms and the superficialities of living. When pent-up passions are released, many hidden problems are also freely exhibited. Sex has a most direct way of sweeping aside surface phoniness, forcing us to see ourselves as we really are. It dramatically demonstrates to a woman what her man is and what his hang-ups are. It also lets him know what bothers her in a profound sense. Character traits show themselves. Tenderness flowers or is sadly lacking. Selfishness asserts itself, as does insecurity and lack of self-esteem. Cruelty, fear, guilt, sadism and masochism are all uncovered. A person's entire life is often capsuled in the course of copulation. Behavior which in the ordinary course of the day might be overlooked, comes glaringly to the foreground. Sex is not only a catharsis, it is also the proving ground for maturity and self-understanding.

This isn't true just of the male, women also reveal their backgrounds and personality hang-ups in the bedroom. Many of them bring to the coital union merely the shell of a female body. Frequently, they assume that if they are merely present, that is all that is required of them as sex partners. Before blaming men, women should check on their own normalcy and then proceed to eliminate the obstacles to their full participation.

Although no two authorities agree on what is "normal," here is a collection of thoughts which reflect the consensus.

A Woman Is Considered Normal If:

1. She has passed through all of the vital stages of her sexual development without guilt or shame, and is physically, as well as emotionally, mature.

2. She demonstrates a strong desire for sex with some regularity. Normal range of frequency of desire can be anywhere from several times a night

to several times a month. The wide variation is due to the extremes of tension in even normal female responsiveness.

3. She participates with joy and abandon in both the foreplay and the actual coital union. She should welcome variations and herself initiate new techniques.

4. She should be ready for orgasm from five to fifteen minutes after the insertion of the penis into her vagina. She should feel orgastic sensation not only in the clitoris, but in the tissue surrounding the vaginal vestibule. She should not be dependent on a single form of stimulation (such as cunnilingus) for reaching a climax.

5. She should assist her lover in maintaining his erection by manipulation or oral stimulation, if he so desires.

6. She can accept the concept of sex without guilt and permit herself to enjoy it purely for pleasure.

A normal woman is one who can relax sexually, blissfully secure that orgasm will take place easily if she so desires. It is also perfectly normal if a woman can function sexually without the accompaniment of romantic feelings of love. When women get to the stage of being sexually guiltless, they will be able to satisfy their sex needs just for its own good sake. Although it shouldn't be necessary to be in love for good sex, a romantic love can add a special dimension to the coital union, above and beyond body needs. Romantic love can add great excitement and raise sexual feeling to the heights of ecstasy. When a man "romances" he enhances the sexual experience for the female. But, it does not necessarily help her to reach orgasm. Many single women feel freer with a man that they don't care about particularly. They tend to hold back with a man they are seriously interested in. When they consider that a man might be marriage material, they often resort to Victorian prudishness in fear that if they let themselves go sexually, he might judge them to be less than "the nice girl that men marry." A woman may actually become passive, submissively frigid, to the one she loves and respond better to a man she cares little about because with him she is not concerned about her reputation. When she has sex with a man she is trying to impress, she often goes out of her way to see that he is satisfied without regard to her own needs. She blocks herself out in her eagerness to bait the marriage trap with a virtuous bride.

This sexual fakery is bound to lead to disappointment for both of them. The unreal, acted-out orgasm is very common among women of all ages. It doesn't help in winning a man. It makes his male ego less secure rather than bolstering it because most men sense the difference between the ostentatious orgasm and the actual thing. He is bound to know that she held back in spite of his expressed and demonstrated consideration for her sexual happiness.

Some Women Expect the Impossible

There are frigid women both in and out of marriage who can tax the strength and patience of the strongest most virile man. The human organic limitation of the male means nothing to them. A frigid woman brings nothing to the sex act but her problems, forcing the unfortunate man to assume her hang-ups in addition to any he may have himself. On the other hand, a woman who has successfully passed through the vital stages of her sexual development can not only bring herself to a satisfactory climax when effectively stimulated, but can also help her lover to become a more virile and self-gratifying male.

The unsure woman often causes a man to become unsure of himself, lose his erection, and behave in a less satisfying way than he might normally. Many a neurotic woman has been the reason for a man to become psychologically castrated. Premarital affairs are the time to discover and correct problems. With kindness and mutual tenderness each partner should evolve to a higher level of happiness as the relationship develops. When this happens, a young woman will become ready to enter marriage with confidence, secure in the knowledge of her own functional health, and not dependent on what her husband will do for her.

EIGHT

Married Sex

---

*The security and permanency of a happy marriage can be the
greatest satisfaction in human life for both a man and a*
woman. Within its context of enduring companionship, a
woman should be at her most relaxed and able to function sexually at her best. A mutually satisfying marriage in which
both partners share all of life's experiences, sexually and otherwise, is what most women dream about from childhood on.
Few women like living alone. They long to belong to and to be
part of a family group. They are strongly propelled by nature's
drive for procreation. Like all other female animals, they
strive toward motherhood, biologically spurred from the beginning of their menstrual cycle.

From the time of the onset of their menses girls are physically ready to have mature sex and motherhood, but nature is blocked by convention. There is an average span of ten years when the needs of the female body are shunted aside and young women are forced to wait until marriage. While the body cries out that it is ready, society forces it to wait a decade. If it were not for the taboos of propriety, females would follow their natural urges between the ages of ten and fifteen years. The shutting off of the sexual outlet during this period of female maturation is the most destructive thing that happens to the female sex drive. Some women take the "no-no's," "don'ts," and "you musn'ts" literally and avoid marriage altogether. When they do bypass it, they are never really content, neither physically nor emotionally. They frantically pursue careers, occupations, avocations, work in various organizations, while frantically pursuing the elusive Mr. Right, whom they do not recognize if and when they find him. All the surface scurrying about is a cover up for the larger striving toward complete sex fulfillment.

Sexual Ignorance

For a woman to be truly prepared for the kind of consummate union that marriage is, she must first eliminate her own sexual ignorance. She must educate herself in the only way that anybody learns anything, and that is by experience. Learning should take place before marriage in order to avoid the stressful conditions that are a direct result of the lack of marital know-how. Unfortunately, neither parents nor the schools provide the kind of education that a marrying woman needs. So she must take up the slack and educate herself by herself. There is no point in forever bemoaning the mistakes that parents made. To do so is to confine oneself to walking an endless treadmill of sexual non-identity, searching for the answer outside instead of inside.

It is foolish to think that a husband, no matter how skilled a lover, will be able to correct all the errors in his wife's early sexual training. To expect him to arouse her from complete lethargy to exalted feeling simply because he is now married to her, is extremely unrealistic. Investigation of thousands of marriages reveals that the odds are against his being able to overcome the backlog of accumulated negative reflexive behavior, unless she does her part.

In order to assure a lasting marriage a wife should have had elementary sex schooling. It also helps if she graduates from the college of pre-marital knowledge. Only then is she ready for the post-graduate demands of marriage. These are the prerequisites that teach her to understand herself and how her sexual machinery functions under all sorts of situations.

One should not expect a man to make a woman out of a child. That is not his responsibility. Many marriages fall apart in this attempt. If a woman marries with a strongly developed sexual identity, she will bring to the union her own fair share of joy and confidence. When you consider the overwhelming weight of responsibilities placed on the shoulders of men throughout their lifetime, it is no wonder that they often succumb to the pressures and die almost ten years sooner than women. Not only must the male provide the economic security for the entire family, but in addition he carries the psychic burden of keeping his wife happy under all circumstances. Women who clamor for equal status should be listened to by

men and assisted in their aims. It could prove to be the answer
to extending the male life-span.

A complete woman, one who is ready for marriage, is also
a person who is ready to help herself improve. If she has sexual expertise, she can even help her husband to raise his own
sexual performance to a higher level. The experience which
outside pre-marital affairs provide makes her a better wife
and lover and more understanding of the problems of the male.

Disappointing Marriages

That most women enter marriage without being fully mature is attested to by the number of unhappy marriages. At
least one out of three marriages ends in divorce, and the figures keep rising. Of the remaining two thirds, half of these
marriages are merely tolerated by one or both partners. Very
often a bad marriage is endured for economic reasons. Women
hang on for a meal-ticket and some men feel it's cheaper to
stay married than to pay alimony. Concern about the children
involved and religious guilt also hold some shaky marriages
together. Suffering while sticking it out is detrimental to
all concerned, especially to the children, who sense the tension in such a situation.

The importance of good sex in marriage cannot be overes-
timated. Men know this. This is a basic reason why men get
married in the first place. Unfortunately, it is more important
to men than it is to women and there lies the rub. A recent
report based on thirty years' study involving about 6,000
couples shows there is a strong disparity in sexual interest between the male and female. This is cited as the reason for

failure in seventy-five per cent of American marriages. "When a couple gaze into each other's eyes with what they think is love and devotion, they are not seeing the same thing," says Dr. Clifford Rose Adams of Penn State University, consultant for the *Encyclopedia Britannica*. In findings presented to the Identity Research Institute in Washington, D.C., Dr. Adams suggests that out of six important factors in a successful marriage, sex ranks second in importance with men, and way down in the last category with women.

"Companionship is the first subconscious factor influencing the male in mate selection," says Adams. "Then in order, come sex, love-affection-sentiment as a single category, home and family, a helpmate to give encouragement, and lastly, security."

For women, the first factor is love-affection-sentiment. She first of all has to feel loved and wanted. The second is security, then companionship, home and family, community acceptance, and *last of all, sixth on the list, SEX.*

"So you see, men and women do not see eye to eye. How can marriages, under these circumstances, last?"

The obvious answer is that they do not. Adams says that the last available government statistics show that 28 percent of all marriages end in divorce. But, he points out, this figure is apt to be misleading.

"If you take into account annulments and desertions, which are not included in the statistics, the figure would be nearer forty per cent. Add to this what we call the morbidity marriage where a man and woman may continue to live with each other just for appearances or convenience while actually hating each other, and you find that only about 25 percent of marriages are really happy. The other 75 percent are a bust."

Adams, whose research includes interviews with college undergraduates as far back as 1939, says the third year after marriage is the biggest divorce year. Half of all divorces take place within seven years from when two people say, "I do". He points out that the basic problem is that men are more interested in sex than women and says, "Wives are inclined to be cold. Some wives had to experiment with another man to find proper adjustment."

In another survey of reasons that motivate men to marry, the following answers were given:

I thought it was about time I settled down.

I got tired of running around looking for sex.

She attracted me sexually so I thought I was in love.

. . . I was getting on in years, so I figured it was about time. . .

Men get regular meals and the advantages of having their clothes taken care of.

Women, on the contrary, stressed the need for love and romantic feeling above all else.

Adolescent Hang-Ups

A woman very often develops strong romantic feelings for a man on short acquaintance. Her feelings cannot be based on what he actually is, but rather on what she wishes he will turn out to be. Because girls are raised with the notion that only "true love" makes sex clean, they overemphasize being loved. If she has not had a free adolescence with its full share of necking, petting, romance and sentimentality, she will carry these unresolved needs into the marriage. Most wives nag their husbands for constant affirmations of love. This clamoring for emotional assurance is a nuisance to many husbands. If they are wise, they know that this neurotic behavior is a result of a wife's inability to reach sexual satisfaction. The repetitive demands for reassurance as to her desirability can, and often does, turn him in another direction. If a woman enters marriage with this problem unresolved, she will be emotionally vulnerable to the slightest, imagined act of rejection.

Romantic love alone makes a flimsy foundation for matrimony and such unions are doomed to collapse. When strangers marry they soon discover that their rose-colored visions of each other pale in the harsh glare of reality. As a couple lives together and grows to know each other, they become more and more disillusioned. The imagined wishful thinking qualities of the other person seem to vanish, and they see each other in shocked dismay. Rather than the wonderful person they each imagined the other to be, they now begin to notice characteristics that they abhor. Unless a man and woman get to know each other intimately over a period of at least several months, (a year is preferable) they marry each other while hiding behind deceptive masks. When the masks drop away and their real selves emerge, they risk not only disliking the other stranger, but what is even worse, being deadly bored with each other's company. They seem to grow duller and less attractive with each passing day.

Boredom

Many marriages break up because people become "sick and tired," bored to death with the sameness of each other. Too much togetherness robs many a marriage of its erotic excitement. Partners become satiated with each other. Everyday mannerisms can become everyday irritants. Spending too much time together is risking over-exposure, both mentally and physically. It is a wise wife who finds interests outside of her home and by so doing holds onto her personal dignity, and a bit of feminine mystery as well. It helps in keeping the home fires burning a little longer.

The great complaint of divorcing wives is that their husbands cheated sexually. It is small wonder that a husband cheats when a wife is neurotically frigid, and the majority of American wives are. The husband becomes frustrated and rebels against the stifling monotony of sex with a woman who contributes no excitement to the union. She may be elegant looking, manage his home and money excellently, but be boring and dull in bed, and for a man, *sex comes first.*

Paradoxically, some marriages last longer via the route of less togetherness. I am neither recommending it, nor do I feel any moral bias against it, but reports indicate that a certain amount of infidelity seems to add a spark of excitement to some otherwise dying marriages. There are increasing numbers of couples who engage in mate-swapping, group-sex and just plain old-fashioned mutual cheating. Changes are taking place in man-woman relationships and strict dogmatic insistence on monogamous marriage is on its way out. Many wives go along with their husbands' desires for mate-swapping in order to discourage his promiscuity outside the marriage.

The inability of the husband to satisfy his wife, and general sexual boredom, pushes many married couples to trying less conventional ways to resolve their problems. Communal sex, wife-swapping, group orgies, are no longer considered shocking to the suburban housewife. It is common practice in small towns as well as big cities to take one's wife to a "swinger's party" where a husband may switch partners and leave his wife to her own devices. It's one way for a husband to relieve himself of the handicap of a frigid or near-frigid wife. All of these diversions are wasted on most wives with sex problems because *no one on the outside can correct what troubles them on the inside of their subconscious thinking about sex.*

There would be less *extra-marital* promiscuity, couples would be inclined to keep their intimacies exclusive if there were, in the first place, sufficient *pre-marital* sexual adventure. When an extra-marital affair is a casual indiscretion it does not affect a marriage seriously, and most wives will forget and forgive. On the other hand, it can make a shaky marriage break up when the attachments become more than just physical.

Where mutual sexual satisfaction does exist in a marriage, each new sex experience acts as a regenerating force and improves the next experience. Good sex is energizing. A complete deep orgasm revitalizes a woman, makes her awaken in the morning cheerful and more kindly disposed to her husband and family. When women fail to enjoy sexual intercourse to the point of being able to reach an orgasm, *it is reflected in everything they do, all day long.* They don't necessarily show their disappointment overtly. Lots of frustrated wives don't get angry—they just "get even." They become the chronic nags harassed husbands have complained about since time immemorial. Dissatisfactions push their husbands to seek a solution outside of their marriage. Single women are plentiful in the major cities and many of them have no scruples about dating married men. For the wife, however, it's not that easy because she usually doesn't have the confidence in her body responses.

When women are totally lacking in sexual self-image, they become passive, submissive servants to their husbands. They are afraid to break away from the marriage entirely because they realize that their problem of sexual incompatability will go with them no matter what new man they may find in the future.

The Search For Equal Status

Many women are searching for answers to the confusion that exists, not only in the lack of harmony within themselves, but in the great confusion peculiar to women as a group. Many learned women feel that the only answer to women functioning properly sexually lies in their complete emancipation as oppressed people. The growing movement of feminists argues that true female liberation can only come when women are liberated economically, politically, and socially. They feel that frigidity has its base in women's resentment against being used as love objects. This is a new breed of women dedicated to the idea that they must destroy entrenched social customs which, they claim, have shackled them for centuries. They insist that the institution of marriage needs drastic overhauling. Many leading sociologists agree in principle, but differ as to the approach to the overhauling.

The feminist position on marriage is as follows:

Marriage is a form of slavery, perpetuating the oppression of women by treating them as a lesser partner.

Marriage and the raising of a family, as they have

been known, are becoming obsolete, no longer suited
to the tempo of the times we live in.

The male supremacist (this includes husbands) must
be toppled from his omnipotent position as the pivot
of the universe.

Women must be liberated from their subservient
roles as wives, mothers, and houseworkers. Wives
should be paid a salary for work done in the home.

They stress that marriage causes housewives to live a
parasitic existence, enmeshed in trivia, forcing their
minds into a state of boredom and their bodies into
inertia.

Although much of what they say is true, they tend to place
the blame for their inequality on the entire population of
males and by so doing retard their own progress. They chas-
tise even the poor, overworked husband who earns the money
the hard way to keep his wife in the "parasitic" existence of
which the feminists complain. It seems to me that we must
differentiate between the male who is in control of the rules
and regulations and the husband who himself is caught in the
web of life's inequities. If, instead of antagonizing all men,
women combined their efforts with the males who are also un-
fairly affected by lopsided marriage conventions, (such as alimony), they would stand a much better chance of reaching
their objective in the speediest way.

While all women may not agree with the revolutionary attitude of the feminist movement, there is no dispute about the
fact that *women are changing*! They may not know in which
direction to make their demands, but *they are demanding*.
They are asserting their desire to fulfill their potentialities as
human beings in every area of work, politics, marriage and

their freedom to function sexually—in and out of marriage.

Liberated Women Can Liberate Man

Men know that when a woman is happy and sexually fulfilled she can make her lover feel ten feet tall. Although some
men may fear the change in women as conflicting with their
male ego, this need not be so. It is the harassed, miserable,
unhappy women who are the enemies of men. Intelligent
women do not intend to take away anything from men. By en-
riching their own lives they will at the same time enrich the
lives of their husbands. We must all realize that we are all
human beings first, men and women afterward. The sexes have
more in common than in conflict. Liberated, fully completed
women do not present a challenge to men. On the contrary,
they offer men a higher level of living by sharing life with a
higher type of woman. If men, instead of ridiculing and re-
senting the new movement of women, will help them reach
their goals, these men will be truly loved in a very special way,
and will share in the joy resulting from such cooperation.

In spite of the rumblings in the structure of marriage, the
foundation of marriage is still very much with us and indications are that it will be here for some time to come. Even in
the numerous cases of young people pairing up and enjoying
sex without the sanction of the state, statistics show that they
do marry if the woman becomes pregnant. Even the most
anti-establishment person recognizes the unnecessary hardships
inflicted on a child that is born out of wedlock. Young people
are marrying. Many of them try each other out first and
there is nothing wrong with that. Perhaps the future divorce

statistics will appear a little less catastrophic because of their foresight.

The urge to mate is basic, and, believe it or not, scientists say that man is naturally monogamous. In various areas of the world, history shows times when men were polygamous due to a surplus of females. At other times and places, where there have been too many men in ratio to the female population, polyandry was practiced, which is the situation in reverse, (one wife, several husbands).

No matter how many wives or husbands human beings have in a lifetime, they prefer the companionship of the same partner for extended periods of time. Scientists cite humans as one of the species that practice "pair-bonding," which is the term used to describe the urge to form lasting relationships. In the all too rare cases where a married couple have a good sexual life and other mutual interests as well, marriage can and does last out their entire lifetimes. The deciding factor, which cannot be overemphasized, is the ability of the woman to fully respond sexually without putting undue strain upon her husband. Human beings do not marry for sexual intercourse alone. Marriage places mankind above all other animals in the mating game. The need for intellectual companionship, understanding, kindness, tenderness, makes homo sapiens different from all other animals. The ability to think and feel emotions makes them yearn for long-term liaisons. Let us keep in mind, it isn't the institution of marriage that is wrong, it's the unresolved problems that exist within its framework that cause it to fall apart. Sexual incompatibility looms as the giant obstacle to good happy marriage relationships, and the inadequacy is, in most cases, that of the woman.

Marriages Can Be Saved

Not all bad marriages are hopeless. If there is a sincere desire on the part of both people to save the marriage, very often they can do so. If the lines of communication have not been permanently severed, sometimes open discussion about their problems can lead to a solution. A wife who finds that she has sexual problems within her marriage should think twice about breaking it up. If she cannot find the answer inside of her marriage, chances of finding it outside of her marriage are slim. There is no "magic lover" waiting to give her instant satisfaction.

There are over twelve million divorced women in America, searching frantically, in most cases, for some sort of answer to the sexual disappointment that they found in marriage. They have dragged out of the marriage fifteen million confused children who, statistically, stand a poor chance of making their own marriages work. When women stop berating their husbands for their own inability to relate, they will be along the road to an answer to their problem.

When a man finds it a constant struggle to bring his wife to orgasm, when he finds that she feels no sensory response when he inserts his penis into her vagina, he will look around to find a woman who is easier to please. Propelled by a sense of inadequacy, he becomes easy bait for any sexually alive woman outside of his marriage. In most cases he would like to keep his marriage intact and still have the privilege of a good sex life. If a marriage has not drifted too far apart, a woman can very often save it by showing signs of sexual awakening.

She cannot fake it, because sooner or later sexual fakery exposes itself. Sexual intercourse is a subtle way of giving and taking love. The interplay of action and reaction causes people to see each other in a deeper dimension than in any other type of communication. When a wife can communicate improved sexual feeling through the flesh of her body, her husband may reevaluate the marriage and see her in a new light.

A long term liaison such as marriage demands that people be prepared to function with some finesse. Otherwise the marriage is really only a protracted testing ground in which both parties are carrying on a stage of development that should have taken place before marriage. If people have not had sufficient experimentation with sexual partners before marriage, they strive to resolve this lack during their marriage. They cheat. Marriage is supposed to be a union for mutual happiness, not a training ground for solving sexual problems.

A Wife's Sexual Frustration

Continuous sexual frustration has a very destructive effect upon a woman and she tends to complain of all sorts of nervous ailments which, upon first examination, appear not to be connected with the sexual experience. Symptoms of extreme physical stress may appear in any area of her body and seem to have no relationship to the genitals.

Bess R. was an interesting example of this problem. She telephoned me for a professional appointment stating that she needed help with a sleep problem. When she arrived she explained further, "I haven't slept through a single night in the last twenty years of my marriage. I keep waking up due to uncontrollable itching on my arms and neck." She showed me her arm which was covered with a mass of red bleeding welts. She said that during the course of twenty years of this affliction, she had visited many doctors, both here and in Germany where she was born and raised. None of them had been able to find anything organically wrong with Bess so she continued to suffer with her strange malady. Her purpose in coming to see me was to learn how to relax sufficiently in order to sleep through the night without mutilating herself.

Bess had emigrated to America with her husband when they were both about twenty years old. Although the itching problem was very slight at the beginning of her marriage, it had grown increasingly more troublesome. Most of the doctors had told her it was a "case of nerves." This seemed obviously true, considering that her nerves had never had the benefit of an orgasm in twenty years of marital living.

Consistent arousal without culmination had left her emotionally as well as physically irritated. At this point she had no awareness that her sexual life was at all connected with the skin problem. She cried as she described the unbearable suffering and embarrassment that the itching and scratching had caused her. Salves and skin lotions were to no avail; some of them had even aggravated the condition. During the day she managed to keep herself very busy. She was a commercial artist and worked in the advertising field. It was necessary for her to leave her desk several times during the day to go to the ladies room and scratch herself in private. She was forced to wear long sleeves and a high-necked dress to cover the unsightly appearance of her arms and neck.

Bess's may seem an extreme case, but skin rashes resulting from nervous tension are not uncommon. Many dermatologists will attest to the fact that large numbers of so-called "unexplainable" skin disorders are *psychosomatic* in origin, which simply means that a physician can find no physical cause. When the cause is not apparently biological (or somatic) it is assumed that emotions are at the root. One wonders if any of her doctors asked her about her sex life. Perhaps she would have thought it an intrusion at that time. Now she came to my studio regularly for lessons in auto-suggestion and relaxation techniques. She wanted desperately to be able to sleep through the night without mutilating herself. I taught her a series of mind/body exercises designed to help her drift peacefully into slumber. She was an apt pupil and almost from the first lesson there was some improvement in her insomnia and a lessening of the scratching habit. She had a long way to go, however. Her condition had existed for more than twenty years, so it was natural to expect that it might take several months of reconditioning to clear it up. When she had mastered the techniques of body relaxation (described in detail later in this book), she found not only an improvement in her skin, but an increased feeling of well-being generally. Then, as she continued the exercises, to her great surprise *there developed a remarkable increase in her sexual responsiveness*. Not only had the nerve endings in the surface skin of her body relaxed with the exercises, but so had the nerves in her genitals as well.

She was experiencing a delayed erotic awakening and, at the age of forty years, was just becoming a mature sexually-oriented female. One day she said, "You know, I feel sure that my sexual restraint caused my nervous itching." In all of the twenty long years of her marriage this woman had never had an orgasm. She explained that she had felt some slight clitoral excitation at times, but it had never resulted in any kind of release from erotic tension.

Bess was sophisticated in many ways, yet never had believed it possible for a woman to have vaginal sensation. At best she hoped to achieve some sort of clitoral climax. Her confusion about how her body worked was due to outdated books she had read as a young girl. She was such a shy person that it was impossible for her to discuss her sexual difficulties with her husband. Fakery was the name of the game that she played. It may have relieved her husband of his guilt, but it didn't relieve her of her own tension. She was the kind of withdrawn woman who had no close women friends, and even if she had, I doubt if she would have felt free to talk to them about her sex life. As a matter of fact, very few women confide their sex problems even to their closest friends.

Outwardly, Bess had become resigned to the idea that nothing could be done; that she would have to go along with their one-sided sex arrangement, but her body rebelled. Her skin cried out in anguish, as her body could stand it no longer and the skin rash resulted.

After several months of diligently practicing the techniques of relaxation and reconditioning, she was able to give up the skin scratching and replace it with normal sexual feeling. She became so skilled at focusing sensation in the genital area that at the present time she is able to have a *complete vaginal internal orgasm*. Her life has taken on more meaning. Not only is she a more cheerful, outgoing person, but her general health has improved vastly as well. She is filled with the kind of exalted energy that only total sexual fulfillment can give a woman.

A Happier Husband

If there were a yardstick to measure delight, I would say that Bess's husband was even more delighted than she was. He was in his early forties and suddenly her new found sexuality made him feel like more of a man than he ever imagined himself to be. Although Bess thought she was keeping her frigidity a secret, men are not that easy to fool. Her husband always saw through her pretenses of making believe that she enjoyed his sexual advances. He assumed that she put on an act of having orgasm to protect his masculine ego. He also, incorrectly, assumed that she did so to keep him from learning the truth about his own sexual inadequacy.

As the years went by, Bess's husband had grown more and more depressed about his inability to help her respond. Her nighttime itching and scratching had become a source of great distress to him also, and had greatly affected his ability to work properly. Now a new life was opening up not only for her, but for him as well.

We must consider Bess an example of the old school of sexual ignorance; she was conditioned by the prevailing code of her generation to believe that *sex is mainly a man's pleasure.* One may argue that women are more knowledgeable these days. Obviously there is greater sexual freedom and more opportunity to learn the facts of life than when Bess was a girl. While it is true that we are seeing some sort of sexual revolution for women, like all revolutions, it has brought with it great confusion and resentments. Women divide their resentments and anger between parents as a group and men as the sex that is in charge.

A Real "Swinger"

Let's take a look at a member of the younger generation, a supposedly liberated female. Let's consider Lucille, who came to see me in order to learn the art of auto-suggestion to cut down on her excessive smoking (which included marijuana). She wasn't primarily concerned about the marijuana, but about the three packs of cigarettes she had been smoking each day.

At the time I worked with her she was about twenty and had been married for a few months. After working with her for a while she suddenly blurted out that she was having her marriage annulled. I suggested that maybe she was being hasty, that after all, a few months was too short a time to resolve the many adjustments that every couple must go through.

She looked at me, then laughed cynically, "If you mean sex experience, forget it. I've had more sex experience than anybody twice my age." Lucille explained that she was considered among the crowd she traveled in as "Super Hip." She said that when the younger crowd heard her name all they could say was "WOW." "People have even accused me of being a nymphomaniac. They call me 'the original swinger'." There was a note of pride in her voice as she recounted the many men she had slept with. They included almost all of her friends and acquaintances, married and otherwise. She boasted that men considered her a terrific bed partner and were pursuing her constantly. She laughed again, "I could get hundreds of affidavits saying what a great 'lay' I am."

Suddenly her mood changed from cynicism to sadness. "There's only one thing wrong," she said wistfully, "I really can't seem to get any pleasure out of it all. I thought that getting married, being so terribly in love with Bob, would change all that, but if anything it's gotten worse. Lately, I just tighten up and it even makes it unpleasant for him. At least before I met him, I could get away with putting on an act. Men always loved my passionate performance. Now I not only can't fake it, but I'm turning off my husband. I guess there's nothing to do but get the marriage annulled. I'm just a fraud."

Lucille had left home when she was barely fifteen years old. She was in many ways typical of the new wave of rebellious youth. Her disappearance had created quite a scandal in the suburban town where she was carefully raised by staid, middle-class parents. Her folks had hired private detectives who located her living in a hippie commune in Greenwich Village. They pleaded with her to come home, offering all sorts of bribes, including a car. She allowed herself to be coaxed back once or twice, but found it intolerable and at the first opportunity left home again.

Lucille preferred the excitement of living in a large city and the anonymity of being lost in a large crowd of her peers. By the time she was eighteen she was completely on her own, working as a waitress and sharing a small apartment with a teenage girl in the same position. Their apartment was the scene of many parties where communal sex was the in-thing. She and her girlfriend shared their food, conversation and bed companions.

She explained that she had been too closely supervised by an overly protective family. Being an only child made matters worse. She felt that she was always in the spotlight and had no personal privacy. Her father was a public official in the small town and her mother the conscientious Sunday-school teacher. She was strongly indoctrinated with quotes from the

Bible and remembered clearly the repeated sermons about "Sins of the Flesh." And, if that were not enough to smother her, she also had an unmarried aunt living with the family. Because the mother spent so much time in "do-good work," the spinster aunt became, in effect, a second mother to further supervise Lucille's activities.

Lucille reminisced, "Wow, did I hate Aunt Claire. Especially since people were always telling me that I bore a striking resemblance to her, which I must admit is true. Every time I looked at my aunt I'd swear I wouldn't become a dried up old maid like her." She described how her aunt often bragged that she had never allowed a man to touch her body. "They love you and leave you," was the aunt's favorite platitude.

In spite of her resentment, this kind of constant conditioning had its effect. Lucille was indoctrinated with the belief that *sex was wrong, sinful, and disgusting*. It may seem paradoxical that she should have become so promiscuous until you take into account her strong rebellious feelings. In her eagerness to strike out and be very different from her background, Lucille went to the other extreme. She claimed to have had sex with as many as five men in a single night and in the next breath admitted that she had enjoyed none of them. She had also experimented with homosexuals of both genders. Lesbians found her very attractive and a challenge to their female "know-how." In spite of the fact that two of them had spent over an hour trying to bring her to a climax, nothing happened for her. Her sense of guilt was so strong that she could not feel genital sensation.

Lucille was even more repulsed by homosexuality than she was by heterosexuality. *Many people classified Lucille as a nymphomaniac, yet she was actually frigid.* When this type of sexual behavior is closely examined one finds that what appears to be a nymphomaniac is only a dissatisfied woman, restlessly searching for a lover who can bring her the tantalizing, elusive orgasm that she yearns for.

In spite of the enormous amount of sexual activity that Lucille had engaged in, she could not remember a single affair that she considered love making, until her marriage to Bob. She had never felt emotion before and now that she did, she was stunned to find that it did not help her to reach orgasm. Lucille was the classic example of a girl who could never say "no." Yet she said "no" to her own body. She was repeating the "no-nos" that her mind fed back to her, information absorbed throughout her childhood.

I asked her why she continued to repeat the same self-defeating sex habits, when she wasn't getting any pleasure out of it. She answered thoughtfully, "I always hoped maybe the next one would be different. I figured maybe the next man would have some technique that the others didn't know. But, I can tell you now, they are pretty much alike. One may have a penis a bit shorter or longer, and some may last longer, but it never seemed to make any real difference." She let out her sharp cynical laugh, "Well, at least I won't die a virgin like my Aunt Claire." It was obvious that her real reason for seeking help was not primarily to overcome cigarette smoking, but to release her accumulated sexual tension. Lucille had visited a psychiatrist for several years and it was with his approval that she had come to see me. She had a deeply imbedded sexual block as a direct result of negative conditioning throughout her childhood. This condition is often reversible by using positive reconditioning methods. We discussed the subject of sex as a *quality experience rather than a quantity experience.* Does having a lot of sex make it better? On the contrary, the repetition of disappointing sex merely serves to reinforce one's inability to function. Before sex experiences can help us evolve to a higher level of sensual pleasure, we must rid ourselves of old crippling suggestion and then replace the old with new attitudes. *Resistant women must reteach their bodies to function properly,* by learning from each successive successful encounter. In order to break the chain of self-defeat, one must start a new habit pattern based on a relationship of mutual understanding and affection rather than the frantic adventurism that Lucille had become a victim of.

It is now almost four years since I met and worked with Lucille. The changes that have taken place are remarkable. She visited me not loo long ago to show me her baby, conceived in mutual pleasure. It amused me to learn that Lucille had reverted in many ways to the early environment that she had so strongly rebelled against. Now that she had her own little girl to rear, she had moved out of the city to a healthy environment. One hopes that mother Lucille will have enough foresight to use her own life's experience to teach her daughter the truth about her body.

NINE

'Frigidity'

Frigidity is contagious. It is caused. It doesn't "just happen."
It is inbred rather than inborn. It is the result of anti-sexual
attitudes that have been indoctrinated from infancy on. It is
an "umbrella" word covering nine out of ten women—at some
point in their lives—the indifferent woman, the one whose genitals are anesthetized, and the passionate woman who has difficulty in reaching orgasm. The term was coined by men and
to them it describes a woman who does not respond properly
to their lovemaking. It is a catch-all word and as such can be
very confusing. Frigidity connotes its own particular meaning
to each woman, depending on the specific problem. It is a mis-
nomer; women are by nature far from cold or frigid as the

word implies. It would be nearer the truth to say that they are *incompleted* women, stymied at some point in their development toward sexual maturity. However, we will use the word frigidity here to signify women whose responses are inadequate.

By and large women seek love and give affection freely. Often they give freely and in their "unselfishness" confine themselves to being used, rather than participating equally. These are the women who are left most disappointed. Although able to reach great heights of excitation, they are unable to accelerate to the point of orgasm. Without scaling the peak of climax they cannot relax into the valley of tranquility that should come after it. It is this disparity between aroused anticipation and lack of realization that is at the core of female sex tension. Residual tension accumulates when a woman who is passionate sublimates her need to reach orgasm and just goes along with the act to please her man. Most women can attest to the fact that they have spent more than one restless night, lying next to a mate who was relaxed and satisfied, sublimely asleep by her wakeful side.

The prime cause of women's difficulties is their essentially different attitudes compared to men. Women are more inclined to bow to propriety and the moral codes set up by an unfair society. Having been taught to associate sex with shame and guilt, their sensory antennae become warped. Almost all women become embarrassed at the thought of aggressively pursuing sex. They associate taking the initiative with being a "bad" woman.

They accept society's image of the "Virgin Princess" waiting patiently in her ivory tower for her one and only Prince Charming to show up on his white horse, remaining chaste until his kiss awakens her to the good life.

Frigid women tend to be super-romantic as a cover up. It is a clinging to past stages of immaturity that says, "not yet . . . I am not ready to be a real, full-fledged woman." It is astounding that some of the most worldly women, who possess a wide education about almost everything else, are strangely ignorant about their own female anatomy.

How Frigidity Developed

For centuries all sex information was controlled by men, and women were led to believe that woman was an imperfect copy of man. This concept stressed the idea that the clitoris is a smaller, less capable image of the male penis. Many books, still widely read, give the idea that the vaginal tract is completely insensitive and lacking in any nerve endings. Books written and distributed by men contend that the center of orgasm is the clitoris and that women were created without the possibility of internal vaginal orgasm. A great deal of women's sexual incapacity for orgasm is directly traceable to the acceptance of this limitation. The newest research refutes this obsolete notion.

Women have also been greatly hampered by being conditioned since infancy to avoid touching the vaginal opening. They have been warned that the hymen might be broken and in so doing they might make themselves susceptible to pregnancy and disease. Female masturbation is considered taboo, particularly in the vaginal area. Many authorities now believe that there would be less female frigidity if there were more masturbation during sexual development. It is neither unnatural nor abnormal for girls to masturbate. According to surveys on the subject, over ninety percent of males masturbate at some time in their lives. The figures on female masturbation vary from forty percent to none, depending on which report you are examining.

Autoeroticism is a natural transitionary phase for both of the sexes. The fact that women have more problems in reaching orgasm than men, may be directly attributable to this disparity. Even those women who do masturbate do so with such shame and guilt that it becomes a negative rather than a positive act. Masturbation for both sexes is an educational experience. It can prepare a woman to function more responsively in a heterosexual relationship. Masturbation is a conditioning activity that can teach a woman how to physically and psychically intensify climatic feeling, and to bring her mind and body into harmony.

The taboos against female masturbation are almost as strong as the taboos against homosexuality. Yet, touching herself is important if a woman is to discover her innate sensory possibilities. If she confines contact with her genitals only to those times when she has sexual intercourse with a lover, she will prolong her frigidity problems. And, if she limits masturbation strictly to the clitoral area, she will be reinforcing her inability to respond vaginally. Mental focusing combined with sensory stimulation establishes patterns of feeling.

Many women who are resigned to being clitorally confined secretly envy and resent men's larger proportions. This is unavoidable if they think of the clitoris as a shrunken facsimile of the penis. Women who accept this man-made premise are bound to feel biologically cheated. These are the vast numbers of women who have internalized vaginal fears and inhibitions. I am not downing the clitoral orgasm. It is certainly better than none at all. But women who have experienced both understand the vast difference. For a truly passionate woman, a clitoral orgasm lets off some of the surface steam, but the kettle remains boiling underneath. Only the vagina is properly equipped with the kind of deep-seated nerves to do the complete job of release.

The next chapter will discuss the continuing controversy over clitoral versus vaginal orgasm. The important thing for all women to be aware of is that they are capable of intensifying sensation in both areas. A completely adequate woman knows that a real orgasm is not localized but that it involves all of the genital tissue; that there is really only one kind of an orgasm and it is felt by the entire sex organs.

Frigidity Can Cause Neurosis

Frigid women are neurotic women. The two problems are the two sides of the same coin. These women exist all over the world and their ailments attest to the cruel price they pay for sexual ignorance and repression. The assorted maladies which result are universal. The elusive, nonorganic pains, tension headaches and other assorted nervous symptoms. Even the obese woman who eats compulsively is very often a sexually frustrated woman who uses food to replace sexual satisfaction.

When women master themselves sexually and learn how to bring about full orgastic release, many of these problems disappear. If they choose to cling to their problems along with their frigidity, they become martyrs to their shaky marriages. Household slaves, subservient to their husband's sexual drives, they push their own instincts into the backgound to die an unnatural death.

Inadequate women often cling to the old notion that man's role is active sexually and theirs is purely passive. Passivity and frigidity are each other's helpmates. Passivity is the greatest female obstacle to reaching orgasm. Sexual inactivity *presupposes defeat by default.*

If a woman does not participate actively in both the foreplay and the act itself, she not only makes it difficult for her lover, but she also eliminates the chance of being aroused sufficiently herself. *Total masculine aggressiveness plus total feminine passivity equals sexual failure for the female.*

If copulation is to be mutually rewarding, a woman must participate actively. She must not only participate, but should initiate the techniques that she prefers. She should feel free to pick the time, the place, the methods and positions best suited for her pleasure. Having been for centuries substandard in the double standard sex codes, she must herself make sure that the best conditions exist for her maximum pleasure.

The greatest handicap in accepting sexual intercourse purely for pleasure is fear. When fear is uppermost in a person's mind sensation must take a back seat. The female mind is too often wary and watchful, afraid of letting animal instincts take over. Women, by and large, resist exposing themselves to pregnancy and all of the social problems and responsibilities that go with it.

Among single women the fear is understandably greater. They fear that if they do like it, they will become dependent on having sex regularly and become attached to a lover who may leave them. It is interesting that many single girls can respond better to a man that they don't have strong romantic feelings for. They rationalize that if they are in love, the possible rejection would be too much to cope with. All sorts of fears beset the single, sexually active woman, especially in those cases where she knows there is no possibility of marrying her lover.

The Pill

Confidence in contraception is of prime importance both to the married and the unmarried woman if she is to free herself of any traces of frigidity. The choice of the kind of contraceptive to be used is most often left to the woman. There is growing controversy about oral contraception and many women have reservations about its use. If a woman does not have full assurance about what she is using, even the act of using a contraceptive can add to her already over-flowing reservoir of fear. There are many types of contraception available. Research is constantly going on to discover more suitable methods. It is wise for women to check with their doctors to determine what is best suited for their individual needs.

Ignorance and innocence are equally responsible for the numerous tragedies which occur in the cases of unwanted pregnancies. A girl who has been shy or careless about protecting herself faces serious repercussions. Many young girls do not even discuss contraception with their lovers. They emotionalize that it takes away from the romantic feeling to be so practical. But, life forces them to think in a more practical way as they anxiously await their menstrual period each month. The stress and tension of counting the days makes many a girl think sex is hardly worth the trouble. She balances the few moments of affection (that's very often all she gets out of it) with the long weeks of watchful worry. Birth control has traditionally been the responsibility of the female. She has suffered the burden of this problem since the beginning of the human race. So far, no society has provided a satisfactory solution. Because of the increasing overpopulation of the earth's surface, the restriction of the birth rate looms as a major concern for all people. Governments must consider the issue as not only essential to the welfare of womankind, but for everyone, man as well as woman, the young and the old. Only now when birth control is recognized as a prime world wide problem, is there a chance women may indirectly benefit. Countries like India and China suffer starvation because of the inability of the land to feed the number of people living on it.

India is a classic example of the kind of suffering that results from lack of knowledge about contraception. The country has become so overpopulated that death from starvation is a common occurrence. Visitors are appalled at the large number of hungry children roaming the streets while their parents continue to copulate and procreate thereby enlarging the problem.

Contraception for the Male

Recently the Indian government instituted a country-wide campaign to introduce contraception to the male as well as the female. The most successful response to the campaign so far has been the project to popularize the sterility operation for males called, vasectomy. It is a simple process which doesn't involve hospitalization and takes just a few moments in a doctor's office. It is by far the surest and simplest method of birth control in existence to date. In the Indian campaign for vasectomy, booths were set up on city street corners, where doctors offered a bonus to each male who would submit to the operation. Men had their choice of prize, either a small sum of money or a transistor radio. The reporter who witnessed the procedure stated that it was a common occurrence to see an anxious looking male go into the booth and come out a few moments later, smiling, with his transistor radio blaring away.

Population control is today's most crucial question. It is the only way to reorder our lives so that we can do our best for the children that are already in existence. The world must face up to the fact that the creation of a new life cannot be left to chance. It has been estimated that only twenty percent, two out of ten births, are planned for on a world-wide basis. That leaves the majority of eight out of ten people accidently conceived and in too many cases, unwanted. The result of such haphazard family planning, or more accurately, lack of planning, affects the emotional as well as the physical health of all concerned.

Our own country is also suffering from the unplanned upsurge of new births. Population explosion brings with it the inherent problems of overcrowding, lack of adequate housing, unemployment, and air and water pollution. The United States Chief Medical Officer said recently, "A change in national mores is needed to keep the nation's population from increasing to the point where we are unable to feed and house ourselves." He further stated that we must, "help the people of this country understand that their vital interests, and that of their country, demand that we control the growth of population."

As a starter, he advised looking into the question of legalized abortion and, since his statement, several states have enacted such legislation. He cautioned that abortion should not be substituted for contraception. The forces working for legalized abortion point out that countless young women die each year from illegal abortions. International legalized abortion is overdue. We must consider it the fundamental right of every woman to choose whether or not she wishes to bear children. This is a basic human right; a woman must be allowed to do with her body what she wishes, according to the dictates of her own conscience. This is not only a humanitarian issue, but a civil liberties issue as well. This unfair legislation prohibits a doctor from helping a woman with an unwanted pregnancy. Removing these cruel laws from the books would eliminate the abortion underworld and save thousands of hapless women from death and permanent injury.

The birth control "Pill" which women looked upon as the long awaited panacea, turned out to be much less than that. It became instead, another reason for guilt, and guilt is something women have too much of already. *Why not contraception at its source?* Why not at the site of the sperm's manufacture, with the male? *Why not a PILL for men?* This would eliminate a great deal of the female problem with responsiveness. And, why not institute a campaign to encourage vasectomy here in our own country, sponsored by our government. Perhaps not for the newly-wed, but at least after men have fathered as many children as they can afford to support. Many enlightened men have already had this very simple operation and report that it was neither painful nor difficult. What greater gift of love could a man bestow upon his wife than to remove this pressure from her mind and body. The love he would demonstrate by such an act of consideration would match the gratitude and affection she would give him in return. Her feeling would make up for any inconvenience that he may have to suffer. Not only would she be overjoyed, but the change in her sexual being would be a metamorphosis.

There Must Be an Answer

It seems inconceivable that United States technology, which leads the world in solving problems, from the deep sea to far outer space, cannot find an acceptable answer to birth control. Our scientists accomplish miracles. We not only managed to land men on the moon, but technicians designed a tiny electrical amplifier no larger than a pin head, to send television pictures from the moon. Isn't it possible to plan pregnancies so that the next generation will not be burdened with the problems left unresolved by our own? Why can't we use our resources to create a more humane world? Surely there must be brains and money available in our rich, scientifically advanced country to solve this crucial problem and allow women to come into their own. Until that happy invention comes to be, women must make the best of the situation as it is. Having taken the best available precautions against unwanted conception, they must then put fears of pregnancy out of their minds and enjoy sex as fully as their male partners.

Only when old fears are *discovered, uncovered and examined in the light of today's morality* will woman realize her true feminine potential. We must understand the beginning, that the original cause of frigidity came from sources outside of our own physical bodies. We must expose the roots, to see the entire structure. When this is accomplished, frigidity is self-curable. You have the *power within you to accomplish this*.

It is a scientific fact that the subconscious acts automatically, based on suggestions fed into its computer-like machinery. The subconscious is a storehouse, a great reservoir of memories. Habits, teachings, from infancy to adulthood lie waiting there. Every day, and every minute it gathers information for our later use. Not all this information is correct.

We all react like robots or puppets, manipulated by past impressions. Women can, however, with diligence, wipe out these restrictive impressions and re-teach their minds to serve their bodies. In so doing, women may discover that they were never "frigid" in the first place.

TEN

Complete Orgasm

In order for a woman to get the most pleasure out of sexual intercourse, she should not be concerned about whether or not an orgasm will occur. Neither should she have any anxiety about whether it will be clitoral or vaginal. She should feel an all over "togetherness" of her sexual self. An informed woman knows that not only is the clitoris very sensitive, but that the inner lips and the vestibule (entrance) of the vagina are also supplied with sensory nerves.

A Sexually Adequate Woman:

1. Enjoys the coital act for its own sake.
2. Gives in to the pleasure of the moment and freely enjoys whatever activities may suggest themselves during the course of lovemaking.

3. Has positive thoughts and expects to be satisfied. Uses her creative imagination to make it happen that way.
4. Is able to surrender her inhibitions and let her sensory feelings build up to a peak.
5. And most important, she doesn't think of her clitoris or her vagina as being separate entities, but as one functioning unit, the center of femaleness.

Difficulties in reaching orgasm are due to a complexity of causes, psychological as well as physical. Most research points to the fact that the psychological often is the cause of the physical. *Every thought, every idea, every mental image leads to a physical result.*

To begin with, let's examine the female sexual organs. Let's see what equipment nature has provided us with, both for procreation and also *purely for pleasure.*

Illustrations are always general. If you find that there is some variation in the size or shape of any of the parts of your own genitals, don't be concerned. This is normal. Just as nature, in its infinite creativity, does not make two faces exactly alike, so does she also vary the parts of the sexual organs.

Therefore, unless your physician has told you that you have a physical problem (such as clitoral adhesions), in all probability your sexual inadequacies stem from poor psychological conditioning. Available statistics support the contention that the female sex problem is correctable in almost all cases.

The female sex organs consist of many connected parts, the center of which is the vagina. It is located between the clitoris, urethra, and the mons veneris on the one side and the anus at the other. It is surrounded with folds, one the outer lips (*Labia Majora*), and the smaller highly sensitive one (*Labia Minora*).

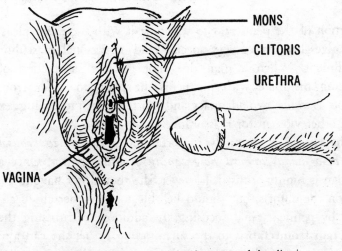

MONS

CLITORIS

URETHRA

VAGINA

While the distance between the center of the clitoris and the vaginal opening vary greatly from woman to woman, all researchers agree that no direct contact is established between the penis and clitoris in normal sexual intercourse.

The secret to increased sensation outside the vagina is to include the inner lips into the existing threshold of the clitoral orgasm. This can be the beginning of expanding clitoral orgasm to include penile-vaginal coitus. These inner lips extend toward the front of the body (*Mons*) and form a hood-like covering over the clitoris, which rests between its folds.

When a woman is truly relaxed she is better able to respond to stimulation. Focused relaxation helps sensation diffuse itself from the center of the clitoris into the hood and through the inner lips where it blends into the vaginal vestibule. Even though a woman may never have felt sensitive anywhere except the clitoris, she does innately possess the nerve endings to bring about this kind of enlarged feeling.

The importance of releasing sensation from the clitoris to the vaginal entrance is more than just her own gratification as a fully functioning female. A woman who is able to feel the insertion of the penis and to welcome it with increased pleasure, gives her man a very special kind of personal masculine fulfillment. When a man does not get the satisfaction of pleasing his mate with his penis, he tends to suffer from doubts as to his own adequacy and is often driven to having sex with other women for reassurance.

The clitoris is infinitely important as *a trigger to arousal and as a means toward heightening orgastic feeling.* Once a woman is highly aroused, however, she should not have to focus on the clitoris, but should be able to bring herself to climax by penile-vaginal focusing. In addition to diffusing the sensation from clitoris to the surrounding tissue, she can also intensify sexual feeling by using the genital muscles.

Undue emphasis on the achievement of pure vaginal orgasm, *without involving the clitoris,* should equally be avoided. When a woman has chronic difficulty in obtaining an orgasm, she should not set rigid rules for herself by being concerned about how, when and where orgasm should take place.

Orgasm, however and wherever it takes place, should be the main objective of every woman whenever she has intercourse, especially if she is inclined to be tense about it. There is nothing to be ashamed of if she can only reach a clitoral orgasm. Many women say that they get great satisfaction out of this release. Some women have several clitoral orgasms and know of no other kind.

It would be foolish to disparage or take away from a woman her ability to climax clitorally, but at the same time she should know that she has the natural ability to increase her pleasure greatly. There is, in most cases, a distance of at least one inch between the center of the clitoris and the opening of the vagina. This factor makes it virtually impossible, in most cases, for direct contact to be established between the penis and clitoris in the traditional "man on top" coital position.

Men have written an enormous amount of material on how to bring women to climax by adjusting position and varying techniques. The greatest struggle through the ages has been men's struggles to please a woman with his penis.

Changing positions may help some women. The "woman on top" is helpful for many as they learn to combine clitoral and vaginal pressures. With many this is the only position in which they can bring themselves to a climax. The important consideration about position and its effect on orgasm is that a woman should have sufficient internal control so that the position her body is in is not a crucial problem. We must accept the logic of biological design and assume that nature intended for the female to feel penile-vaginal contact and to enjoy that inside contact.

The arrangement of sexual parts in a woman's genitals is such that the delicate tissues and nerves centered in and around the clitoris branch out and become part of her vaginal entrance. There is no abrupt shutting off of the clitoris or any other section. Even in cases where the vaginal entrance seems to be desensitized or even atrophied, it is possible to develop and enhance sensory feeling.

It would be unreal to expect an abrupt change over from clitoral to vaginal orgasm, but such a transition is possible with the auto-conditioning exercises found in this book. The diffusing of clitoral sensation into the inner labia and the awakening of the vaginal vestibule can happen. A complete vaginal orgasm doesn't detract from the clitoral orgasm, it rather adds to it.

Freud is often quoted on his theory of "clitoral-to-vaginal

transference." He spoke of this transference as a necessary phenomena in order that complete maturity take place. This theory has been disputed by many leading psychiatrists since that day. The confusion stems from an "either or" dogmatic kind of attitude. The assumption that clitoral versus vaginal orgasm means that all sensation must leave the clitoris and move into the vagina has been discarded. Women are conditioned to respond to external genital stimulation with its accompanying body adjustments. A complete reversal of sensory pattern is difficult and unnecessary for sexual satisfaction. It is not clitoral versus vaginal, but rather clitoral/vaginal equals orgasm.

Too much concern about avoiding clitoral contact is tension provoking. A more realistic goal then is to bring together all possible sensory feeling to make copulation a relaxed joy, rather than a strain, *for both partners*. Orgasm through penile-vaginal friction is the greatest source for mutual gratification, emotionally as well as physically. It is this larger satisfaction that the awakening of vaginal feeling is concerned with. It is concerned with the accomplishing of greater harmony between the sexes.

Simultaneous Orgasm

In speaking about *mutual* gratification, we don't necessarily mean *simultaneous* orgasm. Because individuals differ so widely in their desires and capacities, it is very rare that a couple will be so perfectly attuned as to have simultaneous orgasm take place. When it does happen to happen, it is an exhilarating experience for both people, but women should not strive for this if they are inclined to have problems. A woman should be focusing on the pleasure of the increased feeling rather than holding back or rushing orgasm to meet her lover's tempo. Thinking consciously about when orgasm will take place detracts from its spontaneity. Trying too hard can have a contrary effect and cause an impasse in reaching orgasm. Desire cannot be forced or dragged to culmination. Desire must carry sensation on its own wings of energy. Make love for the sake of making love, not necessarily to reach orgasm. Don't think, "It should happen, it must happen." When you stop this kind of conscious thinking, you will begin feeling easier. De-emphasizing achievement helps this happen.

Much of the strain that women go through in intercourse is associated with their inability to feel sensation in contact with the penis. A woman may have a perfectly normal vagina and yet be completely disinterested in penile-vaginal copulation. Some women simply oblige the man, but abstain from involving their own feelings. This is especially widespread among the older generation, who were misled to believe sex was purely a man's pleasure.

Allowing oneself to be used while staying out of the act emotionally or physically leads indirectly to other problems. Under such circumstances it is unusual if a woman lives through her life without serious nervous disorders. Women have sex organs which are supposed to be used for pleasure as well as pregnancy. There are women who shut themselves off from sexual contact entirely but the practice of celibacy brings with it not only a great variety of illnesses, but also deep psychological scars.

There are many women who are not desensitized or desexualized and yet cannot discharge their tension through any kind of climax. For these women the answer may be to start with clitoral excitation and work toward vaginal involvement as a more advanced sexual development.

There is nothing wrong with clitoral manipulation and a clitoral orgasm is better than no orgasm at all. But a woman who has for years been able to have clitoral orgasms and settles *only* for clitoral orgasms, is missing the deeper, greater fulfillment that includes vaginal acceptance and pleasure through penile activity.

Masters and Johnson, in their book, *Human Sexual Responses,* answer this vital question: "Are clitoral and vaginal orgasms truly separate anatomic entities? From a biological point of view, the answer to this question is an unequivocal "NO." From an anatomic point of view there is absolutely no difference in the response of the pelvic viscera to effective sexual stimulation, regardless of whether the stimulation occurs as a result of clitoral body or mons area manipulation, natural or artificial coition. Or, for that matter, specific stimulation of any other erogenous areas of the female body."

They go on further to state, "There may be great variations in duration and intensity of orgasmic experience from individual to individual and within the same woman from time to time. However, when any woman experiences orgasmic responses to effective stimulation, both the vagina and the clitoris react in consistant physiologic patterns."

Their findings were based on extensive research which involved hundreds of men and women and which extended over more than a ten-year period of investigation. The elusive orgasm is the number one obsession of all sexually frustrated women. Even the so-called nymphomaniac is often just an over-eager female chasing the ephemeral, tantalizing orgasm which seems to slip from her grasp just as she approaches it. Women who think that the answer lies with finding a better lover, never do. Until she looks for the better lover within herself, no real changes will take place. Yet every woman is capable of reaching a profound orgasm if she learns how to do so. It is certainly less difficult than learning to apply eye make-up and a great deal more rewarding. It is amazing how much time and money is spent by women on the superficialities of life. Women of all ages from puberty to the wheel chair are devoted to looking their best and competing for masculine notice. Ninety-nine percent of their energies are devoted to attracting a man's attention and only one percent on enjoying his manliness once they have captured him. Most often the woman who spends hours each day beautifying herself to arouse her man's sexual passion is herself incapable of orgasm. She is left with no returns for her countless hours of effort in trying to achieve that sexy look. Female preoccupation with appearance often has a contrary affect on sexual feeling. Some women worry about how they look during intercourse and counteract the body's need for natural freedom. Many husbands can attest to the fact that their wives complain that because they went to the beauty shop that day they do not want to muss their hair by having intercourse. Some of them even go to bed wearing hair curlers and other contraptions. It is no wonder that they cannot enjoy sex (and even more of a wonder if their husbands manage to).

The average American woman knows a great deal about her "outsideness." She knows about cosmetics, clothes, hemlines and hairstyles, but next to nothing about her inside femaleness, the biological function of her own body. Because of the long existing controversy about female orgasm, few women know what to expect of their bodies. A woman doesn't know if she is supposed to feel an orgasm in her clitoris or her vagina, or both. This ambivalent feeling, not knowing what is right or wrong, is the fuel which feeds her confusion about her sexual identity.

And where there is confusion in thinking, it is inevitable that the body must reflect this confusion. For the body can only be what the mind thinks it is. You cannot anticipate an orgasm in the clitoris and have it take place in the vagina. The human body just doesn't work that way.

A sexually satisfied woman is a healthier, livelier person. The rising excitement and subsequent release of passion is a powerful rejuvenating force. Every part of the body works better when the sex organs function. The eyes are clearer. The face looks more rested and serene. Compulsive over-eating often is diminished and a host of other changes take place. Many of the so-called tension diseases or psychosomatic ailments, disappear or are alleviated.

The prevailing confusion about clitoral-vaginal placement of sensation continues to add to the resistance based on the fear of pregnancy. If that were not enough to turn a woman's motor off, ninety-five percent of the readily available literature compounds the problem by describing her clitoris as a less than perfect vestigial penis. It is described as a classic example of surviving evidence of a time when animals were bisexual and performed both the male and female roles. The nipples on the male are another example of vestigial organs.

When you consider the full meaning of vestigial and its affect on the female sexual identity, you will better realize the importance of vaginal acceptance for a woman's self-esteem. The dictionary describes vestigial as "a degenerate or imperfectly developed organ, having *little or no utility,* but which at an earlier biological stage performed a useful function."

The highest evolution of female sexuality is making the genitals into one unit. Not merely transfering sensation away from the clitoris to the vagina, but wakening up all the tissue inside and outside. Women who experience this are truly assuaged and know the deeper meaning of satiety and infinite closeness to their man. *They know the inner feeling of being . . . The feeling of pride and satisfaction at being the center of creation and at one with the universe.* The joyful repercussions on the male lover can only be understood when one lives through this high plain of sexual intercourse.

The newest research points up the fact that contact between the penis and vagina gives the coital union a much greater depth of meaning. They describe the clitoris as an important means for arousal and stimulation in order to be sure that a woman is ready for entry. In their extended, practical testings involving the activity of the clitoris, they discovered that the clitoris actually retreats into the surrounding flesh of its "hood", when the penis enters the vagina so that penile-clitoral contact becomes impossible.

The retreat of the clitoris is a natural phenomena which researchers had not been aware of until this investigation. It is one indicator of how much has been left undiscovered about the sexual behavior of the human female. Because of long-established discriminatory practices against women in the sciences it is only lately that women have entered this field. Together with their fair-minded colleagues they have brought to light some of the truth about female biological function.

Dr. Marie Robinson, prominent female pioneer in the field of feminine sexuality, has this to say, "The mature female's orgasm takes place within the vagina, the fact that a woman can experience this kind of orgasm generally marks her a fully developed woman in all aspects of her personality." Dr. Robinson's views have since been corroborated by the Masters and Johnson research team.

The clitoral versus vaginal dispute is far from being resolved. There are countless men who are still unaware of the existence of the clitoris and its preliminary importance. Women must begin to acquaint themselves with what it is all about and, if necessary, take the initiative to educate their spouses.

When a woman awakens to the pleasure-giving experience of her vagina, she discovers simultaneously her own inner identity. Her acceptance of her insideness becomes her strength. The woman whose vagina is not only a vessel of receptivity of heightened responsiveness, makes every coital act an act of love. This kind of woman makes a man feel like a real man regardless of his age or penile size. This kind of a woman does not have to worry about infidelity—a man always appreciates the responsive female woman.

Some Call It "Yin and Yang"

Yin-Yang is an oriental concept based on the harmony and dependency of opposites. This ancient principle can help in understanding the maleness of men and the femaleness of women. In this philosophy *Yin* represents the female and *Yang* the male. The penis is *Yang* and the vagina, *Yin*. The earth is described as female and the air around it as male; together they form one entity, each completely dependent upon the other for its existence.

Female is internal and magnetic.

Male is external and dynamic.

Hot makes cold seem colder, just as grief makes joy seem more pleasurable. Just as there can be no left without a right, nor a day without a night, man and woman must cherish their contrasts for the greatest sexual fulfillment.

Only when a woman gets the feeling of being *totally involved* is she fulfilled completely. Nature planned males' outside genitals to merge in perfect design with the inside genitals of a female. This combination forms the harmonious "lock" that is the ultimate creative force; the very essence of *being* and the assurance of the continuity of life.

Having never experienced vaginal satisfaction, some women are understandably more confident about their clitoral response. Many are able to culminate prolonged clitoral stimulation into orgasm by digital manipulation or oral techniques.

Due to very bad early conditioning, most women have accepted a negative image in connection with vaginal function. They associate the vagina with pain and the discomfort and bleeding of their menstrual period, in addition to any other early unpleasant sexual encounters. Most of all, the vagina is equated with the process of child-birth with its traditional fear of pain. It is important to emphasize that above all else, fear of unwanted pregnancy is the greatest deterrent to vaginal pleasure.

What Is a Complete Orgasm?

Very few women can properly describe what an orgasm is because very few women have really experienced it. They are usually amazed to learn that a true orgasm involves all of their sexual parts, both inside the vagina and out. Words are

always inadequate to describe intense feeling and this is especially true of the kind of sensation experienced at the peak of
orgasm. Neither is it something that you can accomplish
merely by reading or listening to a lecture. You can help
yourself, however, by *applying and practicing the retraining
techniques outlined in detail in this book*. Lack of sensation
and slow arousal need not be a permanent handicap.

When a woman wonders if she has had an orgasm, you can
be sure she has not! You *know* it when it happens and it will
happen when you are ready.

What does a complete orgasm feel like? How do you get to
the readiness stage? There are three stages that lead to climax:

Mental and Emotional Communication
   This is a time for lovers to be amorous, to say the tender, kind things that build confidence and sexual security. A time to confide their sexual fantasies and
   their secret desires.

Foreplay: The Stimulation of Erogenous Zones
   A time to fondle and caress each others bodies. A
   time to sharpen a healthy sexual appetite and to increase erotic animalism. Plenty of time should be
   taken for a woman's nipples, clitoris and her entire
   body to become relaxed and receptive. Lovers should
   wait until the woman's vagina is warm, moist, and
   eager for male penetration.

Penile-Vaginal Contact
   This should take place only when she is at her greatest height of sexual stimulation—and not before.
   When her circulation has increased to the point
   where there is an engorgement of blood into the vulva

and the tissue surrounding the vaginal entrance. When the sensation has grown so intense that rhythmic contractions of the genital muscles begin to take place, a woman should then be at a high peak of pleasure and able to bring on orgasm by mental suggestion.

DON'T RUSH. The vaginal zone does not become aroused, normally, until a woman has passed through stages one and two. Complete relaxation and adequate, effective stimulation is necessary before any climax can take place. The husband or lover should, under the best conditions for the woman, postpone the insertion of his penis until she tells him that she is fully ready and eager for it to take place. They must communicate freely through all of the stages.

By the time the lover has inserted his penis, she has an intensified sensory expectancy throughout her entire genitals. Her entire sexual organs respond with equally diffused feeling. There is no forced feeling of trying hard, but rather a melting warmth between the partners. They feel that it is all part of a pattern that is supposed to happen as sexual energies ebb and flow from one to the other.

This vibration of creative energy makes the act more than a physical one. It raises sexual love to a spiritual level. When this kind of male-female vibration is established, both people are keenly aware of it and the woman then feels free to release herself. The muscles around the vaginal entrance then spontaneously tighten and caressingly hold the penis.

This gripping action causes the vulva and the tissue surrounding the clitoris to also get into the act. The muscle action draws the nerves and tissue and pulls them closer toward the thrusting action of the penis. At this point the coital union is at its most satisfying. The penis is stimulating the nerves of the vaginal entrance and the muscles contract more and more as the pleasure increases.

The combined pressure exerted against both the outside and inside of her sex organs gives a woman her most intense orgastic feeling. Even though the clitoris withdraws into the mons area, its hood and surrounding sensitive tissues are stimulated together with the vulva and vagina. Friction between the male and female sex organs causes further tumescence and warmth. The muscular sphincter action of the vaginal barrel matches the thrusting action of the penis as it becomes more determined to reach a peak. For the completely responsive woman, penile-vaginal friction brings about great spasms of sensation extending from the fleshy outside of the genitals to the mouth of the uterus, deep within the vaginal shaft.

The woman who has mastered the techniques outlined in this book can prolong this ecstatic plateau and even time herself to climax with her mate, if she so desires. When the orgastic sensation builds itself to the high level of demanding surcease, she gives up her self-control to the anticipated relief of culmination.

At this point the voluptuous convulsions of pleasurable feeling become overwhelming. The breath quickens, the pulse increases its beat, the body movement becomes uncontrollable. The woman may make verbal sounds of ecstasy, moaning, crying, and perhaps later even screaming as the climax approaches. At the pitch of excitement there is a flush of fresh blood to the face, and the breasts. A surge of revitalization floods the entire body. The entire surface of the skin becomes increasingly moist and ready to release the mounting sexual tension.

The orgasm manifests itself and her entire body pulsates with the rhythm of being alive. There is a rippling sensation across her breasts as the nipples, now fully erect, increase their rosy color. The pulsations pass into the abdominal cavity, down through the pelvis and into her loins.

The gripping of the penis by the vulva is now spasmatic and uncontrollable, each breath is of shorter duration and she breathes through moistened lips. Her thighs quiver as her hips are racked with involuntary spasms which cause her to emit sounds of excruciating delight. As she reaches orgasm her facial expression is tense, her eyes are glassy and vacant and she sounds as if she is experiencing ecstatic pain or even agony. Need for relief overwhelms past resistance as for a moment consciousness seems to cease. At this point time does not exist for lovers, they just drift together into the unfathomable dimension of spacelessness.

It is the sublime moment of creativity as two beings free themselves of all the pressures of daily living, blending their bodies and minds into the kind of unity that makes for the greatest emotional security. When the intensity of passion has subsided and the lovers rest side by side, they radiate a soft glow of love and good health one to the other. A feeling of well-being that is primary to the health of both the male and female permeates every cell of their bodies. This is the time that they let each other know how much they appreciate the love of each other.

The expressions of appreciation and tenderness after sex are called the afterplay, of prime importance in giving the relationship its individual specialness. It also insures continuity and a return match for future mutual pleasure. A woman's gentle caressing after sex indicates to her lover how much pleasure he has given her and increases his ability to do even better next time.

Frequency

Women who experience this kind of deep vaginal orgasm seldom will desire more than one in a lovemaking period. Those that insist that they need two or three (or even ten as several women have stated), can only be experiencing the clitoral type which is usually a more limited, superficial or surface type of feeling. A profound, complete orgasm leaves a woman, as well as a man, sexually depleted and deeply satisfied for a longer period of time.

One woman who had reconditioned herself from clitoral focus to vaginal focus stated, "Even though I used to have three or four orgasms before, I never really felt relaxed. Now when I have a deep vaginal orgasm, I only need one, because I am physically, mentally and emotionally satisfied. More than one would take away from the great experience." She also mentioned that when she does have another vaginal orgasm (after a half hour resting period), "The second orgasm was okay, but not as good as the first. I had to strain to reach it and it left me exhausted."

The average sexually active woman has not learned to use her vagina as the primary source of pleasure. It is more common that she feel sporadic sensation in the clitoris and try to reach clitoral orgasm as quickly as possible before she loses contact with this fleeting feeling. There is a vast difference in the amount of relief from tension that one experiences in vaginal orgasm as compared to the simpler clitoral type. One reason is due to the duration of orgasm. While the clitoral orgasm is intense it is much shorter and generally lasts up to about five or six seconds at best. On the other hand, when a woman learns sufficient control over her sexual machinery, she cannot only double the length of the orgastic peak, but can improve the sensation each time she has intercourse. With practice and focused concentration, a woman can postpone her orgasm as well as her husband's by releasing her muscular grip on the penis and sustaining the plateau which precedes the peak of release. It is all done with the power of the thinking mind. People who practice Tantra yoga can keep the pleasure plateau for several hours. The exercises in this book employ some of these techniques. We all have a control panel sending constant messages to our genitals during intercourse, instructing the autonomic nervous system on how to react to stimuli.

Developing Control

Women as well as men can reach their sexual potential by making full use of their cerebral power. Instead of allowing the wrong signals to shut off sensation or to divert it away from coital contact, you can reverse the message and turn sensation upward. Once you learn the simple techniques of intercepting the negative messages, you will then replace them with the right signals for expanding your sensory perception and gratification. Only you yourself have access to the inner workings of your mental processes. Only you can develop this knack for fully utilizing your mind's power and see to it that you begin functioning properly.

Most men want to be good lovers and when they are encouraged can be. Even those that are inconsiderate, inept, or clumsy make excellent pupils at the hands of a good female teacher who is skilled in the finer arts of female-satisfying. Men can become much better lovers when women are able to teach them what they should know. The trouble is, most women know very little themselves about the female sensory system. Men have been misinformed, just as women have been, about the function of the female sex parts and it is about time that women confidently informed them.

"The Other Woman"

Repeated failures to get reciprocal feelings from his spouse makes a man ask himself, "Is something wrong with me? Am I the man who I was before I married? Is it her shortcoming or is it mine? Is my penis adequate in size, in shape? Am I capable of satisfying a woman? And when he gets to the point of asking himself all these questions, he looks for the answers from the only source possible, *another woman.*

When this kind of situation exists between a husband and wife, honest communication ceases as he tends to spend more and more time away from home. Seeking out the company of other women in the hope of affirming his masculinity sometimes helps him, but certainly doesn't solve the problem of his wife. Most men have a strong need to satisfy a woman *with their penis.* Only when a man can honestly tell himself that he is as good a lover as any other man is he truly content with his over-all masculine image.

Faking Orgasm

When women worry about hanging on to their husbands they often fake orgasm. These sad, frustrated, and neurotic wives get caught in a trap of sexual "role playing". Like an actress, they "make believe" they reach an orgasm to keep their husbands by the old fireside. Almost all women, if they are honest, will admit to having faked orgasm at some time in their lives. When women put on a show of false feeling, they rationalize that they are doing so to protect the man's ego.

Does a woman really fool a man about her sexual responsiveness? Well, to take off on a very old saying, *You can fool some of the men some of the time, but you can't fool all of the men all of the time*. Sometimes men will go along with the deception in order to avoid a confrontation with the woman's problem to which they themselves have no answer. Men may allow themselves to be fooled.

CAN ANY WOMAN BE SEXUALLY SATISFIED? She certainly can, if she applies herself. Read on and find out how.

Sexual Satisfaction
Seven Steps to

The seven steps to sexual satisfaction are tested exercises in EXPERIMENTING and EXPERIENCING. They involve your mind as well as your body. The most important clue to releasing orgastic sensation is to have your mind master your body. Only you can make this happen.

Human beings have two distinct forces at work within them. One is a positive force for self-gratification, the other is negative and often harmful. When a person is confused about sexual identity, these forces pull in opposite directions. We are constantly telling ourselves how we will react under certain circumstances. These self-suggestions can be positive or negative. We are continually choosing between personal success or personal failure. If you are motivated toward happiness, you can learn to disassociate yourself from past patterns which do not serve your fulfillment goals.

Our minds are constantly bombarded by outside suggestions of fears, doubts, and anxieties. The *negative side* of our personalities absorbs this pressure and, consequently, expects failure. It worries, frets, feels sorry for itself, is envious and basically insecure.

The other half of what we are is *positive*. We wish, we hope, *we expect things to work out for the best.* This is the part which looks forward to improvement and strives to reach goals of achievement. It is the positive side that is responsible for the good things which happen in our lives. *It guides us toward fulfilling our hopes and our dreams.*

When we are not aware of this conflict, it is possible for negative responses to take precedent during lovemaking. Negativism makes it impossible for orgasm to take place *because your disbelieving mind has already decided that it will not happen.* You have closed the door in advance, shutting out any possibility of success.

Positive thinking, however, sends a surge of optimistic energy and sensual stimulation to the sex organs. Messages flash back and forth from your mind to your nerve endings—"I can do it!" . . . "It *is* happening!" When you are consistently confident, and refuse to let negative thoughts interfere, there is no other way for your "mind/body" apparatus to work. It must lead you to eventual success.

Your own imagination can make sex an unpleasant experience or it can raise sensation to the heights of ecstasy. Proper images and sexual fantasies trigger sensations and bring on an orgasm. (Test number 5 teaches you a tested technique for channeling your imagination in this direction.)

It is time to make up your mind. Which is it to be?—negative thinking which brings failure, or positive thinking which leads to success. Keep in mind that it is impossible to think negatively and, at the same time, have your sexual organs react in a positive way. Affirmative anticipation is the spark which ignites the body's machinery, and sets it into motion. *Great expectations bring great realizations.* In order for you to realize your full orgastic potential, your mind must believe that *it can and will happen.* These seven progressive steps are designed to lead you in that direction.

There is no reason to think that, because you may have failed in the past, you must continue to fail. Everything in life is in a constant state of change, both positive and negative. This is a fundamental law of nature. If you have been inclined to think in a defeatist way, *why not try thinking like a winner?* A wonderful surprise is in store for you when you do.

The amazing power of the mind over the body was forcefully impressed upon me by the following example: Dolores was a young married woman with four small children whose ages ranged from two to twelve years. She was harassed and irritable. You could see from her weary posture and the look on her small, tight face how much anxiety and tension were burdening her. Although she managed to perform her duties as both wife and mother, she did so with a great deal of resentment. Not only was she unresponsive to her husband's sexual overtures, she could not react affirmatively to most of life's situations.

Dolores was a constant complainer, but there was no doubt that her suffering was real. She complained about her husband, her children, her lack of energy. . . She sounded like a TV commercial—rundown, listless, constant headaches, backaches, etc. Yet her family doctor could find nothing physically wrong with her.

It was her husband who first came to see me, ostensibly to lose some weight. He later revealed that his real reason was to see if I could help his wife. At a later date, they both arrived and it was obvious that they had been quarreling. She came in wiping tears from her eyes and said, "Everything is his fault. He never stays home evenings. As soon as he has dinner he goes out, and only comes home after the kids are sleeping."

She complained bitterly about her loneliness, and his unkind treatment of her. "He never talks to me. We never have a conversation. He reads the paper or ignores me when he is home. Besides that, I'm sure he is running around with other women." Her husband didn't attempt to deny this, but presented his side: "Frankly, I can't stand her constant nagging. It's even affected the sound of her voice, she's always whining. I have to get away from her to clear my head, so that I can go to work the next day."

As they attacked each other, with open hostility, it became obvious that both of them had been unfaithful. Although they frankly admitted the double adultery, neither of them seemed to be happy with their infidelities. Their extramarital affairs were a source of constant bickering. Underneath their conflict, there seemed to be a sincere desire to save their marriage and the security of a home for their children, whom they both adored.

The wife confessed that, although she had become involved

romantically with one of her neighbors, it had turned out to be unsatisfying sexually. "In fact," she said, "he was just as lousy a lover as my husband is." It never occurred to this woman that the problem might be with her. Or perhaps, it did and she was unable to face the reality of her own low level of responsiveness and needed to blame her husband. She claimed the reason she did not enjoy sex relations with her husband was because he really did not love her. As for her lover, she insisted he was very much in love with her—and yet . . . nothing happened. Her frigidity was neither affected by the physical change of men nor by the emotional factor of her conception of love.

Her husband listened and grew angrier as she told her side of their story. Then, without a word, he got up and walked out. She quickly followed at his heels, berating him and piling one accusation upon the other. One could hardly blame the man for spending his time away from such a disgruntled nag. Can you imagine how difficult it must be to make love at night, after a day of such discord?

Some weeks later, Dolores decided, on her own, to take a course with me in auto-suggestion. She said she hoped it would help her to be more relaxed sexually. I explained that she could apply this method in any way she chose. There was no question, but that an improved attitude at this point could bring about improvements in her body. The stress of constant bickering had robbed her of her vitality and sexual confidence.

She was a self-defeating person and it was difficult for her to grasp the idea that her own thinking made her this way. She could not imagine any other way of being. Her thought patterns had been repeated over such a long period of time that they were deeply entrenched which immediately made her spontaneous reactions unpleasant. It took conscientious effort for her to erase her unhappy personality traits, and even more effort to replace them with a set of happier reflexes.

To begin with, I suggested it might help if she acquired a more optimistic outlook on life. She looked at me with mild amusement, "Optimistic? You expect *me* to be optimistic with four kids screaming all day, and a husband who runs around with other women. You expect me to go around smiling?" In spite of the fact that she said she wanted to be helped, she remained scornful of the concept: the mind has power over the body's activity.

Despite this, she was diligent about attending classes. Although she was an apt pupil, she argued and questioned every issue that arose. This attitude continued until one day she came to class looking strangely different, her expression sober and introspective. She described a dream she had the night before. Although she had always had a great fear of horses, she had dreamed that she was a famous western rider, working in a rodeo show "busting broncos."

Dolores sparkled as she described the feeling she had when controlling the wild power of the horse. She said, "It felt great. *I never let him throw me on my back.* It was a thrill to stay on top and make the horse take my commands." This revealing dream helped her to get to the root of her problem in rapid order. She began to understand, challenge, and contradict her own irrational ideas that were causing her sexual dysfunction.

She had understood the sexual connection of her dream. She recognized in it her fear of losing control during the sex act. The pattern underlying her negativism was lack of trust, not only of her husband, but of the power of the orgastic experience. Suddenly she laughed, for the first time, "The most amazing thing about this dream is that I woke up the next morning with terribly sore leg muscles—as if I had actually been riding a horse all night!"

She had not moved from the bed, yet the power of her own imagination had brought about this muscular pain. She proved to herself that the mind is constantly working, even during sleep. With this dream she uncovered some of the inhibiting blocks and was amazed at the extent of her own repressed sexual fears. Once she was equipped with this knowledge about herself, she became more confident in working to change her irrational thinking. We worked out a set of positive auto-suggestions designed to bring her out of the rut she had kept herself in. One of her major problems in struggling to reach orgasm was that she always tried too hard. Over-determination can be a handicap rather than an asset. She had been so ashamed of being inadequate that instead of relaxing, she had strained and struggled and worried about the outcome.

The secret in building up to a successful climax is not to *think* about what is going to happen but to enjoy the immediacy, the "right now", to make the most of the delicious moment. To begin with, you must believe in yourself, that you are normal and have everything biologically necessary to respond to the point of orgasm. You must start with the firm conviction that you are capable in every way and always have been. This is the first step, and it is called positive self-awareness. When you are truly aware, you know that the condition you wish to achieve has always been possible. It is only *your thinking* that has stood in the way.

Awareness assures you that, underneath the seeming inadequacy waits a passionate woman, ready to be released. When you have awareness, you begin to hear what you have secretly been telling yourself, about yourself, and then you change the suggestions, if they need changing. You will begin to improve when you suggest to yourself that there are no "frigid" women; that your sensuality has merely been temporarily obscured. You will realize that normalcy has been lying dormant waiting for the proper expectant attitude.

Positive suggestions (as outlined in a subsequent chapter) will help you erase old patterns, and replace them with sex habits that answer your needs for physical satisfaction.

Changing Habits

A habit *starts* as a spontaneous action and becomes a habit because of repetition. It can also start from someone else's negative suggestion *when it is accepted by you as truth and stored in the subconscious*. It may have been someone else's hang-up to begin with, *but the moment you believe it, it becomes your own*.

The third step that you will learn to master is profound body relaxation. Sexual tension is automatic with most non-functioning women. This is also an automatic behavior pattern and can be systematically replaced with a more meaningful one. The elimination of tension makes it easier to absorb new ideas and new body actions. The tested exercises which follow are based on this premise. Deep relaxation of both the mind and body simultaneously makes it possible for changes in thinking to take firm hold. The removal of old tension permits the body to receive new mental messages of pleasure.

When you learn to relax your muscles deliberately, you are able to ease the pressure on your circulatory system; this enables the blood to circulate freely and, as it surges to the sexual organs, you begin to feel increasing sensation. In addition to relaxing the muscles, you will also learn to relax your breathing.

The technique of relaxed, *rhythmic breathing* has been used for centuries to promote better sexual responsiveness. In the Eastern cultures, such as the Yoga practices, breathing is the core to achieving a depth of tranquility that is conducive to greater emotional and physical happiness.

Relaxation, combined with rhythmic deep breathing, leads to meditation, and it is in the state of relaxed meditation that *sexual self-imagery* is practiced. Meditation has been used since antiquity to transcend environmental conditions and rise above the body's needs. Here we use it to focus on the body's needs in order to increase sexual gratification. We will teach you how to build sexual fantasies to help you to fulfillment. You will learn to focus on maximally exciting things to keep you from being distracted by non-sexual thoughts.

The sixth exercise, which you will enjoy doing, involves the *sex muscles*. These exercises will teach you to have maximum control over the expansion and contraction of these powerful muscles. They will be conditioned to do their part in stimulating the nerve endings within the vagina, as well as making firmer contact with the penis. Doing these natural movements will enable you to grasp the penis and feel stimulated by it (regardless of its size). You can, after diligent practice, develop muscle power to the point where your vagina will feel similar to a fist closed firmly around an object.

The seventh exercise is designed to intensify sensate excitement to its greatest intensity. We refer to it as *sensory awakening*, and it plays an important role both in self-therapy and in mutually reaching greater heights of climatic exaltation.

1. Stimulation of the erogenous zones involves the sense of *touch*.

2. Words of tenderness and love involve the sense of *hearing*.
3. Kissing and oral love-making involve the sense of *taste*.
4. The odor of the lover's bodies involves the sense of *smell*.
5. Looking at one's mate and enjoying every part of him employs the sense of *sight*.

It is the full erotic use of all these senses that makes sex something more than just an act of animalism. You have the ability within your senses to make of the sexual union a more profound union, bringing into harmony the body, the mind, the emotions and the soul.

Before proceeding to the specific exercises given in the rest of this book, remember that the power of sensation can only flow through a positive force. Negativism restricts and constricts, it interferes with the movement of circulation into the genitals. This is true of men as well as women. Negativism causes tension and tension cuts off the ability to function as nature intended.

As you master the seven steps to sexual satisfaction, you will learn to focus and channel your desires toward positive culmination. Repetitive practice will cause your sexual function to assume the condition it would have been in if you had not been sidetracked in childhood and adolescence.

Remember also, there has probably never been anything wrong with your sexuality. Look upon yourself as having temporarily lost touch with your natural reflexes. Most women suffer, at some time, from *temporary sexual amnesia*. The following exercises are designed to bring back your sexual memory.

TWELVE

Step No. 1.
Self-Awareness

Self-awareness requires a journey into oneself. No matter how far we need to travel, every journey starts by taking the first step. One step after the other brings us to our goals. It always helps to know where we've been in order to figure out where we are going and how to get there. Awareness sparks motivation which is fundamental for reconditioning.

The most powerful motivation known is the desire for sexual function. It is a very persuasive force and comprehension channels it in the right direction. A sage once said, "An unexamined life is not worth living." Life without awareness relegates one to an aimless existence, propelled by forces not under our control.

A woman who passively accepts and lives with her unresolved childhood inhibitions clings to an infantile manner of dealing with her sexual difficulties. She has convinced herself that the cause of her inadequacy lies outside of her own realm of control. The answer for her is always to continue searching for the "right man."

No one can make a life for you, and no one else can develop your sexual identity for you. Your successes and failures come from your own unconscious decisions. YOU are the only one who possesses the proper instrument to correct past mistakes—that very personal instrument is your own individual mind that is constantly directing you.

People can and do change, at all ages, *if they are sufficiently eager to do so.*

Without knowing ourselves and what makes our mental machinery tick, we can neither solve our problems, nor adapt and live in harmony with the world around us. To begin the process of learning about yourself you must first look back and ferret out the roots of your self-defeating behavior. Looking back into your past need not be painful *if you realize that the backward look will give you the necessary insight to move forward more speedily.*

Knowledge brings with it the illumination of the causes which hamper our development. Once this information is examined rationally in the light of its usefulness for progress, a woman often takes great giant steps forward. It is not necessary to actually live through each unresolved period of childhood sexuality and adolescence. We have all encountered people, who, as adults in body only, continue to behave in a childish manner where the opposite sex is concerned.

A woman who still thinks like a teenager has a problem

when she meets someone she cares for, because she will tend to behave like one. Adolescent women constantly revert to behavior that should have been *lived through, experienced, and discarded* earlier in their lives. Without awareness, such a woman clings tenaciously to her adolescence throughout her entire lifetime.

In addition to being aware of the inhibiting part that parents play in the sexual growth of their daughters, we must also recognize that civilization itself has proved detrimental to the instinctual drives of the female body.

People need other people, and this is as true for female people as it is for male people. Physical closeness helps us to grow to higher levels of sensory awareness. Countless walls separate people, both literally and figuratively. This makes it difficult for them to communicate in order to work out their mutual needs. Real sexual self-knowledge can only be gained through the interaction between people. Unfortunately, most people lack sufficient opportunity in their growing years to learn about themselves in relation to the opposite sex. They grow up with deepest feelings of insecurity, lack of confidence and loneliness; the self-alienation, no matter how painful, goes unrecognized by the person who is unaware.

Unawareness dooms a person to a life of vacuous despair. Not knowing why, they continually search for an opportunity to relive the lapses in previous stages of their development. Most people move through their lives as if in a dream, totally unaware of the forces which influence them. Like puppets, controlled by strings from the past, they act out the unfinished business of childhood. Unless women discover what influenced their immaturity, they can remain tied to past parental problems indefinitely.

Kahlil Gibran, the Persian poet, said: "Parents are the bows from which children, as arrows, are sent forth." Admitting that parents are often mistaken in their direction, still no good purpose can be served by continuing to blame them forever. Everyone has suffered from some misdirection, yet many people overcome this handicap and reach a higher destiny.

The learning material in this book deals with simple methods of reconditioning our sexual reflexes. There is a simple truth that can help you free yourself for better sexual happiness. It is that NO MATTER WHAT HAS HAPPENED IN THE PAST, RIGHT NOW, ONLY YOU ARE RESPONSIBLE FOR YOUR EMOTIONAL AND PHYSICAL ACTIONS. This is because *we carry within our minds the machinery that can erase as well as place ideas into our habit-patterns.*

Confused Thinking Confuses the Body

Dr. Milton W. White, in his famous book on dynamic awareness: "The Power of Self-Knowledge," stresses the harmful effects that confused thinking can have upon the body. He states: "The difference between helpful and harmful behavior, feelings, and thoughts lies in the fact that the helpful ones develop out of real self-knowledge; that is contribute to sound and effective relationships in which the individual is involved. The harmful ones develop out of a lack of self-knowledge, out of the confusion of relationships. Confusion can arise, as I have said, out of physical disturbances and interruptions, as in the case of the little girl with the over-protective and anxious mother.

"At the time the confusion arises, the individual may not be aware of what is happening. But to deconfuse himself, to make it possible for him to discover and reunderstand his lost relationships and to manipulate them adequately and satisfactorily, he must work at solving his problems and he must work at dissolving this ineffectiveness by learning and retraining."

If you change the "he" to "she", the above quote directly represents what happens to the sexually inadequate female and what she can do to become happier. He states further that "Self-knowledge is defeated by confusion," and that "misplaced fear-reactions lie behind many of our mind/body confusions." When you apply this concept to the accumulated sexual fears which confuse and confound the ability of so many women to relate to themselves vaginally, you will understand this problem more clearly. Right now, only you, yourself, can be held responsible for your immediate emotional and physical reactions because *only you* have the power to satisfy, as well as to defeat, yourself. You can cause your behavior to be negative or positive. You make this choice repeatedly, every moment of your life.

Getting to Know the Real You

Knowledge is the trusty tool which rebuilds patterns of thinking. Knowledge brings the breath of life to sick habits. Knowledge can remold our sexual responses the way we really wish them to be.

Not only must we be aware of what preceded our habit-patterns, but we must be immediately alert to the fact that each thought we think is either helpful or harmful. Awareness and self-knowledge makes it possible for us to systematically sort out and discard old, negative, defeatist thinking about ourselves and replace it with rational thinking about how our bodies function. An unaware, sexually frigid woman constantly reinforces her lack of success. Fear of failure, where orgasm is concerned, is a sure way of making failure happen. Psychiatry points out that worrying about the lack of something brings about that very lack. Whether a woman is extremely "frigid" or just occasionally inhibited, she can greatly benefit from self-awareness.

The most direct way to get rid of sexual hang-ups, is to take a good, honest look at the past. Past false impressions and parental/environment pressures dissolve under the scrutiny of desire for change. Examining the original stimuli which caused sexual limitations makes it possible to break the defeatist syndrome of habit.

Self-awareness is the "do-it-yourself" analyzer of past experience. When we analyze our behavior, we often realize that past attitudes do not always suit present needs. When you decide that you have carried over past undesirable sex habits which cause dysfunction, you can then learn to deliberately remove them. *Preconditioning that limits our sex pleasure keeps us bogged down in other aspects of living as well.*

People who are unsuccessful in satisfying themselves sexually, carry this dissatisfaction around with them in everything that they do, reflecting their shortcomings in the ineffectual lives that they live. When they are self-deceptive and refuse to face the reality of who they are and how they function, they are also unable to relate honestly in other areas such as business, social, and family levels.

Coordination between the forces of mind and body give a person a "self-togetherness" that radiates and instills confidence in every area of endeavor. Our human qualities, our talent for creativity gives us extraordinary advantages over all other forms of life, in getting emotional gratification from our lives.

Whereas animals simply derive a release from instinctual tension, humans are capable not only of this, but much more. The epitome of sexuality is to feel exhilarated physically and exalted spiritually. Once you have risen above the restrictions of your past, you can take yourself up the ladder to a higher plateau of being, by involving all of your sensory attributes.

Your Emotions Effect Your Sex Life

It is important for your general health, as well as your sex life, that you be consciously aware that when you experience good emotions, feelings of happiness, cheerfulness, hope, trust, confidence, your body reacts by functioning at its optimum best. On the contrary, when you feel depressed and moody, or anxious, fearful and guilty, these emotions have a disturbing effect on your body's machinery. In order to feel at your best you must be constantly alert to the fact that your negative emotions come from your own negative thinking. You should know that they disturb your glandular system, your nerves, and digestive organs as well as setting back your sexual function.

When people become consciously aware of the destructive result that their emotions can have upon their general health, this knowledge can help them make a change for the better. When a woman discovers that she suffers from a lack of anatomical knowledge about how her sex organs are supposed to function, she should eliminate her ignorance by learning the true facts.

To change old, non-rewarding habits into better ones, we must be flexible and willing for this change to take place. Wanting improvement is very important in order for the old habit to give way to the new. The older the habits are, the more tenaciously they resist change, but they can be removed. Even the most entrenched persistent bad habits can be overcome with concentrated practice. This latent power for change has always been with you, it is up to you to make the best use of it. Accept your problems as a challenge and do not flinch at the job that needs to be done. You can have fun in the change-over process. The very act of admitting to yourself that you have problems helps give you the confidence to do something about them. There is no point in being dissatisfied and challenged by things that have no cure. In this case, dissatisfaction can act as an emotional spur to make whatever changes are necessary for satisfaction.

Do not generalize your dissatisfaction with your body. Accept yourself as a healthy sexual person whose instincts have been diverted away from the body's needs. Once you know that you are capable and that past fears were unrealistic, you will be able to take the necessary steps toward altering the situation. Once you take the first step, awareness, the others will follow in natural sequence. Auto-suggestion. Body relaxation. Sexual breathing. Self-imagery. Sexual muscles. And the seventh and most gratifying, Sensory awareness.

Enlightenment gives us a clearer image of our future selves and goads us to further improvement. As our minds accept a new image we are encouraged to make the dream a reality. What your mind can conceive and believe, your body can achieve. When you discover how your mind thinks you will, at the same time, discover how your body responds to that thinking. Develop a truer feminine image by becoming fully informed as to how your sexual organs function. Don't be embarrassed about exploring, investigating, and experimenting. Once you accept your sexuality on a mental and emotional level, you will discover that your body has a natural tendency to motivate you toward sexual health.

Once you begin to see and believe that neurotic sexual behavior isn't just externally imposed, but is reinforced by your own mental processes, you will be able to orient yourself in a better direction for happiness. Even though we are originally affected by early acquired resistances to pleasure, we will be cheating ourselves if we continue to blame these early influences for present-day habits. You must be aware of what you continue to tell yourself every day and what you tell yourself at every sexual encounter to maintain these unhealthy disturbances. Your sexual fears may have been originally implanted by forces out of your control, but *you* are the present day perpetrator and as such must be held responsible for your own immediate improvement.

How to Succeed In Sex

The great majority of sexually unhappy people keep reinfecting themselves by selecting, out of the constant flow of suggestions, the self-disturbing, self-defeating ones that fit the original ideas taught to them in childhood. If you find that certain attitudes sabotage your progress toward your goal of self-improvement, reject these negative suggestions whether they are your own or come from outside sources.

The first essential to any kind of success is to know where you want to go, to set a realistic goal. A goal is like a strong rope; it gives you something dependable to hold on to. It helps you to raise yourself to a higher level, to look forward to a clearly defined image of what you are striving for.

Once you are aware of *wanting* to change and have set a rational goal for yourself, the next essential is dedication to the cause for which you are striving. Determination that is fired by a strong emotional desire makes things happen much quicker. Desire intensifies motivation which is the most powerful emotion for bringing about changes. The very fact that you are reading this book indicates that you are motivated to improve your sexual responses. How quickly you reach your objective hinges on how powerfully you desire these changes and the practical relaxed way that you apply the seven steps outlined here.

Self-awareness is a much neglected faculty and can, if used properly, impart a new depth of meaning to even the most mundane things. In sexual matters, it makes the difference between function and dysfunction. With awareness we begin to notice not only ourselves but other people on a conscious level. As we observe their faces, the expression, the tone of voice, the choice of words, even the subtle nuances of their thoughts are somehow communicated. We need only to be alert and open for deeper messages of communication.

An awareness of even the most trivial everyday occurrences makes life more meaningful and widens our scope of "here and now." An alert attention to living and what is happening at the moment doesn't take extra time, it is simply woven into the fabric of existing activity. And the rewards, in the wider expansion of your mental faculties and talents, are manifold.

We can use awareness not only to enhance the present, but to better comprehend the past and its affect upon us. We reach into our memory so that the helpful information that is stored there will come back to us in our need.

Intellect + Emotion = Action

Awareness helps us develop intelligent insight. As we develop this insight, we begin to realize how vast is the realm of our undiscovered potential. While *intellectual insight* discloses this potential to us, doing something about our inadequacies demands that we also possess *emotional insight*.

Adding the emotional quality makes the difference between just seeing what's happening, or doing something about it. Dr. Albert Ellis in his psychological report, "Toward a More Precise Definition of Emotional and 'Intellectual' Insight", states it very succinctly.

"Emotional insight is a multiple barreled process which involves seeing and believing, thinking and acting, wishing and practicing. Quantitatively, it includes more kinds of behaving than does 'intellectual' insight. Qualitatively, it is a radically different, essentially more forceful, effective, and committed kind of behavior. 'Emotional' insight, moreover, includes a complex sequence of thought and action beginning with some kind of 'intellectual' understanding and followed by a whole chain of behaviors which, if cut at any one of its links, aborts itself and never rises above the original 'intellectual' level."

In other words, just knowing that something is wrong is not going to change the situation. What makes the change is action that is propelled by the power of emotional desire for the change to take place. The degree of improvement is in direct ratio to the degree of emotional insight that the person has.

We either get better, or we get worse. The choice rests with each of us.

How to Practice Step Number 1

In order to understand your present condition and plan to make the necessary improvements, you must now take a look at the past. Begin by asking yourself a few revealing questions.

Here are a few samples of the kind of vital questions that prod and probe the recesses of your mind. It may prove helpful to formulate your own in addition to the following:

1. How did my problem start in the first place?
2. In what way was my sexual development interfered with?
3. What was my mother's and father's attitude toward sex?
4. Did any incident occur that shocked or frightened me?
5. What sort of sex education did I receive?
6. What was the source of my sex knowledge?
    a. Was it received at home?
    b. At school?
    c. From friends?
7. How did the various explanations differ?
8. Was my mother eager, interested, and sympathetic?
9. Or was she cold, indifferent, insensible?
10. Am I predestined to be like my mother?

11. Do I know what caused my mother to be the way she was sexually?

12. Has my conditioning affected my present behavior?

It is helpful to write down your answers to these questions so that in the rereading you will gain added insight into your sexual problem. Keep in mind that you must know who you are before anyone else can appreciate you.

When to Practice Self-awareness

Self-awareness is not a "sometimes" thing. It can and should be practiced at all times. In addition to using it to analyze the sexual pressures of the past, self-understanding improves every area of living. It is also important to devote some special time for focusing on the answers to the questions that you must ask of yourself. Eventually you will combine all seven steps into a single fifteen minute reconditioning period. First, read through all of the seven steps before launching on this first one.

When you become aware that you have a body, then you are *somebody*. When you are unaware of your body, then you have no body and are nobody. Expand your every moment with the kind of awareness that gives living its greatest dimension.

THIRTEEN

Step No. 2.
Auto-Suggestion

*After you know what's wrong, auto-suggestion can help you.
Auto-suggestion is the natural ally of awareness. When auto-*suggestion is positive it becomes a very direct method of correcting the problems that awareness brings to light. Assuming that you were led to believe that sex was more of a female duty than a pleasure, being aware of this will not by itself change your attitude. But applying the proper positive self-suggestion can and will change your attitude if you want it to.

When you think of yourself as completely responsive, you merely help yourself become what you always were capable of being. Auto-suggestion is a method of training and remolding mental attitudes through the influence of the imagination.

In using positive ideas for self-improvement, you are harnessing auto-suggestion and putting it to work. It becomes a control method of predicting how you will behave at a given time, because you are instructing your mind to make it so. We are constantly making "predictions" about what we can and cannot do. When you tell yourself that you can't make it, the orders are always accepted and carried out. When you expect more of your body, your body delivers more.

Predictions are, in a way, auto-suggestions, both good and bad. Self-criticism is only helpful if it is constructive and serves a purpose for improvement. Other people's criticism and adverse opinions tend to lower our self-esteem and affect our behavior. When we agree with someone else's opinion about us, the agreement becomes, in itself, auto-suggestion. From that point what we do and what happens to us is our own doing.

Robert Bierstadt, a New York University sociologist, says, "Very often we try to fit into someone else's preconceived idea of what we should be. When people place us into a particular category, it is important to be aware of this." When we are children it is difficult to defend ourselves against negative criticism. However, as an aware adult, we must guard ourselves against the infiltration of defeating suggestion. There is no one who can protect us from this ever-present onslaught but ourselves.

Three Avenues of Suggestion

Here are the three avenues of suggestion that can lead to sexual failure:

1. What we have been told about sex in the past.
2. What people tell us at the moment.
3. What we tell ourselves (consciously and unconsciously.

The third is the most powerful of all suggestions and can make the difference between a fulfilled woman or a frustrated one. Ask yourself, "What am I telling myself about myself? Is it helping me or hindering me?" If what you are saying is less than confidently *positive and affirmative,* then you are probably not living up to your potential of pleasurable living.

Because primitive impulses have been so long considered base, it is no wonder that the subconscious has accepted the idea of sex as dirty, immoral and anti-feminine. While this hasn't stopped people from indulging, it has certainly crippled their instincts, especially where women are concerned.

Outside suggestion, when believed and accepted by our subconscious, becomes internalized. We then reinforce this negative thinking by unwittingly carrying out the suggestions. Once a suggestion is accepted and carried out by the subconscious, it begins its urging to be repeated and reinforced. Eventually what was once a simple outside suggestion becomes an ingrained habit.

No matter how habitual the negatives in your life have become, you can break their grip. You need not be forever dominated by them. You can, as many thousands of others have done, eliminate sex complexes and malfunction by using positive auto-suggestion. This will give you control over your sexual impulses as well as building increased feeling genitally. Positive auto-suggestion will guide you toward acquiring greater sexual gratification. Instead of the negatives such as guilt, shame, and fear, you will see sex as an essential part of good living, joyous and healthy, and natural. It can be done. No doors are permanently closed, no matter how severe the problem may seem to be at the moment.

For the past decade or so, medical doctors and psychiatrists have been warning us about the detrimental affect of negative suggestion. It is cited as one of the causes of mental stress, which can be destructive to our body's functional machinery. There has been a great deal of discussion, in newspapers as well as other media, pointing up the fact that an overwhelming percentage of physical ailments have their origin in negative mental attitudes. It is no longer considered a controversial issue. It has been proven on all sides time and time again. Dr. Hans Selye, father of the theory of "psychosomatic" medicine, makes this very clear in his excellent book, "Stress of Life." He explains that many ailments such as headaches, backaches, and stomach ulcers are directly attributable to mental tensions, anxiety, and worry. Therefore, it should not surprise you to learn that, if your mental attitude can make you ill (sexually inadequate), it can also make you well (and responsive). There is no reason to despair, no matter how tense you seem to be. You can change to a healthy way of functioning in just the same way as you acquired dysfunction, by *repetitive auto-suggestion*.

An Optimistic Attitude Helps

Repeated tests show that pessimistic thinking about one's sexual function makes it virtually impossible for a person to function, while optimistic expectations help a person overcome problems.

Webster's dictionary defines OPTIMISM as:

The doctrine that the good of life over-balances the pain and evil . . . the inclination to put the most favorable construction upon the actions and happenings, to minimize adverse aspects, conditions . . . to anticipate the best possible outcome . . . to have a cheerful and hopeful temperament.

To be optimistic sexually is to anticipate always a gratifying experience. To expect each subsequent act of intercourse to be better than the last one. The optimistic person recognizes that relearning and retraining is always possible.

What has once been learned is not necessarily permanent. The mind is like a tape recorder which records and erases constantly. Learning to the point of habit pattern is called *conditioning*. Getting rid of the habit is called *deconditioning*. Replacing the bad habit with a good habit is called *reconditioning*. That is what you are in the process of doing, right now, as you are reading and absorbing the thoughts in this book. Properly motivated, any optimistic person can be reconditioned to healthy sexuality. Habit that is deeply entrenched simply takes more effort but it can be done and is being done by people every day.

Original conditioning gives way to the reconditioning force of auto-suggestion when it is fired by the optimistic enthusiasm of expected sexual gratification. Sex fulfillment is a powerful factor in human happiness, and is within the grasp of every aware person. You will find that your own negativism tends to collapse and give way to the pressure of applied reconditioning techniques. The fundamental task of your auto-suggestion exercises is to establish a smooth working relationship between your mind as director, and your body as the performer. Proper harmony and communication between the two reflects itself in increased sensory pleasure.

Suggestion does not always happen in a deliberate way. We are all constantly in a state of giving and receiving all sorts of suggestions about everything, some negative and pessimistic, and others positive and optimistic. There are some people who are mostly negative personalities both as receivers and projectors. They are the people who not only defeat themselves, but instill within other people doubts about their abilities to succeed. These people are like dangerous carriers of communicable disease. They may not be aware of it, but they cause emotional as well as physical breakdowns, not only their own, but other people's.

Are You a Negative or Positive Person?

If you are more positive than negative you will see results sooner. If not, you must learn to discard attitudes which do not serve your purpose for better living.

The human mind is the central station of a communication system more complicated than any computer ever created by man.

Long before the development of man-made marvels such as the computer, nature designed a system far superior. The brain is a structural masterpiece and while it is still largely unexplored, we do know some things about how the human mind works. We are continuously discovering new dimensions of the human potential. Although we like to think of ourselves as "having a mind of our own," the fact is that our minds are not private and personal at all. In fact, in the truest sense, our minds have no independent existence at all. They are the receiving stations for a huge amount of information constantly fed to them from the outside world. Awareness gives us the independence to reject those ideas that do not fit into our self-image. Much of our involuntary physical activity is a result of ideas planted there a very long time ago. This is especially true of our sexual activity and unless the obsolete messages, which we are apt to keep receiving, are cancelled out, we cannot hope to reach our goal of full sexual potential. You must decide for yourself between a negative or an affirmative way of life. And then do something concrete about it. Be decisive and enthusiastic. Notice the slightest improvement and nurture and encourage it within yourself. Practice being definite, positive and decisive in every avenue of your daily living. Welcome every possible chance to say, "yes" instead of "no." Don't teeter-totter on the brink of every decision with "but," "if" or "maybe." Instead of constantly debating every issue, stop confusing yourself and take the most direct road to success. Don't make a ponderous problem about sexual function. Learn the facts and face them with courageous insight. Letting your mind stew in a quandry only serves to make stronger your inability to use it as a strong directing force for your body.

There is one thing that all people have in common, whether they are rich or poor, male or female, black or white. They can choose for themselves between an affirmative, positive way of life, or a defeating, negative one. Everyone has this choice. In addition, we possess twenty-four hours a day in which we can make the most or the worst of living.

Make a Choice

You must choose whether you wish to perpetuate outmoded, unsatisfactory attitudes and responses or whether you are ready to embrace life fully. If the latter is true there is nothing to stand in your way but yourself. Every time you think and every time you speak, you should know that each thought and word brings with it a physical action and a possible effect upon your body. Suggestion has unlimited power in both directions. If your thoughts are of a defeatist nature, you are surely going to be defeated. However, if you think and speak as a winner, you cannot help but act like a winner and win out over adversities. Your wonderous brain is constantly exercising control over both the involuntary and voluntary systems of your body. It determines all of its action based on records and memories of past suggestion. When you think like a loser, your clever brain digs up all the old defeatist associations to further hamper you. There are also some helpful memories to recall if you really wish to do so. Everyone has both. Check and notice your responses. Check and notice what you are telling yourself about your sexual function.

Always keep your mind open and eager, enthusiastically curious about new ideas that might be of help to you. Your mind is like a huge tape recorder of unlimited capacity. If you wish to become more positive than negative you must develop a system for wiping off "the tape" and replacing misinformation with proper directions for living. Unless you do this you will be cheating yourself out of the kind of life that can only come from running your machinery on all its cylinders.

Open the Shutters of Your Mind

More than 300 years before Christ, the philosopher, Aristotle, said, "If the body were to take the mind to court, the judge would find that the mind had been a most ruinous tenant of the body." The truth of his statement is even more evident today as mankind's over-active brain exerts ever more tension upon the body.

Your mental warehouse has not only vast accumulations of helpful information, but also a great backlog of useless debris. The sooner you give your mind a good house cleaning, the better you will feel. Concentrated auto-suggestion is the "broom" which can sweep it clean.

While it is important to always think positively and be alert and aware of negative forces around us, in order to clear out imbedded germs of negativism we must make a special kind of concerted effort. The auto-suggestions must be planned and repeated often. Emptying the mind of extraneous thoughts and focusing on the new suggestions makes them become a reality sooner.

Your regular relaxation and concentration periods are the most productive times for giving yourself corrective suggestions. It takes special attention to change from pessimistic to optimistic. More than mere attention, it takes *concentration,* for they are not really the same thing.

Concentration is the ability to shut out disturbances and *focus on the central idea,* in this case sexual fulfillment. Even though other thoughts might filter into the mind, in focusing there is an automatic tendency to drift back to the auto-suggestion being worked on. Despite temporary interference, your thoughts are pulled back to the problem at hand. A woman who finds that she is unable to concentrate on corrective auto-suggestions is one who is unsure of her ability to improve. She has been sold a self-image which rules out the possibility of success. This kind of person feels doomed to failure not only as a sexual being, but as a human being as well.

Positive auto-suggestion not only helps rid us of sexual problems, it also helps in countless other ways. An increased feeling of well-being, of energy and expanded creativity comes with the very beginning of the acceptance of positive suggestion. Abundant hope takes over despair and inertia.

A woman who has led a crippled sexual existence, bogged down by a morass of guilt and fears, must be ready to throw it all out and participate in sex for the sheer joy of it, *purely for pleasure*. The woman who cannot give positive auto-suggestion to herself may subconsciously deem herself unworthy of sexual happiness. If this is the case, she should seek help from a psychiatrist, as this book is written for those women who are psychically ready to accept their birthright of sexual normalcy.

The best and most effective way to get speedy results from self-suggestion is to be systematic about it. Setting aside a special study-relaxation time, and being consistent about it is the only sincere way to affect the necessary changes. Getting into the habit of self-help is just as easy as perpetuating the habit of self-hurt.

Changing Habits

The human personality is made up of a collection of reflex habits. All of our activities center around these patterns of automatic habit. In order for you to reach your goals, you must be wide awake to your own entrenched habits and keep asking yourself, "Is this action helping me get where I want to go, or is it hindering me?"

Remember that you always have the opportunity to decide between a negative or positive reaction to stimulus. Think about where a suggestion is coming from. Examine the source and search out its motivation. Know what your true desires are and do not choose to continue a habit if it is contrary to your needs.

There is an ancient Buddhist maxim which states, "What you think upon, grows." Auto-suggestions become self-motivators and cause physical changes to take place as well as personality changes. Dysfunction increases if you dwell upon it. By the same token, sexual happiness can also grow if you focus good thoughts upon it.

Auto-suggestions are *self-commands*. If they start the mind and body moving in the right direction, they are the right kind of suggestions. They are the activators that can bring about all affirmative improvements. Not only are self-suggestions self-commands, they are also builders of self-esteem, self-confidence, and self-love. It has often been said that to be truly loved by another, one must first feel lovable. To reach this high level of self-acceptance, we must be constantly on guard against the onslaught of verbal put-downs and non-verbal put-downs.

Remember that all hetero-suggestion, past and present, is transformed into auto-suggestion by your failure to reject it. If you desire to be more than a puppet of outside direction, you must carefully examine suggestion before making it your own. Awareness of the past should not make you bitter against family and environment. There is no point in castigating parents for mistakes in your sexual education. Sexual ignorance is universal and your parents were a natural part of that condition. You must learn to accept the fact of past conditioning without emotional trauma, in the knowledge that the effects upon you are correctable, *by you*.

How to Practice Step Number 2

If you consistently repeat any of the following suggestions fifty to one hundred times, both morning and evening, you can expect to see a definite improvement in just one short week. However, if you "program" yourself by combining all seven steps into a complete reconditioning period and stick to it regularly, the results will astound you.

You can give the suggestions to yourself either verbally (out loud) or non-verbally (silently). Both methods are effective in breaking down the wall of negative resistance to orgasm. Many advocates of auto-suggestion claim that when suggestion is spoken out loud it has an especially effective result on the subconscious. They say that the spoken word cuts into the mind more decisively via the sense of hearing.

However, it is not always practical to verbalize sexual auto-suggestion. So keep in mind that both methods are extremely helpful. If you have privacy during your daily reconditioning practice periods, by all means, state your auto-suggestions verbally. If not, focus your thinking upon them and use the following techniques to instill the suggestions as deep as possible.

While silently mouthing the suggestions (or merely thinking

them), *tap your forefinger* with each repetitive suggestion. This technique brings together the mind and body, while at the same time tapping the thought into the automatic motor system.

Silent sexual suggestion can be practiced effectively no matter where we happen to be, without anyone being aware that we are doing it. This is important because the more often you suggest sexual success to yourself, the sooner it will happen. Each time you make a success suggestion to your mind, you accumulate the power of this activating force and teach your mind to flash the right messages to you in time of need.

Almost everyone is susceptible to this scientific process of change. There are, however, two types of women who will not be able to benefit from this program. They are:

Those who are intellectually incapable of understanding.

Those who are unwilling to improve.

Of all kinds of suggestion, sexual suggestion is the most powerful and shows the most spectacular results. It can expand the feeblest sensation to the greatest heights of orgastic ecstasy.

Here is a sampling of auto-suggestions which have proved helpful to many women in increasing their sexual responsiveness:

1. I am sexually normal and have everything it takes to feel genital sensation and respond to the point of orgasm.
2. I enjoy intercourse and am looking forward to increased pleasure each time.
3. Every time I have sex it turns out to be better and better.

4. I feel sensation in both the clitoris and vagina and can reach a *unified orgasm*.
5. I am free of guilt, shame and fear. All inhibitions are gone. I will let myself go and intensify pleasure.
6. I keenly enjoy penile-vaginal contact. I can and I will have an orgasm in any position I choose.
7. (Spoken out loud during intercourse) It feels so good to just relax and enjoy sex. I know I am going to have an orgasm. I am not resisting it. The feeling is growing more intense. It is happening ... Now. ...

The exact wording of the suggestions is unimportant as long as it expresses your personal desire. Use your own words and expressions for greater effectiveness. If the so-called "naughty" words help free you from restraint, use them by all means. Anything that helps you reach an orgasm is morally right, as long as no one is hurt by it.

The following general suggestions are helpful to make sex more relaxed and mutually satisfying.

1. I am going to be clean and well groomed for sexual adventure.
2. I am not squeamish about variety in lovemaking.
3. I will communicate my secret desires and be tolerant of his.
4. I will participate and take the initiative in foreplay.
5. I will compliment my lover on his lovemaking.
6. I will be more demonstrative and exuberant about sex.
7. I am free of fear, shame and guilt.

When to Practice Step Number 2

Affirmative auto-suggestion should be practiced at all times. This is not something which you turn off and on. If you have chosen to be successful, then you must be aware that you are always being bombarded by harmful suggestions all around you. When a negative thought presents itself, reject it immediately. Replace the rejected thought with a positive suggestion that will bring you closer to your goal. In addition to always being positive, it is important that you use your regular periods of reconditioning for the specific ferreting out of the old and the reinstating of the new. Daily conscientious disciplined auto-suggestion will do the job. You must first of all convince yourself that orgasm is possible. Just as you have convinced yourself previously that it was impossible. Repeating the thought again and again will help to bring it to fruition. Reconditioning through auto-suggestion does not take extra time from your daily schedule. Positive suggestions's special techniques are worked during the two practice periods. They consist of fifteen minutes before falling asleep and the first fifteen minutes when you awaken. These times have proven to be the most relaxed for most people. However, do not limit yourself to just thirty minutes a day if you can devote more time to reconditioning your reflexes. The more time you focus on this pleasurable study, the sooner you will see remarkable results.

FOURTEEN

Step No. 3.
Body Relaxation

The root of the word RELAX *comes from the Latin,* LAX-ARE, *which means to let go. We know that a certain amount* of tension is healthy and spurs us on to do necessary tasks. This is constructive tension and acts as a propellant, giving us muscular spring and bounce, without which we would be lazy and listless.

When does tension stop being healthy and become a problem? When people strive to succeed, and find themselves frustrated in the attempt, the unused, unresolved tension remains with them. This residue of accumulated stress exerts a muscular pressure on the alerted nerves of the body. The resulting constriction causes the natural processes of the body to lose their

214

natural rhythmic pulsations. Every tension-ridden muscle or organ represents emotional conflict left unresolved.

Tension not only hampers the general functioning of the body, but also specifically cuts off the flow of sexual vibrations to the genitals. There are people who are able to discharge tension in the regular course of their work. If you are one of these, you are lucky. If not, do not despair, because relaxation is an art that can be learned even by the most resistant. This book has been designed not merely to be read, but to guide you in that direction. You will find that any effort or time expended in learning to release your tensions is well spent, not only in being rewarded with a better sex life, but in all other areas of endeavor.

Trying Too Hard

The reason so many people suffer from excess tension is that they go beyond the requirements of healthy striving for the human body. While straining to succeed they are too often frustrated in their attempts and tension ensues. In their struggle to exist economically and keep up with the Joneses, they over-try and the stress is transferred to the muscle tissues of their bodies.

The desire to be superior and rise above the environment also can cause undue tension. Many things cause stress, but the negatives head the list: Fear, Anger, Jealousy, Vindictiveness, and a host of other destructive emotions wreak havoc with the body's nervous system. Unless a person knows how to throw off this burden of accumulated tension, it can cause breakdowns, both physical and emotional.

On the other hand, a positive, optimistic outlook is a direct aid to relaxation. When one thinks in terms of: Hope, Serenity, Peacefulness, Tranquility, and Joyfulness, the body responds in kind. You cannot think tense thoughts and feel relaxed.

Admittedly, it is very often difficult to feel serene in a world that is troubled by mass tension, but this is even more reason to have a method of remaining calm and objective, so that one does not become a victim of this environmental pressure. The ability to transcend conflict does not necessarily make one ignore the responsibilities to change environmental problems; on the contrary, it makes a person better able to increase emotional control.

When tension piles up exceeding the limits of its usefulness, it is not only harmful to the general health, it is especially injurious to the pursuit of sexual pleasure. When a man tells a nervous woman to whom he is trying to make love, "Just relax and enjoy it," he is repeating what his forebears have said since the beginning of time. Unless she can follow his advice, she is doomed to remain only a receptacle for his sex needs. Women are notoriously tense when it comes to sexual receptivity and they have reason to be so. They have been harangued and hammered about the assorted pitfalls of sex and by the time they do indulge, they bring with them a huge backlog of sexual resistance and tension. This handicaps not only the woman in her quest for fulfillment, but makes it virtually impossible for the man to satisfy her. Tension and resistance go hand in hand. Tension builds resistance, enforces tension. It is a vicious cycle of self-defeat, leading nowhere.

Not only is relaxation essential for good sex, it is also imperative for normal healthy living. Resting and relaxing are the means of revitalizing the mind and body to carry on with its day-to-day activities.

In order for people to keep their balance, nature has decreed that periods of repose compensate for periods of motion. This helps maintain the inner, subtle equilibrium of harmony with our outside environment. When you refresh yourself through sleep and relaxation, you are helping to restore the expenditure of energy. If you give in to the "movement and rest pattern" you will then be able physically, as well as mentally, to cope with recurring demands upon your faculties.

People who are out of balance with the demands of nature for restoring energy through regular relaxation and sleep are usually out of rhythm sexually as well. Your sex life can only be as good as your general condition. If you are a relaxed person, you will be inclined to be more receptive to sexual feeling.

In addition to relaxation being indispensable for all-around health and well-being, it is also indispensable as a state of receptivity to receive reconditioning auto-suggestion to improve sexual responsiveness. The relaxed mind is like a sponge, open to new ideas. You must teach yourself how to deliberately relax for this reteaching purpose. Once you have learned the method described here, you will be able to use it for many purposes in addition to improving your sexual pleasure.

You will receive many other dividends besides being able to tap the deeper resources of your sexual being. Not only will you be able to relax under stressful conditions, but you will learn to breathe deeply and more healthfully, fall asleep easier and sleep more soundly, as well as cope with the tensions of the people you come into contact with.

A tranquil mood sets the stage for the constructive meditation which makes one aware of the need for improvement. The ability to relax has almost become a lost art in our hypertense, pressured, keyed society.

We know that too much civilization has scrambled our basic instincts with its tempo of hurry-scurry. The advanced human mind has in many ways betrayed the best interests of health by creating too many demands on the body. This is especially true on a time basis. Keeping up with the establishment's blueprints of what a successful person should be leaves little time to enjoy the simple pursuit of relaxed living. Few people, except the very rich, can find the time to simply enjoy leisure, to just luxuriate in the good feeling of it. Most people rush around every day of the year, except for two weeks' vacation and by the time it arrives, they have forgotten how to "let go." Consequently, most people are helped much less by a vacation than they would be if they learned to relax for one half-hour each day; it is urgent that people take time to relax regularly in order to protect themselves from the tension that saps their ability to perform in all areas of life.

Relaxation Speeds Learning

For the special purpose of this book, the retraining of the sexual reflexes, relaxation is a must. Without the use of relaxation techniques, the process of sexual reconditioning would take a very long time and might prove discouraging. Relaxation speeds up the process of learning. You will soon be able to demonstrate to yourself its amazing effectiveness when combined with the other techniques described subsequently.

You will discover your own deeper levels of untapped energy, unused and awaiting your release. You have the power within you to make this a reality. The purposeful, methodical practice of all of the combined *seven steps to sexual satisfaction,* makes it possible not only to correct obsolete thinking patterns, but to free your sexual machinery to function maximumly. Relaxation opens the door to increased feeling—to learning and accepting a new way of doing things. It has long been recognized by people in the teaching field that it is much easier for students to absorb knowledge when they have a relaxed state of mind. When people feel calm, they find it easier to concentrate. They are able to focus their entire attention and absorb information on a more profound level. When a person is in a state of meditative relaxation, the powers of concentration are greatly expanded. Relaxation makes it possible to rally dynamic attention on self-improvement. It helps in projecting a new self-image, in visualizing yourself as you really should be, without last years' hang-ups. Relaxation is indispensable for building a true feminine sexuality where there once was an unsure and wavering one.

For the past decade we have been learning a great deal about the importance of calm, emotional stability in order to prevent psychosomatic illnesses. Lack of awareness of mounting tension can lead to aggravated personal harm. It is common knowledge that such things as ulcers, migraine headaches, and assorted other maladies are directly influenced by tension conditions. As far as sex is concerned, people cannot be at their sexual best when tension puts their nerves in a bind. Sex must begin with a relaxed state of mind and body, otherwise, it becomes, in itself, another source of unresolved tension.

We must consciously protect ourselves by building "umbrellas of awareness" to shield us against the constant downpour of negative tension. Without being alert and protecting ourselves against these outside forces, we can be reduced to non-functioning organisms.

It should not surprise you to learn that if tension can make you feel distressed, the removal of tension can make you feel exhilarated. No matter how tense you may consider yourself to be, you can learn to relax if you really want to. The only difference between the tense and the relaxed person is conditioning. The tension-inclined person can overcome this with reconditioning.

You will have to devote a few minutes, twice a day, to accomplishing this, but you will find it well worth the effort. It will repay you in innumerable ways. You will become not only more cheerful emotionally, but also keener mentally, and these are just bonuses in addition to the reward of sexual normalcy.

How to Practice Step Number 3

To begin with, select a place where you have privacy, one that you can return to again and again. Using the same room and familiar surroundings has an assuring, comfortable effect. You will find that repetition of environment builds and reinforces relaxation. Each time you practice you will become more and more conditioned to letting go tension.

When once you have mastered these simple techniques you should be able to feel relaxed under less exacting circumstances. But at the beginning of your self-help program, make it a habit to return to the same couch or bed and repeat the same procedure each time to ensure a build-up of relaxed feeling.

How you recline is also important. The familiarity of your body's posture helps the muscles to release their tension.

The more often you induce a tranquil state, the quicker your body and mind will drift into it at the next practice period. *Be sure to first eliminate possible distractions from interfering with routine practice.*

Next, loosen all clothing which might restrict or hamper you: buttons, belts, girdle, brassiere. Remove your shoes, glasses, jewelry, and anything else you wish. Now, settle down into a comfortable position with your arms resting loosely at each side, palms turned up, elbows softly bent. Your legs are separated and relaxed, knees slightly bent, with toes pointing in opposite directions.

Experiment with a pillow. Some people can relax easier with it tucked under their knees or thighs, as well as under the back of the head. Others, like myself, prefer no pillow at all, but respond better to a flat surface. When your body is adjusted to as comfortable a position as you can manage, forget about it for the time being. Just let it go. Pause for a moment to become aware of a general looseness throughout your entire frame. Think of all of the joints of your body as very limp, like a puppet on a string, dangling aimlessly. Think of a melting feeling in the large muscles of your body.

Next, you must deliberately set aside all conscious thinking about the problems of the day, or the problems of yesterday, or even problems that may occur tomorrow. Think only of this very moment. Of the HERE and NOW, of how good it feels to release the body of tension.

Just lay all thoughts aside. Postpone decisions. Leave judgments to another, more suitable time. Take into yourself an *inner quietness* . . . a peaceful feeling *inside your mind*. Let your conscious perception of time drift away and just relax all over.

Now focus your attention upon your eyelids. Slowly and softly close your eyes, like a flower which closes its petals at the end of the day, having seen enough of the bright sunlight. Rest your eyes, for the resting eyes rest the mind and the resting mind rests the rest of the body.

Next take three deep breaths. Say to yourself, "I am breathing in a relaxed feeling and breathing out tension." (The next chapter will give you detailed instructions on how to develop sexual power through controlled breathing, but for now, just breathe deeply and naturally.) As you breathe, be aware of the power of the outgoing breath to carry out with it stress and tension. Expel the air out of your lungs forcefully and then allow it to drift back in easily. Think of the outgoing air as a huge sigh, carrying with it emotional tension, and making room for tranquility to enter in its place.

As you continue to breathe deeply and slowly, think of all of your body growing very loose and progressively relaxed. Starting with your scalp think into each area of your body a loose, limp feeling of easiness.

Say to yourself, (silently) "My scalp is loose, limp and very relaxed. My forehead is smooth and free of tension. My entire face is smooth and serene, like a newborn baby's. My eyelids feel very heavy and restful. All the little nerves and muscles around my eyes are very relaxed."

Think into the tissue and nerves a feeling of easy looseness. Say to yourself, "My cheek muscles are loose and relaxed, the hinges of my jaws are open, loose and limp. My lips are barely touching and my teeth are apart. My tongue is resting in the lower part of my mouth, it feels so soft, so limp, so free.

My neck is relaxed, shoulders feel so heavy. My arms feel heavy, loose, limp and deeply, completely free of tension. I am breathing slowly and rhythmically and my entire chest and torso is heavy and relaxed. My hips are very heavy. The buttock muscles seem to melt with their heaviness right into the couch. My body feels as if it is becoming part of what I am lying on. My thigh muscles are relaxed and very heavy . . . and my knees are loose and limp, like a puppet dangling on a string . . . free of all pull . . . free of all tension.

Just letting every part of my body go deeply and completely. Now my feet let go, they feel heavy, loose, and limp. Toe by toe I let all tension go. Now my entire frame feels completely limp and loose, from the very inside of my bones to the outside of my skin. I feel no tension, just a loose, limp, pleasant heavy feeling of well-being."

Now you let tension go from the entire back of your body, up the back of the legs. Focus on a feeling of freedom extending and expanding up the back of the thighs into the lower back. Feel the base of the spine let go, and then a looseness throughout the spinal column as if each vertebrae were wide open, allowing cool, soothing air to pass through unhampered by tight muscle pressure. Feel the heavy ropes of muscles on both sides of the spine become loose and limp allowing the feeling of air to pass through the entire spine, soothing, easing and pleasing every nerve in your body.

Think of your backbone as if it were a loose, heavy length of chain, lying limply on a large, very soft pillow. Let your spine go, let it become part of whatever it is resting on. Feel the contact as your spine blends into the friendly support of your bed, underneath your shoulder blades. Think of your shoulder blades as two doors and open them wide and let a pleasant loose feeling into your entire back. When you open the doors of your back all the tension goes out and tranquility creeps in. Let it happen.

You have the power to think into your body either tension or repose. Tension is an enemy of sexual feeling, so consciously determine to rid your nervous system of this inhibiting force and replace it with the kind of "staying loose" that brings with it fulfillment.

To relax even more, empty your mind of all conscious thinking. Thoughts bring with them the tension of making decisions, so let them float away. Suspend, postpone all judgments. Lay them aside. Problems can wait. Let a quiet feeling pervade the inside of your mind as you breathe slowly and rhythmically. If an unwanted thought drifts in, let it drift out again. Don't browbeat your mind. Don't force or suppress the ideas. Think of them as fluffy puffs of white clouds on a blue summer sky. Let the thoughts, like clouds, drift aimlessly by, blown apart by shifting summer winds so that the thoughts lose shape, become whispy and melt, dissolving into the blue of the sky and into the blue of your resting mind. Let all thoughts and ideas pass by as if they belonged to someone else. Don't lay claim to any thinking. Be aware of only one thing, how good it feels to let all accumulated tension go from your body. How delicious it is to luxuriate in a feeling of loose, limp restfulness.

Let old memories flow away. If memories of old negative sexual experiences come to mind, empty them as you would refuse which serves no useful purpose. Relaxation of mind and body causes the old, ingrained habit patterns of thinking to become less secure. Relaxation and positive suggestion will wipe them out and replace wrong thinking about your body with positive success images.

Become aware, as you relax, of an inner feeling of tranquility both in mind and body as you let all thinking flow through the river of your mind, emptying itself into the sea of life and then blending, dissolving, melting, and becoming one with all experience both good and bad.

When to Practice Step Number 3

Practice this exercise for fifteen minute periods at bedtime and upon awaking in the morning. Be certain to give as much time to these seven steps prior to foreplay as it will assure you of greater responsiveness.

In the morning allow fifteen minutes for relaxation plus self-suggestion. End the relaxation suggestions with a thought of waking up and facing the day filled with energy and vitality, happy and cheerful; that every day in every way your body becomes more and more relaxed and responsive. Each time you practice self-relaxation it will be easier to achieve this state of tranquility. The more deeply you relax, the stronger your self-suggestions for improvement will be imbedded into your subconscious mind.

Remember, relaxation can bring back lost feeling. It aids in awakening all of the sensory responses.

FIFTEEN

Step No. 4.
Sexual Breathing

Living fully demands breathing fully. Breathing serves a two-fold purpose:

    To bring sufficient oxygen into the body so that every cell of every organ can renew itself.

    To give the proper rhythmic pulsations to all of the organs of the body, not only the involuntary ones such as the heart, but the sexual organs as well.

  Deep, healthful breathing involves the entire body, which was meant to move totally and in unison to the overall tempo which the lungs set. Have you ever noticed an animal's breathing? Have you ever watched a lion or a tiger resting in the zoo? Or the household dog or cat lying in repose? When natural breathing has not been curtailed, the abdomen as well as the entire muscular system vibrates as each breath invigorates and revitalizes his energy.

Sexual performance is greatly influenced by the way a person breathes. The inability to reach orgasm, for example, is directly connected with the withholding of the outgoing breath. Fear of letting go orgastic feeling makes people literally "hold their breath." This is true of men as well as women. Some people are immediately helped just by discovering this simple fact. Check with yourself and see how you breathe during sexual excitation. You should be involving the large diaphragm muscles, which run around the center of the body. Breathing regenerates energy. The input and output of oxygen is the crux of vitality.

The diaphragm muscles are connected to other muscle complexes of the body and when they are brought into play, the entire body is activated. Leonardo da Vinci, in writing about how breathing affected the musculature of the body, put it this way:

"The diaphragm is moved by its own muscles, but it is necessary that these muscles be moved by other muscles more remote from the middle of the diaphragm."

When an inhibited woman learns to use her diaphragm muscles to exhale freely and forcefully, she also frees herself to reach a higher peak of sexual excitement. Not only does she release tension with the outgoing breath, but very often the orgasm as well.

Through the centuries in many highly evolved civilizations (such as the Chinese and the Indian), rhythmic breathing has been considered the key to inner peace and tranquility. It is still studied and practiced as a fine art (Yoga) not only in the Eastern cultures, but throughout the entire world as well.

Not only is proper breathing helpful for improved physical well being, but it is indispensable as a means of reaching a higher level of emotional and spiritual being. The oriental concept of using rhythmic breathing for mental detachment and meditation works wonders for the people so dedicated. "Transcendental" meditation implies, and often is in fact, a separation of the mind and spirit from the needs of the "animal" body.

WE ARE GOING TO USE BREATHING IN A DIFFERENT WAY

The breathing exercises described here are designed for the opposite result. You will learn how to use breathing together with relaxation and imagery to bring body and mind together in harmony so that your emotional and sexual desires will be fulfilled.

In modern civilization we tend to live a hurried, harried, overly tense existence. The hustle and bustle of daily activities tie up the mind and distract it from the body. Pressures and responsibilities blot out the demands of the basic instincts. The demanding standards of "status-success" set up anxiety reactions which work contrary to the leisurely vibrations that a healthy body demands.

Breathing Should Be Slow, Deep, and Regularly Paced

Our anti-natural way of life shows itself in the uneven pace of our breathing. This happens without our even being conscious of it. The discord creeps up on us and seeps into the nerves and organs of our bodies. Our musculature becomes taut, and the taut muscles tighten around the nerves, as we become cogs in the racing wheel of the machine age.

From the highest to the lowest, we are caught in the speeded up tempo that our bodies were not meant to cope with. People react to this pressure by becoming increasingly tense and out of touch with the rhythms of their bodies. The tension caused by spasmodic breathing results in a constriction of the muscles around the chest and lower abdomen. This tensing up of the torso muscles slows down circulation to the sexual organs as well as interfering with the pulsating action of the nerves.

In order to avoid falling victim to the mechanical speed-up surrounding us at all times, we must be alert to our body responses. We must avoid shallow breathing and consciously take into our bodies our full share of oxygen. Without realizing what is happening, many people fall into the habit of breathing with only a fraction of their lung capacity.

A person who is a "partial-breather" is in effect, only partially alive, because we can only function to the extent that oxygen propels us to. Every cell of our bodies demands its full share of revitalizing oxygen. Though oxygen is colorless, tasteless, odorless, and invisible, it has the power to fire the mind and body to great feats of accomplishment or, if lacking, to shut off our machinery completely.

Air, such as it is in our polluted atmosphere, is just about the only free thing that is left. Perhaps that is why we do not appreciate it. If air were bottled and sold commercially we all would appreciate its merits. In all probability we would have been urged to over-breathe if someone were profiting by our breathing. Why not profit by it yourself with the reward of generally increased health and sexual vitality?

The Power of Your Lungs

Proper breathing is the secret of learning "mind-body" control. If you first learn to control your breathing apparatus, you can move on to the other organs of your body and do likewise. Your lungs are the largest organs of your body and require the greatest muscular activity to keep them in motion. This respiratory motion is fundamental to every need of your body.

It has been estimated by researchers that the average person, unless taught otherwise, uses only about *one fourth* of his or her breathing capacity. This percentage includes smokers as well as non-smokers. It should be obvious to even an inveterate smoker that smoking is not only detrimental to the lungs but deters sexual circulation as well. Consider the master plan of the loving body. If the body was designed with a need for four-fourths, or total capacity of oxygen, living cells must die if we are partial, one-fourth, breathers. (Smokers further reduce the efficiency of their respiratory system by adding toxic carbon monoxide.) When people, both men and women, give up smoking there is a general improvement in their sexual energy.

Nature created our bodies with organs of size and shape to do specific jobs and do them well. Every cell, every bit of tissue that is part of every organ of our bodies demands its full quota of oxygen or it grows weak and dies. Oxygen cleanses and renews cells. It rejuvenates us. People often ask me, "Well, what about pollution? What's the use?" My answer is that precisely because of pollution we must be doubly on guard to see to it that our lungs are given ample opportunity to do their job.

Shallow breathing, plus pollution, doubles the danger of

respiratory problems and insures sexual malfunction. Athletes know the importance of deep breathing to increase energy.

Breathing Is Indispensable To

1. Prevent muscular fatigue and increase stamina.
2. Aerate the brain cells for clearer thinking.
3. Regulate digestion through diaphragmatic action.
4. Relax the midsection to increase circulation to the sexual organs.

When lack of oxygen stifles the renewal of body cells the ultimate result is breakdown of some part of the body. If breakdowns of organs do not result, the slowdown and sluggishness can be equally debilitating. Breathing is the only activity of the living body which cannot stop. Deny the body oxygen and in one to three minutes death ensues.

We know that people can remain alive even after their hearts have stopped beating. They have been known to continue breathing afterward for as long as an hour. They are even able to live and function normally with the implantation of an artificial heart or one belonging to another person. Not so the lungs. They are truly an indispensable part of the anatomy. Unfortunately, few people recognize their unique importance. Of all the organs we possess, the lungs are the most abused and misused.

Oxygen is the one element which the body cannot store for possible future use. We store fat for fuel and our blood supply can easily be replenished if need be. But life is from one breath to the next and if you only half breathe, then you can only be half alive.

It is the job of the lungs to purify our blood, and if you do not see to it that this happens, it will show itself in decreased ability to function. On the other hand, if you apply the lessons in this book to your own body, you will be rewarded with improved all-around health and find that the acquired diaphragmatic action makes orgasm take place much easier.

Most people when asked to take a deep breath, will respond by sniffing or sucking in air into the upper part of their chests. This is in effect, a short, strained, shallow breath and only adds to the accumulated tension that already exists.

When we suggest that you breathe deeply for relaxation, we mean slow, methodical, measured breathing, using the muscles of the lower diaphragm. Not only is how you inhale important, but the exhalation is even more so. It must be controlled and forceful to expel not only carbon dioxide, but tension as well.

The respiratory system is complex. It is comprised of the two large lungs and the air passages leading to them and away from them. The heart rests between the lungs and is connected to it by arteries, and veins. Because it is so closely connected, it is also deeply affected by the action of the lungs.

The lungs are of a spongy, porous material and have an elastic quality. This makes the "stretch and release" action of their motion not only affect breathing, it can soothe and regulate the heart as well.

Their bellows-like motion acts as a pace-setter for the entire body and gives us the pulsation of life. If the lungs were flattened out, you would have 1100 square feet of lung sac tissue and every square inch was created for a precise purpose, to feed and replenish some particular part of our anatomy.

A newborn infant emerges into the world and the first thing it does is draw into itself a long deep breath of air, which gives it the power to emit its first announcement of being.

From the first to the last, how fully we live can be gauged by the way we breathe. We all have four avenues that express how we exist. They are breathing, thinking, eating, and physical motion. The quality of our particular life is keenly projected through these media. We are as we think, as we breathe, as we eat, and as we use our bodies.

Sexual happiness is influenced by all four. The rhythm of breathing is of utmost importance. Not only has it a calming affect upon the nervous system, it also rocks the sexual muscles and awakens them. To begin with, breathing is essential to eliminate the negative. Nothing surpasses a deep sigh to release residual accumulated tension. A sigh is nature's way of saying, "Slow down!" It is a biological way for the lungs to expel accumulated carbon dioxide and stress. It is a signal that the body is tired and needs a full supply of new oxygen for a spurt of energy. Proper breathing can relax and refresh every fiber of your body. Unlike food, you cannot get too much air. A full amount of air affects in a positive way the entire circulation of the body. This is especially true of the sexual organs, because in order for them to function fully, they must become engorged to a tumescent state, and this can only happen with increased oxidation.

The forceful expulsion of air while breathing, intensifies sensation during orgasm. The diaphragm muscles extend to the lower abdomen and as one focuses on the rising and falling of the abdominal muscles, relaxation spreads to the entire body.

How Improved Breathing Benefits Your Sexual Health

1. It purifies our blood and increases circulation to the genitals.

2. Its rhythmic action soothes the nervous system.
3. It revitalizes sexual energy.
4. The diaphragm muscles activate the sexual organs to pulsate.

How to Practice Step Number 4

When you have fully relaxed with step number 3, focus on your breathing apparatus. To start, rest your hands on your lower abdomen or belly. Look, listen, and feel the rhythm of your breathing. Now learn proper rhythm for sexual fulfillment.

Breathe in slowly to the count of five, hold for one count and breathe out to the count of five, hold for one count. Say to yourself, "1, 2, 3, 4, 5, *AND* 1, 2, 3, 4, 5, *AND*" etc. After this pace becomes easy for you, increase the count. The size of the lung cavities and your own personal capacity will tell you what is comfortable. You may increase it to sixteen or more as do many practitioners of Yoga breathing.

After you have mastered the rhythm of your breathing, begin to focus your thoughts on areas of your body.

Skin Breathing to Relax the Nerves: Having already relaxed your body in general by way of the previous exercise, now think of your body as if it were a *large sponge,* eager to soak up as much air as possible. With your eyes closed, focus your mind on the surface of your body, concentrate on the image of your skin being very porous.

Now take a very deep breath and imagine the air coming in through the pores of your skin. Slowly let the air out holding on to the same image. Take into the body sensory feeling and let out tension.

Relaxing Hands and Feet: Think of your hands and feet as being very heavy, loose and limp. Now focus your breathing. Imagine the air coming into your body through the fingertips of your right hand. (You may feel a tingling sensation and that is a good sign that you are learning how to increase circulation through concentration.) As the breath comes into your hand, trace its course up your arm, across your shoulders and down the left arm as you breathe OUT. Breathe in through one hand and down and out through the other. The thought of breath is a relaxing thought, hence the physical response.

Now focus on your legs and repeat the same procedure. In one foot, up through the leg and exhale as you concentrate on the path of the exhalation, down through the other leg.

Spinal Breathing: Concentrate on the back and feel a loose, limp sensation in the muscles across the shoulders and down the spine. Now as you inhale, focus your attention on the thought that the air is coming into your body through the anal opening and passing up through the spine, up the back of the neck and into the head, now hold for a count of two and exhale, letting the air pass again down the neck, through the spine and out the anus. Repeat three times and rest.

Breathing with Heartbeat: Concentrate on listening to the beating of your heart and as you breathe in and out, time the inhalation and expiration to the contraction of the heart muscles. Use the following tempo; breathe in for six heartbeats, breathe out for six heartbeats, pausing in between. The number of heartbeats can be varied according to your own body rhythms. Meditating while concentrating on the beating of the heart is very beneficial for general relaxation. Repeat as often as possible.

Breathing "Through the Genitals": In the same way that

you fantasized the air coming into the body through the spine, imagine that as you breathe in, the air is coming in through tiny holes in the ends of your ten toes, the air comes up into the legs, passes up the inside of the thighs, enters the vaginal opening and proceeds up through the body into the head. Hold for the count of two, then exhale down through the hollow torso, escaping through the nipples, through the womb and continuing down out the vagina, down the inside of the thighs. Repeat three times and rest.

When to Practice Step Number 4

Naturally you must always practice good breathing to ensure yourself of optimum health. You can start right now to improve your feeling of well-being by breathing deeper and more leisurely. Be aware of the size of your lungs and use their full potential. The specific exercises outlined in this chapter should be practiced in conjunction with the other six steps. Your daily periods of controlled breathing and relaxation will speed up your progress toward the goal of *Complete Womanhood*.

In addition to the two fifteen-minute practice periods (morning and evening), you can strengthen your respiratory system at all times.

While Taking a Leisurely Walk: Pace your breathing to keep time with your steps. Five steps; inhale, hold, one step. Five steps, exhale, etc.

While Sitting In Buses, Subways, Etc.: Make all your breathing diaphragmatic. In this way you will improve the general capacity of your lungs for top-level service under all conditions.

While Participating in Coitus: Do not count your breathing, as this would prove a distraction from sensory feeling in the genitals. Instead, do the genital breathing exercise, focusing on good sensory feeling. You will find that if you are breathing slowly and deeply (having trained yourself prior to sexual intercourse), you will be better able to concentrate on the increase of pleasurable sensation in and around the vaginal opening.

Genital breathing is an ancient oriental exercise. It will help you reach a stronger orgasm whether you focus on the clitoris or the vagina. Because women find vaginal orgasm so much more satisfying once they learn the technique of bringing it about, I suggest you try it and convince yourself. If you think that the air is passing through your vaginal opening, the thought serves as a mental lubricant for the intensification of sensation in the nerve endings. Train yourself to think of the breath coming in and out of the body in this way. Repeat again and again. Remember, you are not just training your body, you are *reconditioning* it to repair damage that has been done. So be very diligent.

After several weeks of concerted practice, you will find that the interaction of the mind and body makes sensation come about automatically. No conscious effort becomes necessary after reconditioning sets in. Remember, you were always capable. You can control, through focusing your mental breath, the pitch of orgastic sensation, until your own natural instinct takes over. A panting, forceful, outgoing breath will carry you over the threshold of orgastic climax and into the valley of tranquility which follows.

SIXTEEN

Step No. 5.
Self-Imagery

When you have learned to relax your body by practicing the exercises described in the previous chapters, you should now be ready for Step number 5, Self-Imagery. Sexual function is not solely dependent on physical stimulation. It is, to begin with, a cerebral function. Sexual pleasure is accentuated or decreased as a result of what a person imagines while he or she is engaged in lovemaking. If a woman lets her mind wander to problems of children, shopping, or other extraneous thoughts, her sex drive will diminish; but persistent focusing on objects or incidents that entice or excite her will do the opposite.

Imagery is the art of using your creative imagination to

bring about self-induced dreams or fantasies in which you picture yourself as enjoying sex without problems about reaching orgasm. The passionate visions you conjure up grow out of the emotional power of positive anticipation of success. This is the force of motivation. It is a kind of burning desire which fires the mind to transfer the fantasy into reality.

Every Reality Was Once A Fantasy

Fantasy wells up from the unconscious. It has the power to release dynamic erotic excitement. Your mind is a boundless storehouse of many mental images, some helpful, some harmful. All previous thoughts, emotions, verbal and non-verbal suggestions have been recorded there in minute detail. The repetition of innumerable mental messages, flashed back and forth, again and again, makes them sink deeper into the subconscious mind where they become first embossed and then engraved into what we call memory. The dictionary defines memory as "the capacity or faculty of retaining and reviving past impressions and previous experiences."

The problem that confronts the non-responsive woman is that she tends to recall only the unpleasant memories. Even though she may at some time have had some degree of sexual pleasure, the negative woman will obliterate this memory and consistently dwell on the failures. She gets caught in the treadmill of defeatist imagery, because having failed before, she *expects* its recurrence.

This phenomenon accounts for almost all failures to successfully culminate the coital act in orgasm. While a woman may be consciously striving very hard, struggling physically to reach orgasm, she is not expecting it to happen. Sexual imagery is a method of self-training which provides you with the proper helpful memories at the proper time. In cases where a woman may not have successful sex memories, she can fantasize the scene, creating a vision of erotic satisfaction to make the reality of the moment more exciting for herself.

Once she invents a positive fantasy, she can super-impose this vision of positive success to wipe out her old negative self-image. Human beings are the only animals who think about sex. They think about it too much and their thinking is often worry rather than happy anticipation. Men worry about whether they will be virile enough and women worry about whether they will be able to reach orgasm. And as soon as a man or woman worry about how they will function, they impair their sexual ability.

Concentrate On Success

The human mind cannot concentrate on two things at the same time. When a woman focuses her thinking on how she looks, or what is happening to her lover, she is not focusing on feeling pleasurable sensation. This is at the core of many women's inability to reach orgasm. Their minds wander to other things that distract from the coitus itself. When they do think about the intercourse they are in the midst of, they tend to focus too intently, they force and press, and the harder they try, the more they worry about the degree of sexual feeling, the further it slips away from them because of the negativism that worry presupposes. There is only one way to get the most out of sex, that is to concentrate with confidence on the simple act of mutual satisfaction.

Mutual fantasies are a great help to women during copulation. There is less guilt for women if they think sex and talk sex combined with "togetherness." Sometimes mutual fantasies involve other people, and if that helps, why not? Acting out fantasies of infidelity may keep them from becoming reality. They release unconscious suppressed desires and can be very exciting for both people.

Women often conjure up their own private sexual scenario which is a projection of their inhibited interior dream. This is a proven way to increase one's ability to reach orgasm because it releases pent up tension and gives a predetermined, self-determined direction for personal achievement. Rather than allow habit-entrenched, unpleasant thoughts to intrude and overwhelm sensation at the crucial moment of approaching climax, you will learn how to hold fast to your success image and bring yourself to orgasm.

This method trains you to paint an improved portrait of yourself as you should be. It shows you how to thrust aside interfering pessimistic ideas and to focus and concentrate on the best of past sexual encounters. First of all, you begin by seeing yourself in your mind's eye as normal and sexually perfect in every way. You can only accomplish what you can picture yourself capable of doing. Every inhibited woman has become, unwittingly, what her distorted mental image has forced her into being.

Fortunately, thinking can be changed, and with this change, physical improvement invariably results. The first and most basic aid to orgasm, is to see yourself as already being able to reach this heightened state of sensation. Each time sexual lovemaking starts, assume in a most casual mental manner that *of course* you will reach orgasm. It has been proven over and over again that this sort of sham causes the pretense to become reality.

Sensory Nerves Respond Kinesthetically

The "Kinesthetic Sense" is sometimes called the sixth sense. It enables the body to carry out the image that the mind has conjured up. Specific sexual ideation, no matter how far-fetched and shocking to one's grandmother, is a basic necessity for the nonorgasmic female who wishes to improve. She must think of something sufficiently exciting so that it will obliterate all other conscious thoughts from her mind. She must also allow herself to visualize herself trying varied coital positions and sex play, which she may have once considered shocking. When a woman can accept an image of herself being sexually free enough to experiment with sex play that she thinks is wicked or sinful, she will also be accepting herself as being wicked and sinful enough to have an orgasm.

When a woman, through prudishness or ignorance, can only picture herself as having an orgasm through "normal" man-on-top-of-woman, penis-in-vagina, sexual intercourse, she is condemning herself to a life of frigidity. Shame may cause a woman to shut out the thoughts of pleasure from fingering (called digital manipulation), self-masturbation, mutual masturbation, and oral-genital excitation. Through improvised fantasy a woman can overcome sex shyness in telling her lover what she enjoys. She can imagine the act taking place, feel the responsiveness increase, and then tell her lover to carry it through to reality. This method of using imagery compounds sensations in both the clitoral and vulva regions.

Just like an IBM computer, your mind feeds back to your body and into your sensory motor system the exact thoughts that you have been feeding into it. Your body machinery always reflects by its behavior just what your mind thinks is proper. Your subconscious mind takes you at your own face value. How have you been evaluating yourself about sex? What have you been telling your mind about how you function sexually? If you imagine yourself to be a failure, how can you possibly succeed?

There is no area of endeavor in which creative intelligence does not play an important part. Even a person with intelligence far below the normal range has some degree of constructive imagination which could be expanded and enlarged upon for self-help. There are those gifted people who have exceptional intelligence and with it the special talent for using their imagination to improve the lot of all mankind. That kind of super-intelligence is not essential to improve the functioning of your sexual machinery. All that you need is the motivation and normal range of intelligence to make this happen through use of the techniques of self imagery.

To activate helpful sexual images is only half of the reconditioning process. The other half is to eliminate the negative images which obstruct the flow of sensory feeling. Negative sex experiences leave their psychic residues, just as bad food leaves its toxic waste. Just as toxic waste can clog the proper functioning of the digestive system, contrary sexual memories can interfere with sexual perception. Among the most destructive image distortions are those inflicted upon women due to their lesser status. They are identified as being weaker, less sexual, dumber, prudish, fearful, embarrassed, all of which are at variance with the facts. Whether the suggested images are covert or overt, subtle or explosive, they are a tremendous persuasive and pervasive force.

Every physical action, including orgasm, is first seen in the mind's eye where it is calculated, then accepted or rejected. This happens very quickly and without our being consciously aware that it is happening. There is a constant viewing of past experience by the subconscious mind, a series of flashbacks review themselves, and a silent commentary goes on within us as to whether to make use of them or push them aside. Imagination always chooses the picture that triggers the action which follows. It is our hopeful mind which sets the goals through images and these goals become the direction toward which we strive. Imagination also provides the map and the guideposts to help us reach our goals. Knowing where we are going, through imagery, gives us the strength to pull ourselves forward, when we might otherwise weaken due to confusion. Sexual fantasy enables you to select your very own choice of what you wish the reality of sex to be.

Don't sell yourself short of complete sexual satisfaction. Begin right now, start painting a picture of yourself at your sexual best and forcefully reject anything which does not enhance that picture.

Planning your progress can be fun. You will be able to set the stage, see yourself in action and preview the orgasmic experience as if it were already accomplished, easily. When a woman uses her power of imagery to see herself as already passionately involved, she is taking the first step in the direction of linking her body to her mind. This affirmative acceptance of culminative climax ignites the emotions which in turn fire the nerve endings in the genitals and make the wishful thinking a real happening. Sexual imagery is especially effective for that large percentage of women who manage to reach orgasm sometimes but not always. These are the women who are left the most disturbed and dissatisfied. Very often they hover on the brink of climax unable to follow through. They strain themselves, teetering and tottering on the verge of orgasm, sometimes making it and sometimes either giving up in despair or exhaustion. When they don't make it, it's because they either allowed a negative thought to take over or else they tried too hard to succeed.

Once a woman has had the feeling of orgasm, she has a positive image to recall from her reservoir of sexual memories. She can steadily improve her control by remembering the very best previous experience and embellishing it for greater self-gratification. If orgasm can take place once, it can take place again and again. No matter at what level a woman functions, she can step up to greater heights of ecstasy.

If she is "frigid" to the point of having little or no sensation, she can build clitoral sensation by relaxation and focusing on a sexual image of clitoral awakening. If she has clitoral sensation, but cannot reach clitoral orgasm, imagery can make her reach orgasm. If she reaches clitoral orgasm, but cannot feel anything vaginal, imagery can diffuse and spread the clitoral feeling all through her genitals. If once she begins to feel the pulsation of nerve endings in and around the vagina, sexual imagery can make her have a deep complete internal and external orgasm simultaneously.

People are programmed to behave according to the fantasies they have fabricated about themselves. If you refuse to imagine yourself relaxed to the point of orgasm, it cannot happen. Your body, as well as everyone else's, awaits instructions from your ruling mind, which is the master of your body's successes and failures.

One summer while visiting friends at a lake resort, I found myself watching some young people learning to water ski. Two young girls stood near me discussing the possibility of taking lessons. One of them said, "Oh, it scares me. *I could never imagine* myself doing that!"

The other one said, "I can. It looks like a lot of fun. I'd like to try a lesson." The one who said, "I can't," didn't. She tensed up, and as she shouted, "I can't, I'm falling," she did just that. She fell into the water immediately. As she tossed about in the water, her friend of the optimistic nature, continued to sail serenely around the lake.

We have all noticed negativism in others, but are less inclined to recognize it in ourselves. Meditating on an improved sexual image will bring your negativism to light where you can examine it and then dispose of it for a more rewarding pattern of thinking. In practicing sexual fantasy you must screen out past images which may shut off sexual pleasure.

Raise Your "Passion Potential"

Even if you consider yourself perfectly normal and able to respond easily to effective stimulation, you will find that practicing these exercises raises your "passion potential" and assures a longer-lasting, more fulfilling orgasm. It has been estimated in studies conducted on the creative imagination, that people use only about ten percent of their capacity to enlarge on life's experiences.

Men have a decidedly different attitude toward sex imagery than women. They will freely admit to having had innumerable sex dreams both while sleeping and while awake. One of the reasons that adult women avoid confrontation with the needs of their bodies, is that they closed their minds as well as their eyes to all things sexual during adolescence. Whereas teenage young men freely use pornography to fantasize, girls of the same age withdraw in shock and shame. Most young men fantasize while masturbating and by so doing prepare themselves for later heterosexual relationships.

Many adult women find that masturbation during sexual imagery is a positive aid in locating and strengthening orgastic sensitivity. Most women need to go through this stage of self-assertiveness if they have not done it at an earlier time.

Whether you use self-imagery while alone or during the sex act itself, you must see yourself as being in control. Visualizing is the surest way to eliminate anxiety which becomes overwhelming to the woman who fears the power of the orgasm. If during masturbatory fantasy, a woman imagines that she is having sex with a lover, it then becomes simply a matter of carrying the feeling over to the actual heterosexual union.

When a masturbatory fantasy is firmly established the woman goes into the sex act with her lover with the support of this necessary transitory "crutch." Sometimes a crutch is essential for progress and this is one of those times. If heterosex has kept her from reaching orgasm in the past, she now can use her sexual fantasy to shift her attention from what is actually happening to the imaginary situation, which she has learned to control. It is possible for this type of woman to derive orgasmic gratification with her lover while using her reverie.

After self-imagery has served its useful purpose of giving a woman sufficient confidence to follow through to orgasm, she will convert her technique to *mutual fantasies*. She will then include her lover into her erotic, sexual scene. Whether you are using visual imagery alone or with your lover, you will see yourself relaxed and enjoying the foreplay. You will see yourself having stronger sensation with penile-vaginal contact. You will see yourself reaching a keener orgasm without strain. You will see yourself feeling serene and tranquil and satisfied. You will see yourself looking forward to the next experience as being even better. You will engrave these new images into your subconscious mind through repetition until they firmly erase the old self-defeating impressions which led to sexual failure in the past. Remember, the mind is like an electronic computer. Feed it positive pictures and you will get positive answers in return.

How to Practice Step Number 5

Very little effort is required to practice this exercise. The same environment is helpful as in the previous lessons. Assuming at this time that you have mastered:

1. Self-Awareness
2. Auto-Suggestion
3. Relaxation
4. Rhythmic Breathing

You should now be ready to carry your retraining program a step further along the path leading to your goal: *complete orgastic satisfaction*.

Here are some practical suggestions on how to make fantasy serve your purpose:

1. Having already selected an environment conducive to tranquility, you are relaxed on a reclining chair, couch, or bed. The room is quiet and not too brightly lit and you have arranged things so as not to be disturbed.

2. You breath deeply and rhythmically, while emptying the mind of all extraneous thoughts. If an outside idea comes to mind, let it pass right through and flow out again. Give it no harbor. Treat distracting thoughts as you would unwanted strangers.

3. Your eyes are softly shut to keep out any intrusion of unwanted visual stimulation. You bring the focus of your thinking from outside of yourself to deep within the quiet of your resting mind.

4. You focus on an aware feeling throughout your body, especially concentrated on the nerves in your genitals. You feel life coming into your body, as you use imagery to eroticize your entire body. All of the nerves tingle in the erogenous areas, the nipples of the breast, the clitoris, and vulva.

5. As you breathe rhythmically and deeply now, your entire body very relaxed and content, you focus your concentrated thinking on the entrance to the vagina, the vestibule. You think of all of the nerve endings converging into the vagina. You meditate on this fantasy.

Picture—Imagine—Visualize

Now imagine that you see before you a blank movie screen or television set. You are going to project onto this screen a visionary dream, which becomes in effect, a "prophecy" of your next sexual experience. If any negative thoughts drift in, or shame or fear, kick them out, give them no resting place. Deliberately and consciously suggest to your subconscious that you wish to respond to the utmost. Visualize yourself actively participating in the foreplay. See yourself being made love to and enjoying it. See yourself active and aggressive, without embarrassment. Let yourself go into your fantasy and allow a luxurious feeling of voluptuousness to spread its radiance throughout your genitals and directly into the vagina.

Now the clitoris diffuses its heightened, hypersensitive feeling throughout the entire genital area. The sensation spreads from the clitoris to the sensitive tissues of the labia in and around the vaginal vestibule. Your imagination releases a surge of anticipation as you visualize the promise of contact with the male's organ. In your mind's eye you picture yourself as strongly desiring the insertion of the penis. See yourself as being eagerly passionate for this male-female contact. The penis having made entry into the moist and eager opening, you now focus all your attention on seeing this contact. Picture, imagine, visualize your vaginal walls warmly welcoming the penis with sensory response. Continue to use all of your mental power to enlarge upon this feeling and it will become more and more intense. Use your fantasy to increase this good feeling until it permeates every cell and every tissue of your sexual organs.

While you are imagining this contact, this feeling of hugging the penis with your vagina, actually begin to contract and relax the muscles which ring the opening of the vaginal entrance. (The next chapter will give detailed instructions on how to make full use of your muscle power.) The pressure of the muscles against the nerve endings intensifies the sensation and soon the sensation is equally divided between the clitoris and vaginal opening.

Think of the male and female organs, linked in harmony, a creative, magnetic force. Feel this union vibrating vitality into your body and giving you an exhilarated glow of health from head to toe. Meditate as long as you wish on this image. Think of the penis as a pleasure instrument. Think of your acceptance of it as providing the maximum gratification. Picture your "inside" receptivity as being in harmonious concert with the "outside" male force of giving pleasure. See yourself as being ready to combine your body and emotions with your lover to carry yourself into the heights of orgasm.

Each time you practice sexual imagery you will find it more effective in arousing and increasing your sensory responses. Create your own personal sexual images for success. Picture, visualize, fantasize sex positions, techniques, and anything else which you might find stimulating and satisfying.

Each improvement builds further success.

When to Practice Step Number 5

Most people find that bedtime is the most conducive time for relaxed meditation and reverie. It is very pleasant to drop off to sleep at the completion of the combined exercises of all seven steps. Sexual imagery is most effective when practiced in conjunction with the relaxation period, as well as during the coital act itself. During sexual intercourse, it becomes a very effective way of communicating your desires to your mate. Share your fantasies and encourage him to tell you his own secret dreams. Perhaps suppressed curiosity about coital positions and new techniques will enable both of you to communicate and become closer through shared fantasies.

When you practice sexual imagery as a reconditioning discipline, you will employ all the other techniques discussed in these chapters. The combination will raise the effectiveness of the entire self-improvement program to a higher level of achievement.

There are four times when sexual fantasy is most effective:
1. Morning
2. Bedtime
3. During the Foreplay
4. After the Insertion of the Penis into the Vagina

Remember, your very own imagination sets the stage for increased orgasmic sensation. Your imagination focuses and localizes sensation in the vaginal entrance.

SEVENTEEN

Step No. 6.
The Sex Muscles

In the preceding chapters on Awareness, Auto-Suggestion, and Self-Imagery, we stressed the role that the mind and emotions play in female sexual arousal. In the chapter on Breathing we emphasized the importance of using the diaphragm muscles to activate the sexual pulsations of the body. Now you are going to learn how to bring the sex muscles into the act. If you have never been aware of their existence, you are in for a very pleasant surprise. The full use of these muscles can make the difference between straining to reach orgasm or easily controlled sensation where you want it, when you want it. When a woman masters this technique, she gives to herself not only the power to reach orgasm, but the power to prolong coitus, both for herself and for her partner. Virtually all research points out that most of the human female's dysfunction stems from psychological factors rather than from her biological structure.

The act of thinking causes a chain reaction as every thought brings with it its emotional charge and that emotional charge causes a particular muscle reaction. Thoughts of avoidance of the internal part of the female genitals (the vaginal shaft) is the reason for its lack of muscle tone. This lack of muscle tone is the greatest obstacle to reaching vaginal orgasm. The reason so many women do not believe that internal sensation is possible is because they are unaware of the hidden power of their sexual muscles to stimulate the deep nerve endings.

Those women who do know about the vaginal sphincter muscles generally think of them in relation to childbirth. The reason for this surprising anatomical ignorance is that most women have never tried to use them other than for childbirth. Exerting muscle pressure during coitus is, in itself, an assertive declaration of sexual involvement. It is this passivity which has kept these stimulators lying dormant and unused over long periods of time; sometimes throughout a woman's entire lifetime.

Increase Frictional Contact

Fortunately, the problem of flaccid sexual muscles can be easily rectified. Once a woman accepts their existence and learns to strengthen their activity through exercise, sensation begins to develop where it never existed before, in the inner labia, vaginal vestibule, and anterior wall of the vaginal shaft. Without the gripping action of the vaginal sphincter muscles, it is impossible for a woman to have internal sexual feeling. Lack of penile-vaginal frictional contact correlates with lack of sphincter muscularity. In order to awaken them to their biological task, the muscles must be strengthened progressively by exercise.

The first stage in bringing these muscles back to life is to isolate them mentally; to become conscious of their physical existence.

The second stage is to deliberately and systematically exercise them while giving yourself auto-suggestions about increased sensory feeling.

The third stage is to use these muscles, during the sexual act, by exerting pressure on the penis. This will not only help accelerate your climax, but it will increase the man's pleasure as well.

The flaccidity of the interior vaginal walls can be overcome and increasing muscular power developed in a comparatively short space of time. One week of daily practice will show remarkable improvement. Increased control will be noticed by the degree of natural expansion and contraction of the sphincter muscles during coitus.

A normal condition of the genital muscularity can be established by practicing the preceding exercises, relaxation, breathing, etc. in unison with the vaginal muscle contractions. Discover the primary source of sensations by discovering the power of these muscles.

Clitoral Expectancy

The woman who is very tense and has acquired consistent resistance to vaginal contact may find that she has difficulty in focusing on the vagina, and may automatically shift her attention to the established, habitual clitoral expectancy. If she does this, she will be reinforcing the clitoris as the center of sensation. If a woman is entirely satisfied to respond only clitorally, fine; that is her free choice. However, she should be aware that she is herself bringing about this condition and that she can change it if she so desires.

Women who do not know how to use their internal muscles generally have difficulty in coordinating their sexual movements as well. It has been observed that clitorally oriented women imitate the male's pelvic action and in so doing often lose contact with the penis, which tends to slip out of the vagina at the most crucial point of impending orgasm. A woman with strongly developed vaginal tone uses her sphincter muscles as other female animals do to ardently grasp and hold onto the penis.

She needs less outside hip/pelvic activity because her sensation comes from the penis itself; not by forcing feeling by exerting friction on the outside tissue of her genitals. The intensification of pleasure-sensation, when it is caused by the penis making close contact with the vaginal walls, make the male/female sexual relationship something much more than a mechanical release. The "outsideness" of the penis satisfying the "insideness" of the vagina makes for the kind of harmonious closeness that no other kind of sexual practice is capable of giving. It is the unity of two halves becoming one entity, each supplying the need of the other for completion.

The woman who has never developed internal sensation has very little regard for the male's ability to satisfy her. Clitoral women insist that they get better orgasms when they masturbate; they merely endure the insertion of the penis. One highly sexual clitoral woman expressed it in this way: "I had to teach my husband how to manipulate my clitoris to bring me to an orgasm. Before I got the courage to be that aggressive, he would just insert his penis and get his pleasure. I couldn't care less if it were inside or not. All I kept thinking about was that I didn't want to become pregnant. I would rather feel safe than have an orgasm vaginally."

She is typical of the vast majority of women who are highly sexual yet prefer not to respond through penile/vaginal intercourse. The main reason for the lack of internal desire is the inability to understand the vast difference. Woman who have not responded vaginally, secretly believe it is impossible.

Only in the past few years has it come to light that vaginal sensitivity is directly influenced by muscular nerve pressure. Masters and Johnson explain that lack of sensation is due to lack of internal pressure on the deeply imbedded nerve endings lying dormant under the thick, insensitive tissue which lines the vaginal shaft.

This view is further supported by Ronald M. Dentch, researcher on sexual subjects, in his book, "Key to Feminine Response in Marriage." He explains that the pleasure factor in vaginal muscular control was brought to light accidentally in work done by Dr. Arnold Kegel, a prominent professor of gynecology at the University of California. The "Kegel Exercises," as they have become known, were first developed by this doctor as an aid to easier childbirth. He also investigated their use to prevent the sagging of the internal organs, such as the bladder, that are supported by the same muscle complex.

Women who used the exercises to aid themselves in the above problems discovered that they also derived an added bonus; the ability to control the contractions and expansions of these sphincter muscles caused them to experience a new kind of sexual sensation, internal vaginal sensitivity to pressure. There are comparatively few women who use these muscles naturally during coitus. They are the extremely rare, (one out of ten) women who have not been sexually crippled by their environmental conditioning. These are the fortunate women who reach orgasm easily, clitorally, vaginally, or both in unison.

A woman who has managed to rise above the inhibitions of the past finds that she can use these vaginal gripping muscles automatically. She is that magnetic, profoundly sexually woman to whom men are greatly attracted. The wife who learns to control her sexual muscles not only to please her husband, but to bring on her own orgasm, is cherished by him. There is much less chance that he will stray from this kind of fully-flowered woman than from the clitorally oriented one.

Men are constantly driven to try to prove their masculine capabilities. It is the wise woman who knows that the highest form of "Male Appreciation" is to appreciate his penis. The average man regards his penis with pride and joy and wants to know that it can bring a woman to a climax. In cases where he isn't able to do this with his wife, his injured male ego will often compel him to seek out another woman who can reassure him that he is normal, and perhaps, better than that, that he is a good lover.

Every woman can master this technique, and when she does, she will discover that a minimum of muscular exertion will give her the maximum erotic pleasure. There is always some degree of improvement if a woman applies herself to practicing the strengthening of her sphincters due to the fact that she is responding with machinery precisely designed to do its specific job of intensifying frictional contact. When this machinery is properly turned on and functioning the need for clitoral stimulation becomes unnecessary for orgasm to take place.

Natural Rhythms and Pulsations

The effective use of the sphincters with their pursing and tightening action carries a woman forward on an easy, natural wave of vibrations which must inevitably lead to a peak of climactic release. While this is a simple and natural procedure, it is amazing that these proven facts have had so little exposure to the mass of frustrated women. To many, it may even seem difficult to accept, due to the barrier of repeated negation, not only during childhood, but during sexual intercourse itself. The fact that women have for centuries been striving to imitate men in the sexual act doesn't mean that nature intended it to be that way. The limited information (mostly misinformation) that women have acquired has been through their sexual contact with men, who lacking the facts themselves, look upon women as a less than perfect imitation of themselves. Literature abounds in references of this fabrication of man's imagination, such as the Bible reference that woman was fashioned from the "rib of Adam," and countless other fairy-tales.

It is logical to assume that nature, in its infinite creative wisdom, planned for a woman to enjoy the acceptance of the penis into her vagina if for no other reason than to propagate the species.

More Proof

The lack of apparent nerve endings on the surface of the vaginal lining has made people assume that women are incapable of internal orgasm. That theory is now obsolete. Among the people who investigated the problem are Drs. Terence F. McGuire and Richard M. Steinhilber, who conducted extensive research at the Mayo Clinic: "According to our data, the muscles beneath the vaginal mucose are well supplied with proprioceptive endings (nerve endings which respond to pressure). These are adequately stimulated during intercourse and could well represent the primary sensory apparatus. It would appear that vaginal orgasm is a reality.

If this seems like a new idea to you, you are not alone. Until very recently researchers were not aware of this latent ability because they had confined their testings only to the surface lining of the vagina. More testimony to the established fact of vaginal sensitivity is brought out by the research conducted at the American Institute of Family Relations. Dr. Paul Papanoe of that organization reported that out of the 1,000 cases of "female frigidity," 65 percent or 650 women, were clearly helped to achieve greater sexual gratification through increased internal sensation. These were the women who learned how to use these vaginal muscles.

"It is a rare woman," says Doctor Papanoe, "who cannot heighten her sexual adequacy through this technique, usually to a considerable extent." While some women respond to the exercises almost immediately, others who have become so atrophied that sensation is apparently non-existent, take persistent, prolonged exercising. There is no case so extreme that the problem is irrevocable. Every woman can show improvement if she so desires.

These muscles are amazing in their ability to become regenerated when they are put to use. If you consider that they are the very same muscles used in propulsive action of childbirth, you will understand the control that they can exert during the sexual act. A woman can draw the penis into herself, or she can expel it if she so desires. This control power adds to sexual confidence which is so lacking in a very large percentage of our gender. Acquiring this kind of confident control makes a woman not just a second class sexual replica of the man, but a very special, highly evolved kind of being.

The action of the female sexual muscles causes a pulsating motion that puts her body into the basic rhythm of life. Expansion and contraction is the basis of everything that is alive. The bellows-like action of the lungs which brings oxygen into our bodies functions on this principle as does the heart and the entire circulatory system. Pulsation vibrates in every form of life, from the simplest cell to the most complex of creatures.

It is interesting to note the differences in sexual pulsations between the male and the female. Once the male has inserted his penis into the vagina he instinctively moves back and forth in a rocking motion. His is a thrusting action and differs from the kind of movement that is basically feminine. Most women have been taught to imitate the man and rock back and forth attempting to accommodate the motion of the male thrust. Rather than helping to increase frictional contact, this very often causes the loss of genital contact as too much *outside* motion makes the penis slip out of the flaccid, non-gripping vaginal tract.

If a woman holds her hips steady instead, and uses her internal muscles to grip the penis on its forward thrust, she will be assuring both herself and partner of maximum sensation. The gripping action of the vaginal sphincters is built into the basic biological structure of the female sexual organs. Nature intended that the female respond with an involuntary, spontaneous action from within. The awakened, responsive vagina is like a fine musical instrument, vibrating with controlled resonance. A depressed woman is one whose sexual vibrations have been "pressed down," without vital movement, like the sphincters of her vagina.

Does Genital Size Affect Pleasure?

Among the many fallacies that confuse both men and women is the misconception that the size of the anatomical parts of the genitals (male and/or female) is a crucial factor in reaching orgasm. There are some women who complain that they are too small to accommodate a normal or large penis. Still others reject men who are not endowed by nature with a larger than average penis in the belief that a small penis cannot make sufficient contact with the walls of their vagina. The facts prove that it is neither the size of the vagina nor the length or width of the penis that makes the real difference in sexual satisfaction for the woman. The woman who thinks of her vagina as too small should consider that, after all, no penis has been recorded to equal the size of a newborn infant. The woman who has trouble allowing the penetration of a penis, should first of all see her doctor. If he tells her it is merely tension, the exercises found in this book will help her immensely. In any case, natural use of these muscles cannot possibly harm her and will add to her general well-being.

Whether a woman is anatomically tight or merely emotionally tense, sufficient foreplay should take place before the male attempts penetration of the vagina. In order for any woman to reach orgasm she requires anywhere from fifteen minutes to an hour of preliminary lovemaking. Many women are too ill at ease about sex to insist that this take place. A woman who allows a man to put his penis into her vagina before she is ready to accept it and enjoy it, is assuring herself of not reaching orgasm.

Importance of Preliminary Lovemaking

For a woman to reach vaginal orgasm, she must not only have a relaxed mental attitude, but must see to it that her lover provides effective preliminary stimulation. If he does not know what to do, she should teach him. There are some few lucky women who are sufficiently passionate by nature so that a minimum of stimulation is necessary. No matter where in the wide range of sexual responsiveness a woman may consider herself (from anesthetic frigidity to easy vaginal orgasm) all women need cuddling, coddling, and sufficient fondling before penetration.

This is not easy for all men to understand, because for many, foreplay may be pleasant but not really necessary to bring about orgasm. The act of sexual intercourse is basically simple for the male. He places his penis into the vagina, and by the friction which his agitated motion brings about, stimulation builds up within a few moments. He provides his own build-up of sensation by rubbing the nerve endings in his penis on the walls of the vagina.

Due to the fact that men are in better control of their sensory feelings during coitus, they have 90 percent success in reaching orgasm once they have an erection, which is essential for penile-vaginal intercourse to take place. The tumescent pressure on the nerves in the penis causes arousal and the intensification of orgastic sensation.

If a woman is to achieve control of her own orgastic sensation she too, must know how to bring it about. The vagina is a hollow tube which leads from the external genitals (the female lips) into the uterus (or womb). When not in use, the vaginal channel is usually collapsed and its walls are dry. In a non-aroused state the vagina is not receptive to penetration.

If a man does not wait for sexual readiness on the part of the woman but tries to force entry, it can cause her unnecessary pain as well as prove unsatisfactory for the male. A woman must communicate and see to it that she is prepared for sexual intercourse. It is no longer considered proper for a woman to just lie back and expect her lover to do all the work of preparing her for coitus. Not only should she contribute her creative ardor to the lovemaking, but she should stimulate herself internally by exercising her vaginal muscles during the foreplay.

Effective preliminary stimulation presupposes that the lover has caressed and manipulated the outer labia as well as the clitoris (in addition to the self-stimulation conducted by the female). This preparation is necessary to lubricate and prepare the vagina for the subsequent entrance of the penis. The stimulation of the erogenous zones of the female body, the lips, breasts, thighs, ears and throat, bring on the flow of secretions from the labia as well as the interior walls of the vagina.

Within the vaginal shaft itself are many tiny glands that secrete a lubricating fluid as the female becomes more aroused

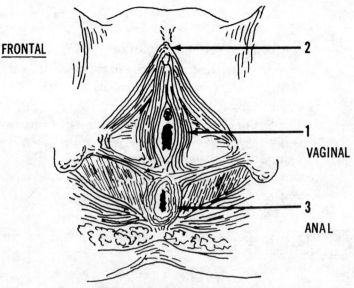

FRONTAL

2

1

VAGINAL

3

ANAL

THE SEXUAL MUSCLES
The three sets of sexual muscles are intertwined and
the action of each affects the others.

and nears orgastic readiness. This is often referred to as the
"sweating" of the walls of the vagina and it takes place on an
involuntary level with the normally passionate woman. However, any woman can assure herself of proper lubrication by
using her built-in muscle contractors. Once she is sufficiently
lubricated to permit easy penetration of the penis, she can then
heighten the ecstasy of sensory contact by a squeezing motion.

There are three sets of muscles which play an important
part in making the sex act what it should be for the female.

1. The Vaginal Sphincters: The internal tube-like or-
    ifice of the vagina is ringed by interlocking, ex-
    tremely strong muscles, called sphincters. When
    you consider that they can expand and enlarge to
    permit childbirth and yet can also contract to grip
    an object as small as one's finger, you may realize
    their astounding flexibility.

Although these muscles have the inherent ability to accomplish these extremes, not every woman can master their control without being taught a specific method of doing so.

The loss of this natural function can be attributed to the following causes:

a. Ignorance of the female biological structure.

b. Guilt and fear of sexual involvement.

c. Lack of confidence and assertiveness.

The exercises which follow, however, if carried out properly and regularly, can cause this natural action to take place without undue stress or strain.

2. The Frontal Muscles: These are located in the clitoral area and when used properly draw the surrounding tissue (hood of the clitoris) down closer to the vaginal opening. This tissue is liberally sprinkled with nerve endings and can help in bringing about heightened feeling during penile-vaginal contact.

There are actually no completely separated nerves just as there are no disconnected parts of the female genitalia. The clitoral tissue blends and becomes part of the inner labia, (vaginal lips), which ring the vaginal vestibule. The action of these frontal muscles is to draw sensitivity closer to the vaginal entrance. (See illustration.)

3. The Anal Sphincter: This group of muscles is located inside the anal opening at the base of the anus. Their action is similar to the action of the vaginal sphincters. The term sphincter simply designates muscle that is found inside a hollow organ.

We have intestinal sphincters as well that help in the digestive action of our bodies. In spite of the fact that most people cannot isolate the action of the three groups of sexual muscles, their combined use for sexual feeling helps in female arousal.

By concentrated focusing on the anal muscles pressure can be exerted on the anterior wall of the vaginal orifice and add to the frictional contact during copulation. This action combined with the "pulling down" action of the frontal muscles causes a puckering or pursing of the labia as well as increasing the gripping action of the vagina shaft.

How to Practice Step Number 6

In order to make vaginal orgasm a reality for yourself, as soon as possible, concentrate on mastering the following exercises. Their regular practice will help to restore and rejuvenate the entire muscle complex from below the naval through the genitals and into the buttock areas. You will find that it is not difficult once you have convinced yourself that the muscles exist and respond to your wishes.

First: Contract the frontal muscles (in the clitoral area). Tense them as though you are holding in the urge to urinate. Focus on keeping this contraction while you count to five, during the inhalation. Then let go of the muscle contraction as you exhale to the count of five slowly. Now rest for the count of ten, as you focus your awareness on the next set of muscles.

Second: Practice pulling the anal (rectal) muscles together tightly, as if you were trying to retard a bowel movement. Hold this contraction as in the above exercise and then release the tension as you exhale to the count of five. Pause for the count of ten, as you turn your attention to the activation of the vaginal muscles.

Third: The secret of localizing the vaginal muscles and building their power is to focus on a feeling of pulling together all the external tissue and drawing everything inward and upward into the vaginal cavity. Experiment with the lips of your mouth as this will give you the concept of what this simple exercise is supposed to do. (While the outer tissue may not actually move inward, the nerves will react as if it were happening.) Once you get the feeling of internal gripping, hold your muscles very tight for the count of five, then release again for the count of five. Rest for the count of ten and repeat as often as you can.

Then combine all three exercises into one highly focused tensing action. Feel as though you are pulling your entire outside genitalia together and drawing all of the nerve endings toward the center into the vaginal opening, making contact with the penis. The sum total of this "Exercise of Experience" is to give you the power of contraction and expansion of the vaginal passage at will. This studied control of sexual pressure will release and increase orgastic sensation.

It is interesting to note that vaginal tone is not at all related to the general musculature of a woman's outside body. Great athletes may have flabby internal sex muscles, while a small weak-limbed woman can have excellent internal muscle tone. The reason given by doctors for this seeming paradox is that the sexual muscles are not connected to the general muscular structure of the rest of the body. The muscles with which we are concerned are suspended from the front of the pelvic bone to the back without crossing or attaching themselves to the overall outside muscle system. (This may also explain why some very large-boned women have tiny vaginas which seem out of proportion to their size, while a tiny wiry woman could have a loose, distended vaginal passageway.) Keep in mind that both problems are readily correctable with the exercises described here.

When to Practice Step Number 6

Eventually you will do these exercises any time and any place. However, at the beginning it is best to learn them at home during your regular practice periods. This makes it possible for you to concentrate free of outside disturbances. Once the techniques are learned, they can be practiced almost any time or any place and under any conditions. Their action is invisible. When you practice it is most effective to use all seven steps together at set times of the day, morning and evening.

Because no one can tell that you are doing these internal exercises you can practice at home, going to or from work, sitting at the movies, standing waiting for a bus, while taking a leisurely walk, or even when playing bridge. Work on them as often and as vigorously as you can. You cannot expect occasional use to compensate for years of disuse. So use every possible moment around the clock. This includes, of course, the foreplay before intercourse, and during intercourse itself. If you are conscientious, you will find that the increase in sensation is phenomenal. Remember that by developing your internal femaleness, you are not only assuring yourself of a most basic kind of biological satisfaction, you are also freeing your man to be as naturally masculine as nature intended him to be without straining and becoming anxious as to whether you will be able to reach orgasm.

EIGHTEEN

Step No. 7.
Sensory Awakening

People use only a tiny speck of their sensory potential. Women suffer even more than men from sensory deprivation, because they have been taught to believe that giving full vent to their sensory desires is hedonism or debauchery. Things are changing, however, as even the most orthodox of the religious denominations have softened their attitudes about the concept of sex being "sinful."

Aware people are transcending these imposed limitations and challenging the validity of obsolete concepts. Sensory deprivation can drive people mad, whereas freeing the senses can bring euphoric exaltation. Accepting a new set of beliefs and freeing the senses they can mobilize the forces of the

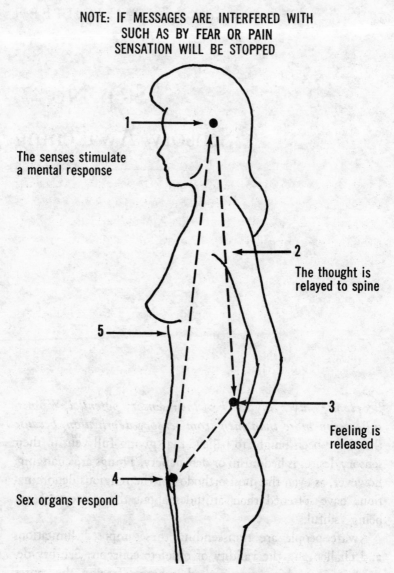

NOTE: IF MESSAGES ARE INTERFERED WITH
SUCH AS BY FEAR OR PAIN
SENSATION WILL BE STOPPED

1

The senses stimulate
a mental response

2

The thought is
relayed to spine

5

3

Feeling is
released

4

Sex organs respond

SENSORY STIMULATION

Your sensory organs send messages to the brain,
which relays them to the central nervous system.
Your mind can accelerate or diminish sexual pleasure depending on this inter-communication.

mind and body to affect speedy changes. There is no limit to the amount of changing for the better that can take place.

To ignore the senses, as so many people do, is to relegate sex to banality, a vulgar mechanical exercise, or mutual masturbation. Without the poetic involvement of the senses, sex can fall into a rut of boredom. On the other hand, when you take sex out of the commonplace, it can be uncommonly good. Sensory eroticism makes one relish sexual intercourse with epicurian delight. It frees the entire nervous system to luxuriate in the coziness of skin-to-skin contact; to titilate to the taste of a soulful kiss, and to do all of these things unashamedly and joyfully.

The language of love is communicated through all of the senses. It is not just what one says or listens to, but how one touches and feels, the aroma of a lover's body, the taste of his lips. All these things aid to the completeness of the coital union. Men are usually very responsive to sensory arousal, whereas women resist due to past conditioning when it was considered proper for women to be shy about sexual passion.

Women were expected to be looked at, but not to look. They were to be felt, but not to feel. They were to listen to erotic words, but not to speak them. The so called "good woman" was an object pure and simple. That time has passed. Good women now are neither pure (in the old sense), nor simple. They insist and sometimes even demand the right to get into the sensory act.

Women who have left the twilight zone of sexlessness, are now eagerly looking, speaking, as well as listening—they are touching, tasting, feeling and enjoying the entire aroma of sexual love. They are no longer plastic people, but flesh and blood females, vibrantly alive.

People generally have built in a protective shield over their senses, a shell to mute the tumult which results from the constant bombardment of civilization's sights and sounds. We tend to automatically protect ourselves in this way from the kind of hyper-tension that surrounds us in daily life. Unfortunately, by shutting off our sensitivities to outside tension stimulators, we often deaden our senses and become calloused to the affect of pleasurable stimuli as well.

Organs of Stimulation

There are special groupings of sensitive nerves which are concentrated in certain areas of the body, the nose, ears, eyes, tongue, and skin. The full conscious use of all of these organs can impart a deeper meaning to lovemaking than just instinctive animal release. Each of the five senses, smell, hearing, sight, taste, and touch, has an individual and unique effect in arousing and enlarging sexual pleasure. They bring with them an emotional quality which is essential to the fullest release of the female sensual potential. The sensate capability lies dormant throughout most women's lifetimes. At best, we use only a small fraction of what we are intrinsically capable of. The impulse to expand sensory reaction is triggered by the awakening of a thought. Thoughts stimulate emotions, which in turn spur the particular sensory organ into involved activity. Every sense organ gives rise to its own specific sensation and in turn affects the degree of sexual excitation in the others.

In order for the organs to do their optimum job as sex stimulators, old limitations must be discarded. When women toss aside the old sensory restrictions including, "don't touch, don't look, don't listen" they will be on the road to real sexual liberation, not just in theory, but in the deepest physical sense.

A liberated woman can open her own doors wide to new dimensions of sensory gratification. It is the purpose of these tested sensitivity exercises to teach you how to examine your sensations and bring them under your control and to serve your own individual needs for full orgastic pleasure. You will discover that your innate capacities are more potent than stimulants such as alcohol, marijuana, and assorted other sex-stimulating drugs, most of which have harmful side affects. You need nothing outside of the excellent equipment with which nature has endowed us all for sexual arousal and satisfaction. You will find that you can awaken your senses and turn them on and upward to the natural power of mind-body harmony. There is no limit. Using the senses properly and fully can lift sex to the greatest level of creative artistry.

What happens when you don't use your senses? They often become unusable and have to be taught of their own existence. Whether abuse, misuse, or disuse, dulls the senses, they can be stirred back to life by awareness. The human senses have to be "updated" like everything else that falls behind the times.

You must ask yourself if you are allowing yourself to use all of your senses fully for sexual pleasure—without prudish hangovers from the past. If the answer is no, find out why you are denying yourself your birthright, the pursuit of a most fundamental happiness. The sexual release of mind, body, and emotional tension.

When you learn to freely feel, to see, to touch, to hear, to taste, you will raise the limited threshold of your conditioned sensory feelings to undreamed of heights. Using positive auto-suggestion combined with self-imagery and relaxation, as outlined in previous chapters, will make you more receptive to a new set of habit patterns. You will then be sufficiently liberated to communicate with your lover in a new and much more profound way. Your emancipated body will then be a true receiver of unhampered sensory pleasure. Not only will you receive heightened sexual feeling, but you will be able to transmit and exchange with your lover ecstatic vibrations on a phenomenal level.

Most people limit their thinking sexually to the sense of touch (that of skin to skin), but there is the kind of touching that comes when we touch one another with the sound of the voice, or touch in an infinite way when we look deep into each other's eyes. We are sexually *touched* a great deal more than with the surface of our skin. There is a great deal more to satisfactory sex than mere genital skin contact. The amount of sexual pleasure depends on the degree of sensory awakening. Because women have been conditioned to equate sex with romantic love, their sensory awakening is tied directly to their emotional involvement. Feelings of being loved and cherished must precede female surrender to sexual intercourse. Proof of this is evident when your examine the behavior of professional prostitutes and forced sex, such as rape. Where women are not emotionally involved, their senses also remain uninvolved. Except for monetary gains, they are seldom moved into sexual participation without some emotional feeling.

Mae West put it succinctly, when she said, "Sex is an emotion put into motion." Sad to say, too often women have lots of "emotion" but find that they are unable to put it into "motion." Men have much less trouble enjoying sex without the rationale of "being in love." While they are to a great extent freer than women about using their senses, many of them also need to be taught how to expand their senses more fully in order to enhance sex—not only to help their woman, but to add to the variety of their own experience.

If the man knows less than he should, there is no reason why a woman can't teach him, rather than expect all the initiative and instruction to come from him. There is no question but that both men and women are a long distance from their pleasure potential, but the fact remains that the problem is more female than male. Women who know that they have been retarded should start doing some concentrated catching up.

Men complain about the large percentage of women who will not consider having sex unless the lights are off. Many women not only insist on darkness to hide their own bodies, but cringe at the thought of looking at the male genitals as well. These are the same kind of women who become embarrassed at hearing descriptive erotic words. There are even some women, more than a few, who feel reluctance about touching their own bodies; the thought of masturbation disgusts them. When a woman is inhibited about her own body, she certainly cannot be expected to feel free about her lover's.

We hear the expression, "You've come a long way, baby!" but the aware woman says, "Baby, we've still got a long way to go!"

Your sense of sight: A sexual experience starts with the first lingering glance exchanged between a woman and a man. Somewhere, deep in the recesses of her mind, a woman knows if she will eventually make love to this man. That biological awareness, that animal instinct shows in the special way that she looks at him. A glance is a subtle way of communicating even at a distance. It opens the way for the other senses to enlarge upon the initial reaction to another person. When glances meet and two lovers look searchingly into each other's eyes, emotions are immediately intensified. This heightened feeling adds a new dimension of ardent desire which can lead to much greater intimacy. Eye-to-eye contact reveals the mutual depth of passion. It is a powerful way of communicating non-verbally during lovemaking. Therefore, the insistence on total darkness can rob the relationship of this subtle method of male-female interaction of desire. The interplay of imagined thoughts is sent from one to the other. Softened light, rather than complete darkness, can be of great help in arousing a woman. It has been said that the eyes are the mirrors of the soul and, where a woman is concerned, soulfulness adds a special dimension to the sexual excitement.

While women, generally, love being seen and admired (and the enormous amount of money they spend on looking attractive proves that point), when it comes to actual sex, many of them prefer darkness. They fail to realize that being seen but "not seeing" separates them from real sexual contact with their male partner. The average woman tends to think of visual sex in terms of pornography, and retreats into a shell of Puritanical taboos.

Women who have difficulty reaching orgasm very often also have difficulty looking at the sexual act. They carry over into the sexual act an aversion to seeing themselves doing something which was once called, "not nice for a girl to do."

When women cling to this outmoded barrier they lose something that is very important to the realization of full orgastic satisfaction. They lose an affirmative sexual image of themselves. Seeing one's self having sex and enjoying it, triggers orgasm in many cases.

One woman who violently objected to her husband's having the light on during sex explained that. "I freely and fully enjoy sex in the dark, but when I see what my husband looks like, I can't bear it and either the light gets turned off, or *I* get turned off."

She was echoing the sentiments of many people who prefer to dim the lights for sexual activities because they feel that their imagination can do more to stimulate them than the person they are with.

Sight is a powerful message conductor and can interfere with sexual focusing, if what one sees is not conducive to arousal. We have all been conditioned to be dominated by what we see. The sense of sight always takes precedence over what we are told. "Seeing is believing" and "I'm from Missouri and have to be *shown,*" are the kind of old American sayings that we have all been nurtured on. The power of sight is not only a positive factor, it can also be a deterrent where sex is concerned. If a woman is visually sensitive she should express her feelings openly and insist that she have the proper kind of atmosphere that suits her needs. It's a simple law of life that if you don't ask for what you want, you won't get it.

One reason that some women react negatively to their sense of sight during sex is because they have been conditioned to expect their lover to look like Prince Charming in a fairy tale. Let's face reality, girls. If he is less than stimulating visually, by all means, dim the lights. But, if the opposite is true, if looking at him turns you on, rather than off, look him over and enjoy it. Seeing can add to the erotic illusion rather than disillusion the sensuous woman. If you have a man who is worth looking at sexually, make the most of your sensory reactors and leave the lights on. You might find that it helps you to overcome your Puritanical hang-ups.

Eyes Speak a Language

Even if you prefer darkness or semi-darkness for coitus itself, make the most of your sense of sight during the foreplay. Try looking directly into your lover's eyes during lovemaking instead of closing your eyes. Your facial expression can convey to him all of the subtle messages that you might not be ready to communicate verbally. When your eyes hold his glance a little longer than usual, they transmit vibrations of desire. Your face has an infinite vocabulary of expressions that can only be appreciated when your lover can see how you feel and see how you are reacting to his touch. The same is true for him. If you look at him, you may learn much more than just the meaning of the words he is saying. Seeing and being seen lends an air of excitement to lovemaking that is further increased by the creative involvement of the senses. So take a good look, don't count your sense of sight out of the picture.

In spite of the fact that most women need a pleasing visual atmosphere to relax and enjoy sex, you will find that as you become more sexually evolved you will be able to respond under less exact conditions and enjoy sex even more.

While it has been said that there is more sex going on in automobiles than in the comfort of the boudoir, most women prefer the proper surroundings for their best response. Candlelight bathes the body in a special kind of soft glow, and women need to know that they look their best to their lover. Try visually stimulating affects.

There are wives who turn off their husbands as well as their own chances of enjoying sex by going to bed with hair curlers on, cold cream, shabby night gowns, and so on. They use the senses in a negative way to ensure themselves of not being sexually attractive to their husbands. Many a man turns away from a woman who could be naturally lovely, but appears at bedtime looking like a monstrosity.

Some psychologists believe that frigid wives make themselves look unattractive in order to avoid the amorous advances of their husbands. Other women try too hard to look super-sexy. They get into bed wearing hair pieces, wigs, artificial eyelashes and assorted transformations that hamper their own ability to function freely.

A woman needs to feel comfortable in order to enjoy sex fully. Researchers say that when a man is aroused he has blurred vision. He couldn't care less whether or not you have false eyelashes on or not. He is more involved with the rest of the body. Men are very visual—they love to look at the nude female form. This is in sharp contrast to the way women feel about looking at the nude bodies of men. Most of them shy away from the experience, cringing at the thought of looking at the male genitals. This is a hangover from the early suggestion that there is something threatening about the penis. Sexually liberated women need to systematically wipe out this detrimental concept. Look him over and enjoy doing it. Nature planned it that way. Abandon prudishness once and for all and let the sight of his body entice your desire. Let him know that you are changing for the better. Why not undress him for a change? Let your sense of sight get into the act to increase and expand your pleasure.

Your sense of hearing: Your ears do a lot more than listen to the words that are spoken. They are like sponges which soak up the feeling of sound, the emotions behind the words. As a result of too much of an overload of noise which surrounds us constantly, many of us learn to subconsciously ignore much of the sound that could bring us pleasure and relaxation. Communication between lovers does not consist of merely listening to the meaning of the words. Words are the least important part of sensuous sound.

It is the vibrations of the voice as the words are uttered that give it the emotional quality that stirs our imagination. Language consists not only of words, but of tone, pitch, volume. Human language is what makes us essentially different from other forms of animal life. But words alone do not say what we are thinking and feeling. A man may repeat cliches and rote phrases of flattery to a woman and impress her less than the incoherent murmurings of a sincerely aroused, non-verbally expressive man. Murmurings of sexual feelings have an "extrasensory" faculty of transmitting more truth to a person than the most carefully chosen words of amour.

Noted psychologist, Albert Mehrabian, has devised this tested formula: "Total impact of a message:

   7 percent verbal
  38 percent emotional quality
  55 percent facial expression"

(Again we see the importance of the visual impact of seeing a lover's facial expression during lovemaking. Its combination with the sound of the softly spoken word is highly stimulating.)

Let restrictions go and express yourself freely. Tell your lover what you want and how you want it. SOUND OFF! TALK IT OUT! He wants to help you, let him! It will please him and make him more of a man to please you. Whisper into his ear your secret desires and see what happens.

The human ear is an amazing mechanism and because of its proximity to the brain carries its message to our motor re-actors quickly and forcefully. The human being can distinguish between 300,000 to 400,000 variations of tonal vibrations of sound. When you consider that all sound picked up by our ears carries with it an emotional reaction, you will understand how potent is this gift that we all possess and how we can increase sexual pleasure by putting it to good use.

The need for lovers to communicate with each other is basic to good sexual relationships. Speaking draws people closer and adds a dimension of emotion as one reacts to the message that the ears pick up. What we say and how we say it can build or destroy a relationship.

Verbal suggestion is highly combustible and one badly chosen word can wreck a love affair before it has had a chance to get started. Even the tone of voice, its quality of pitch, can freeze the warmest person instantly. The sound of words colors their meaning and can titilate or dampen desire.

When you think of the three words "I love you" while expressing feelings of love, you will better understand the impact of emotions on mere words. Subtle vibrations that result from our true feelings give our message more meaning. Quoting the world's most erotic poetry in a sexless voice would be less stimulating than reading the phone book with a voice full of sexual passion.

Passionate love is often possible between people of different languages because of this factor. The soft sound of breathing of a satisfied lover says much more than lengthy declarations of satisfaction. It is a wise lover, male or female, who makes good use of all of the senses, and in particular the sense of sound because it has a very quick effect on the sexual stimulators.

Your Own Voice Can Arouse You

The sound that has the greatest affect upon us at all times is the sound of our own voice. Because it is the closest sound to our mental receptors, it influences our behavior greatly. In the chapter on auto-suggestion, you learned many positive suggestions that you can tell yourself during coitus. Notice how your own declaration of positive anticipation of sexual satisfaction affects the degree of sensation that you feel. Say the right things to yourself. You are always listening to the sound of your own voice and are very prone to accept your own advice.

A man who knows how to convey to a woman through his choice of words and manner of speaking that he has selected her above all others for this precious moment, opens the way for her to raise her level of sensuality to greater heights. Words and sounds can kindle the flame of passion and the right words at the right time can bring a woman to orgasm, or shut off all sensation. One way of assuring herself that she will hear the right verbal suggestions when she needs them the most is to freely tell herself what she needs to hear in order to reach orgasm. There is nothing wrong or sinful in telling a man to say erotic words that may help you at your peak, but if he gets carried away by his own drive toward orgasm, say it yourself. Your ear is a powerful conductor of messages to the brain, and you need that mental directive to reach the peak of climax.

The act of hearing takes place when the motion of sound waves vibrates the inner ear, which is close to the brain. The inner ear is composed of a thin membrane stretched tautly over the end of a tunnel-like structure leading in from the outer ear. The sounds of words make this drumlike structure quiver its exciting messages to the brain. The brain in turn relays its answer to the entire nervous system of the body, building anticipation and desire for sexual fulfillment. Because the brain is so close to the receiving end of the hearing instrument, every word we say instantly affects how we function. Keep this in mind and be sure to say the right words at the right time, not just to him, but most especially to yourself through auto-suggestion.

Your sense of taste: The involvement of our sense of taste starts with the first kiss. The very first taste of another's lips can be the beginning of a lifetime of love or can turn a person away in disgust. The first kiss can be the indicator of what sort of lovemaking will follow.

Sometimes a kiss can be almost a sacred ritual, complete and satisfying in itself, on a deep level of sensuality. Kissing is probably the most expressive form of mutual acceptance that is possible between lovers. It can be the forerunner of total mind-body involvement, not just because there are so many erogenous zones which can be orally stimulated, but because the lips, mouth, and tongue have infinite varieties and subtle nuances of sensory interaction. Next to the sexual organs themselves they are the most sensitive parts of the body.

The erotic kiss signals the beginning of the forthcoming coital union. A kiss can reveal what words try to conceal. A poet once called a kiss, "The silent language between lovers." How you kiss and how you are kissed in return (and also *where* you are kissed) can indicate what kind of a sexual relationship to expect from a particular lover. Kissing can be more stimulating erotically, spiritually, and esthetically than the most meaningful verbal conversation.

If a kiss is prolonged and unhurried, it can help a woman reach new and constantly heightened plateaus of pleasurable anticipation. There is no place that should be considered out of bounds for a lover to kiss. A clean, healthy body is entirely lovable and kissable. Reluctance to accept a loved one's body totally is a sign of conditioned negativism, and may indicate a problem on the part of the reluctant one. However, where and what one kisses during foreplay is an entirely personal thing and there should be no anxiety about whether one or another kind of kissing is normal or not. Everything is normal if it meets with the approval of both people concerned.

Whatever one's preference may be, the fact remains that kissing is an essential part of the foreplay leading to satisfactory sex for women. It sets the stage for what is to follow, by giving a woman confidence in her desirability as well as effectively stimulating her sensory reflexes. Mutual desire expands as the erotic excitement increases, spurred by the ebb and flow of effervescent vibrations.

When lips cling cherishingly with full reciprocal acceptance, the level of feeling can rise to a spiritual communion between two lovers, above and beyond mere sexual union. Kissing is a builder of understanding on a more profound level that words are capable of. The lips and tongue not only taste, but they are super-sensitive to touch and the reception of the most subtle vibration.

A wit once said, "I kissed my first woman and smoked my first cigarette the same day and I have never had a cigarette since." There may be more to the above statement than meets the eye. A sexually satisfied person doesn't need destructive habits. Frustrated lovers often are compulsive smokers and overeaters. Research shows that most alcoholics are driven to drink because they are unable to enjoy their sexual capacities. Many psychologists and psychiatrists attributed oral compulsion to sexual immaturity, and there is a great deal to support this theory.

The intangible, spiritual exchange that is experienced in a deep kiss, does more than arouse lovers sexually, it can be the means of assuring one another of deeper values. It can bring with it the kind of exhilarated elation that awakens not only the physical body, but creative awareness as well.

How Kissing Turns You On

A well-known chemist released the results of experimentation recently that involved the body's chemical reaction to kissing. It showed that both men and women react with increased blood pressure, heightened circulation, quickening of pulse, and deeper breathing. The only marked difference between the male and female was that the women reacted much more strongly if they also believed that they were in love with the man. In the case of the male subjects, their automatic motor system responded equally, which points up again the fact that women are strongly directed by their romantic feelings.

Some people are more adept than others at kissing and many a man has turned off a woman from the very start by kissing her in such a way that she became disgusted rather than aroused. It is an accepted truth that once a woman grants a man the privilege of deep, soulful kissing, she is also saying that she is not adverse to his trying for all the rest.

The erotic kiss differs from the kind of kissing that takes place between mother and child or platonic friends. Deep sexual kissing plays an indispensable role in stimulation of sexual excitement. Its importance lies in the fact that the lips, the mouth and the tongue comprise what is known as an erogenous zone, and whenever erogenous zones are stimulated the excitation spreads to the other sexual areas. The kissing of the area around the genitals, or the genitals themselves causes the lips of the vulva to swell, become lubricated, and open in readiness for the penetrating thrust of the penis. Without necessarily being aware of it, many women equate kissing of their mouth with their vagina being entered by the penis. The male tongue going into their mouth sets an image for the genitals to follow.

Techniques of kissing vary with each lover and those unfortunate people who limit themselves are missing a great source of stimulation. A woman should know the variations of foreplay in order to teach her lover, if he is unaware of them. Men who have been conditioned by non-responsive women, do very little kissing of any kind. Some do not like the taste of a woman's body, and they have a problem. They are the users of the female genitals as a receptacle. Some kiss only her lips. Some kiss only her lips and breasts and are repulsed by her genitalia. On the other hand, some men love the entire taste of a woman's body and women should know that there are such uninhibited men.

If she is clean, takes some time for grooming and keeps her body fresh, a woman should know that she is lovable all over and she should not accept the "non-kissable" body image of a man who may have some sort of a problem himself. Psychiatrists tell us that men who insist on a hospital-sterile kind of woman need help. While cleanliness is not necessarily godliness, as some of us were taught to believe in childhood, still lovers should demonstrate to each other not only their passion for each other's bodies, but also their respect for each other's senistivities by presenting their bodies in as inviting a way as possible. Be kissable all over and make it a mutual pleasure for both of you.

Your sense of touch: Skin-to-skin contact awakens the most intimate of all the senses. One can close one's eyes, say nothing and let the hands roam over a lover's body sending exquisite messages of love. The tender emotion in a touch can dissolve all manner of barriers. A lover may not mean the words he is saying, or he can, if he is a skilled actor, look as though he adores you, but the touch of his hands will tell the true story about how he really feels.

Those people who were taught *not to touch* as children, must learn that touching is a meaningful exchange, a sharing of good feeling, a way of giving and at the same time of taking. Touching can remove the walls we build around ourselves. It can let loving in. There are countless ways to touch and to be touched. It can be as deep, as high, as wide, as your own boundless imagination. It can be a source of comfort and reassurance to the shy or timid. It can be an indication of the best that is yet to come. It lets a woman know what sort of man she is getting close to. How eager he is, how tender; how thoughtful, how ardent.

So many of us have been cautioned against touching in childhood that the tendency is to avoid too much intimate contact in adulthood. When we stop touching each other, we not only alienate our bodies, but wreak havoc with our nervous systems because touching is very important for mental health. When people do not touch (themselves or other people), they tend to dull their deepest feelings and become alienated from life itself.

The human skin has a massive network of tactile receptors specialized in receiving messages of heat, pain, pleasure, pressure, and so forth. We react a special way to the soothers, the relaxers of touch. The stroking, massaging, petting of the skin sends a vibration of meaning to the brain and prepares our body for the sexual act.

All of the many subtle facets of a person's personality are unconsciously revealed by his or her touch. Each and every part of an individual's body carries with it "touch messages" of that individual's special desires and innermost intentions. Luckily, the spirit of instinctual animalism still survives in the nerves and muscles of our bodies and from this force springs the need to draw closer to someone of the opposite sex. This motivation precipitates the mounting desire for sexual intercourse and its profound closeness. There are countless methods of sensory arousal through the sense of touch. It is imperative to optimum arousal that both take plenty of time to touch each other.

In foreplay, it is the man who inititates the first caress in most cases. This has been the case for too long and when women take the reverse role, it often helps to release their pent-up sexual feeling. The custom of a woman just lying still while the male does all the preliminary work of lovemaking is a major reason for female lethargy. Standard literature describes foreplay as a time for the male to prepare the female "so that her juices will start flowing in order that he can make entry into her vagina." Research indicates that women become much more aroused and lubricated if they enter into the foreplay and use all of their senses to help arouse themselves as well as their lover.

Men Welcome An Active Partner

Men welcome the sharing of this pleasurable responsibility of preliminary stimulation. A woman who is a self-starter and gets off her back and into the act becomes a special kind of sexual partner that a man cherishes. This kind of woman does not have to worry about transgressions because chances are he would have difficulty in finding another like her—sexually active women are not easy to find. They too often have been trained to be overly modest about their sensory feelings and are afraid that their lover will think less of them if they surrender to feeling and seem to enjoy sex too much. This must be checked out with the rest of the obsolete fairy tales told by grandmas throughout history.

If you want to reach your highest peak of orgasm, freely and deliberately use your sense of touch to arouse yourself. Touch and be touched all over. There is no place on the human body that is out of bounds. Touch his toes, his hands, run your fingertips over the inside of his thighs, scratch his back, touch his testicles, hold them in your hand (gently), contemplate the wonder of them, note the variations in texture of each part of his body.

Be freely aware of all of nature's wonders as you enjoy the results of your own touching and the feel of his masculinity in contrast to your own feminine feeling. Run your hands over his buttocks. Don't avoid or miss a spot. Get to know every hair and pore of his body and invite him to do the same with yours. *Become sensually aroused through participation.*

If your partner is one who becomes overstimulated too quickly, it is sometimes best to direct your needs toward your own arousal at the beginning. With practice and experimentation he will become more adept at his own control and be able to cooperate in your further arousal. If he has this problem, direct his attention toward stimulating you. Don't be prudish about it. We only get in life what we ask for, and it is no longer chic to be used by a man as a receptacle in one-sided selfish sex.

One of the most effective ways for him to relax and arouse you is through a leisurely, soothing massage. There is tender loving in the art of stroking and manipulation of the body. Massage stimulates and increases circulation. There are as many variations of massage as there are people with creative minds to think them up. Play "touching games." Take turns patting, petting, stroking, teasing, and pleasing each other. You will find it a new experience in being alive. Being fondled and caressed sets up a kind of trusting communication between a woman with problems and her lover.

Some people find that a rougher kind of massage excites them more than the soothing style. You might try starting out with the gentle kind of massage and including a few light slaps for the excitement of it. The variations can include everything from a light, gentle tapping of the finger tips, to squeezing and delicate pinching.

Lovers must communicate their thoughts about this and feel free to ask for what they want and to say no, if that's the way they feel. The sense of touch is dormant in most people. Discover what your own potential is.

Your sense of smell: Your sense of smell has always been recognized as having a strong influence on sexual reactions. You may remember in the story of Cleopatra and Marc Antony how she, "Ensnared him and kindled his passions with the aroma and fragrances emanating from her person." Shakespeare described Cleopatra as, "So perfumed that even the winds became lovesick."

The art of exciting the senses through perfumery has existed since the very beginning of mankind. Sorcerers of ancient Egypt were in great demand to compound and invent formulas of new fragrances with which to stir the libidos of decadent kings and their royal flocks.

Many of these aromatic concoctions were so powerful and well-conceived that in recent archaeological excavations, their aroma was found to be still very profound. Time after time when ancient tombs of kings and pharoahs are opened, sealed jars and vessels are discovered containing assorted essences, culled from plant and animal life. Although buried for thousands of years, they still retain their strong recognizable aroma of spikenard, balsam, and musk.

Interestingly enough, these ingredients are still used in the making of many of today's commercial scents. Many perfumed offerings were associated with the religious rites of their times as well as for their erotic value. It may shock the sensibilities of present day prudes, but history shows a strong correlation between sexuality and religious fervor.

This is exemplified by the great sexual religious fertility

rites still held in many types of primitive societies around the world. Incense, for example, was used not only as a burnt offering to a deity, but also as a means of sexual arousal in most of the Eastern cultures. With the new feeling which has developed in the past decade toward oriental cultures, the use of incense for sex purposes is having a new upsurge.

Both men and women in every part of the world, throughout history, have used fragrant ointments and sweet smelling spices to help them get and keep a mate. They have anointed their hair, their skin, their mouth, and their clothing for the prime purpose of snaring and involving a lover. It has been used as a secret offering to get the gods to return an errant lover as well.

Literature abounds with stories of great courtesans who owed their amazing erotic power over men to some magic aromatic formula dreamed up by medieval alchemists. There are still sects in India who practice sexual rites in which they take turns anointing each area of their partner's body with a different variety of aromatic essence. Each type of smell is designed and endowed with a special ritual significance.

In ancient times exotic aromas were not only used for the enhancement of the erotic senses, it was also used to mask the natural odors of both female and male bodies. Lack of modern plumbing, as we now know it, must have made such masking a necessity. This concern—to the point of anxiety—with one's natural body odors is peculiar only to the human species. All other animals are attracted rather than repelled by body odor.

These days, with the new open attitude toward all things sexual, more and more cosmeticians and chemists are exploiting the sexual possibilities of perfumery for their aphrodisiac affects. There are male as well as female products, and more are being introduced every day. At this very moment an aerosol spray is being displayed at fashionable department stores in major cities, the purpose of which is to spray the male genitals with an inviting aroma.

Because of the constant bombardment of TV and radio product propaganda that we are subjected to, we have been deeply conditioned to respond favorably to artificial rather than natural odor for our bodies. We have witnessed a strong campaign on the part of commercial chemists to remove all trace of human odor, to fumigate and embalm our bodies prematurely. There are at present hundreds of products on the market designed to remove all traces of smell, from the mouth, the hair, the hands, the underarms, the feet, and the genitals. If someone can dream up some other area of the human body to deodorize, I'm sure that person will quickly become rich. Don't let yourself become too carried away with the de-animalization of your body.

Because of wide-spread anti-smell conditioning the present day man has come to expect a woman to use these deodorizing products and it stands to reason that you cannot go against this training if you want a relationship with him. Men expect that a woman will be clean and smell fragrant, and women should make sure that they do so for their own comfort as well as his. Bathe frequently, experiment with various aromas until you find the one that suits both of you. Perhaps you will prefer more than one fragrance, as they do in the secret sexual sect in India. Experience, experiment, exhilarate your senses to the fullest, and you will exalt in the expansion of pleasure for both of you.

In Conclusion

If this book is to perform the service that is intended, to help you reach your highest potential of sexual satisfaction, you will have to apply yourself to its teachings. You may at times feel like skipping the practice periods, and if you do, you will be retarding your own progress because it is the consistent repetition of the exercises that brings results.

On the other hand, if you work at them diligently, with real devotion to reaching your goal, I can promise that you will be delighted at the rich rewards. Remember that your reconditioning program involves not only the building of good sexual habits, but also breaking away from the old, self-defeating ones.

Keep in mind that:

1. A fundamental of good sexual response is faith in our ability to function as nature originally intended.
2. No matter how severe your negative conditioning, it can be corrected with applied positive auto-suggestion.
3. People can and do improve at any age and at any stage of their lives. One is never too old to love or to be loved.
4. Good feeling between people has no limitations; the range of sexual experience in infinite.

Remember that emotional motivation sparks and ignites your innate power to reach upward toward your true potential. Learn to expect more of yourself and you will deliver more. Be aware that the art of positive sexuality requires that you *assert your needs*. Having discovered what you want and that you are capable of achieving it, set about getting it as quickly as possible!

The plan of correction that you have read in this book will work for you as it has for thousands of others. Start by doing the exercises individually and then combine them into one masterful reconditioning period. You are starting the greatest adventure of your life—the exploration of your full feminine sexual identity.

Practice the exercises regularly as often as possible and you will find that sex will no longer be an exasperating experience, but rather an exciting and exhilarating one.

PRACTICE, PRACTICE, PRACTICE, Until positive, affirmative sexual reflexes become automatic.

Index

A PERSONAL WORD FROM MELVIN POWERS
PUBLISHER, WILSHIRE BOOK COMPANY

Dear Friend:

My goal is to publish interesting, informative, and inspirational books. You can help me accomplish this by answering the following questions, either by phone or by mail. Or, if convenient for you, I would welcome the opportunity to visit with you in my office and hear your comments in person.

Did you enjoy reading this book? Why?

Would you enjoy reading another similar book?

What idea in the book impressed you the most?

If applicable to your situation, have you incorporated this idea in your daily life?

Is there a chapter that could serve as a theme for an entire book? Please explain.

If you have an idea for a book, I would welcome discussing it with you. If you already have one in progress, write or call me concerning possible publication. I can be reached at (213) 875-1711 or (213) 983-1105.

Sincerely yours,

MELVIN POWERS

12015 Sherman Road
North Hollywood, California 91605

MELVIN POWERS SELF-IMPROVEMENT LIBRARY

ASTROLOGY

____ ASTROLOGY: HOW TO CHART YOUR HOROSCOPE *Max Heindel*	3.00
____ ASTROLOGY: YOUR PERSONAL SUN-SIGN GUIDE *Beatrice Ryder*	3.00
____ ASTROLOGY FOR EVERYDAY LIVING *Janet Harris*	2.00
____ ASTROLOGY MADE EASY *Astarte*	3.00
____ ASTROLOGY MADE PRACTICAL *Alexandra Kayhle*	3.00
____ ASTROLOGY, ROMANCE, YOU AND THE STARS *Anthony Norvell*	4.00
____ MY WORLD OF ASTROLOGY *Sydney Omarr*	5.00
____ THOUGHT DIAL *Sidney Omarr*	4.00
____ WHAT THE STARS REVEAL ABOUT THE MEN IN YOUR LIFE *Thelma White*	3.00

BRIDGE

____ BRIDGE BIDDING MADE EASY *Edwin B. Kantar*	7.00
____ BRIDGE CONVENTIONS *Edwin B. Kantar*	7.00
____ BRIDGE HUMOR *Edwin B. Kantar*	5.00
____ COMPETITIVE BIDDING IN MODERN BRIDGE *Edgar Kaplan*	4.00
____ DEFENSIVE BRIDGE PLAY COMPLETE *Edwin B. Kantar*	10.00
____ GAMESMAN BRIDGE—Play Better with Kantar *Edwin B. Kantar*	5.00
____ HOW TO IMPROVE YOUR BRIDGE *Alfred Sheinwold*	5.00
____ IMPROVING YOUR BIDDING SKILLS *Edwin B. Kantar*	4.00
____ INTRODUCTION TO DECLARER'S PLAY *Edwin B. Kantar*	5.00
____ INTRODUCTION TO DEFENDER'S PLAY *Edwin B. Kantar*	3.00
____ KANTAR FOR THE DEFENSE *Edwin B. Kantar*	5.00
____ SHORT CUT TO WINNING BRIDGE *Alfred Sheinwold*	3.00
____ TEST YOUR BRIDGE PLAY *Edwin B. Kantar*	5.00
____ VOLUME 2—TEST YOUR BRIDGE PLAY *Edwin B. Kantar*	5.00
____ WINNING DECLARER PLAY *Dorothy Hayden Truscott*	4.00

BUSINESS, STUDY & REFERENCE

____ CONVERSATION MADE EASY *Elliot Russell*	3.00
____ EXAM SECRET *Dennis B. Jackson*	3.00
____ FIX-IT BOOK *Arthur Symons*	2.00
____ HOW TO DEVELOP A BETTER SPEAKING VOICE *M. Hellier*	3.00
____ HOW TO MAKE A FORTUNE IN REAL ESTATE *Albert Winnikoff*	4.00
____ INCREASE YOUR LEARNING POWER *Geoffrey A. Dudley*	3.00
____ MAGIC OF NUMBERS *Robert Tocquet*	2.00
____ PRACTICAL GUIDE TO BETTER CONCENTRATION *Melvin Powers*	3.00
____ PRACTICAL GUIDE TO PUBLIC SPEAKING *Maurice Forley*	3.00
____ 7 DAYS TO FASTER READING *William S. Schaill*	3.00
____ SONGWRITERS' RHYMING DICTIONARY *Jane Shaw Whitfield*	5.00
____ SPELLING MADE EASY *Lester D. Basch & Dr. Milton Finkelstein*	3.00
____ STUDENT'S GUIDE TO BETTER GRADES *J. A. Rickard*	3.00
____ TEST YOURSELF—Find Your Hidden Talent *Jack Shafer*	3.00
____ YOUR WILL & WHAT TO DO ABOUT IT *Attorney Samuel G. Kling*	3.00

CALLIGRAPHY

____ ADVANCED CALLIGRAPHY *Katherine Jeffares*	7.00
____ CALLIGRAPHER'S REFERENCE BOOK *Anne Leptich & Jacque Evans*	7.00
____ CALLIGRAPHY—The Art of Beautiful Writing *Katherine Jeffares*	7.00
____ CALLIGRAPHY FOR FUN & PROFIT *Anne Leptich & Jacque Evans*	7.00
____ CALLIGRAPHY MADE EASY *Tina Serafini*	7.00

CHESS & CHECKERS

____ BEGINNER'S GUIDE TO WINNING CHESS *Fred Reinfeld*	4.00
____ CHECKERS MADE EASY *Tom Wiswell*	2.00
____ CHESS IN TEN EASY LESSONS *Larry Evans*	3.00
____ CHESS MADE EASY *Milton L. Hanauer*	3.00
____ CHESS PROBLEMS FOR BEGINNERS *edited by Fred Reinfeld*	2.00
____ CHESS SECRETS REVEALED *Fred Reinfeld*	2.00
____ CHESS STRATEGY—An Expert's Guide *Fred Reinfeld*	2.00
____ CHESS TACTICS FOR BEGINNERS *edited by Fred Reinfeld*	3.00
____ CHESS THEORY & PRACTICE *Morry & Mitchell*	2.00
____ HOW TO WIN AT CHECKERS *Fred Reinfeld*	3.00
____ 1001 BRILLIANT WAYS TO CHECKMATE *Fred Reinfeld*	4.00
____ 1001 WINNING CHESS SACRIFICES & COMBINATIONS *Fred Reinfeld*	4.00
____ SOVIET CHESS *Edited by R. G. Wade*	3.00

COOKERY & HERBS

____ CULPEPER'S HERBAL REMEDIES *Dr. Nicholas Culpeper* 3.00
____ FAST GOURMET COOKBOOK *Poppy Cannon* 2.50
____ GINSENG The Myth & The Truth *Joseph P. Hou* 3.00
____ HEALING POWER OF HERBS *May Bethel* 4.00
____ HEALING POWER OF NATURAL FOODS *May Bethel* 4.00
____ HERB HANDBOOK *Dawn MacLeod* 3.00
____ HERBS FOR COOKING AND HEALING *Dr. Donald Law* 2.00
____ HERBS FOR HEALTH—How to Grow & Use Them *Louise Evans Doole* 3.00
____ HOME GARDEN COOKBOOK—Delicious Natural Food Recipes *Ken Kraft* 3.00
____ MEDICAL HERBALIST *edited by Dr. J. R. Yemm* 3.00
____ NATURAL FOOD COOKBOOK *Dr. Harry C. Bond* 3.00
____ NATURE'S MEDICINES *Richard Lucas* 3.00
____ VEGETABLE GARDENING FOR BEGINNERS *Hugh Wiberg* 2.00
____ VEGETABLES FOR TODAY'S GARDENS *R. Milton Carleton* 2.00
____ VEGETARIAN COOKERY *Janet Walker* 4.00
____ VEGETARIAN COOKING MADE EASY & DELECTABLE *Veronica Vezza* 3.00
____ VEGETARIAN DELIGHTS—A Happy Cookbook for Health *K. R. Mehta* 2.00
____ VEGETARIAN GOURMET COOKBOOK *Joyce McKinnel* 3.00

GAMBLING & POKER

____ ADVANCED POKER STRATEGY & WINNING PLAY *A. D. Livingston* 5.00
____ HOW NOT TO LOSE AT POKER *Jeffrey Lloyd Castle* 3.00
____ HOW TO WIN AT DICE GAMES *Skip Frey* 3.00
____ HOW TO WIN AT POKER *Terence Reese & Anthony T. Watkins* 3.00
____ SECRETS OF WINNING POKER *George S. Coffin* 3.00
____ WINNING AT CRAPS *Dr. Lloyd T. Commins* 3.00
____ WINNING AT GIN *Chester Wander & Cy Rice* 3.00
____ WINNING AT POKER—An Expert's Guide *John Archer* 3.00
____ WINNING AT 21—An Expert's Guide *John Archer* 5.00
____ WINNING POKER SYSTEMS *Norman Zadeh* 3.00

HEALTH

____ BEE POLLEN *Lynda Lyngheim & Jack Scagnetti* 3.00
____ DR. LINDNER'S SPECIAL WEIGHT CONTROL METHOD *P. G. Lindner, M.D.* 1.50
____ HELP YOURSELF TO BETTER SIGHT *Margaret Darst Corbett* 3.00
____ HOW TO IMPROVE YOUR VISION *Dr. Robert A. Kraskin* 3.00
____ HOW YOU CAN STOP SMOKING PERMANENTLY *Ernest Caldwell* 3.00
____ MIND OVER PLATTER *Peter G. Lindner, M.D.* 3.00
____ NATURE'S WAY TO NUTRITION & VIBRANT HEALTH *Robert J. Scrutton* 3.00
____ NEW CARBOHYDRATE DIET COUNTER *Patti Lopez-Pereira* 1.50
____ QUICK & EASY EXERCISES FOR FACIAL BEAUTY *Judy Smith-deal* 2.00
____ QUICK & EASY EXERCISES FOR FIGURE BEAUTY *Judy Smith-deal* 2.00
____ REFLEXOLOGY *Dr. Maybelle Segal* 3.00
____ REFLEXOLOGY FOR GOOD HEALTH *Anna Kaye & Don C. Matchan* 3.00
____ YOU CAN LEARN TO RELAX *Dr. Samuel Gutwirth* 3.00
____ YOUR ALLERGY—What To Do About It *Allan Knight, M.D.* 3.00

HOBBIES

____ BEACHCOMBING FOR BEGINNERS *Norman Hickin* 2.00
____ BLACKSTONE'S MODERN CARD TRICKS *Harry Blackstone* 3.00
____ BLACKSTONE'S SECRETS OF MAGIC *Harry Blackstone* 3.00
____ COIN COLLECTING FOR BEGINNERS *Burton Hobson & Fred Reinfeld* 3.00
____ ENTERTAINING WITH ESP *Tony 'Doc' Shiels* 2.00
____ 400 FASCINATING MAGIC TRICKS YOU CAN DO *Howard Thurston* 4.00
____ HOW I TURN JUNK INTO FUN AND PROFIT *Sari* 3.00
____ HOW TO WRITE A HIT SONG & SELL IT *Tommy Boyce* 7.00
____ JUGGLING MADE EASY *Rudolf Dittrich* 2.00
____ MAGIC FOR ALL AGES *Walter Gibson* 4.00
____ MAGIC MADE EASY *Byron Wels* 2.00
____ STAMP COLLECTING FOR BEGINNERS *Burton Hobson* 3.00

HORSE PLAYERS' WINNING GUIDES

____ BETTING HORSES TO WIN *Les Conklin* 3.00
____ ELIMINATE THE LOSERS *Bob McKnight* 3.00
____ HOW TO PICK WINNING HORSES *Bob McKnight* 3.00
____ HOW TO WIN AT THE RACES *Sam (The Genius) Lewin* 5.00

____ HOW YOU CAN BEAT THE RACES *Jack Kavanagh*	3.00
____ MAKING MONEY AT THE RACES *David Barr*	3.00
____ PAYDAY AT THE RACES *Les Conklin*	3.00
____ SMART HANDICAPPING MADE EASY *William Bauman*	3.00
____ SUCCESS AT THE HARNESS RACES *Barry Meadow*	3.00
____ WINNING AT THE HARNESS RACES—An Expert's Guide *Nick Cammarano*	3.00

HUMOR

____ HOW TO BE A COMEDIAN FOR FUN & PROFIT *King & Laufer*	2.00
____ HOW TO FLATTEN YOUR TUSH *Coach Marge Reardon*	2.00
____ HOW TO MAKE LOVE TO YOURSELF *Ron Stevens & Joy Grdnic*	3.00
____ JOKE TELLER'S HANDBOOK *Bob Orben*	3.00
____ JOKES FOR ALL OCCASIONS *Al Schock*	3.00
____ 2000 NEW LAUGHS FOR SPEAKERS *Bob Orben*	4.00
____ 2,500 JOKES TO START 'EM LAUGHING *Bob Orben*	3.00

HYPNOTISM

____ ADVANCED TECHNIQUES OF HYPNOSIS *Melvin Powers*	2.00
____ BRAINWASHING AND THE CULTS *Paul A. Verdier, Ph.D.*	3.00
____ CHILDBIRTH WITH HYPNOSIS *William S. Kroger, M.D.*	5.00
____ HOW TO SOLVE Your Sex Problems with Self-Hypnosis *Frank S. Caprio, M.D.*	5.00
____ HOW TO STOP SMOKING THRU SELF-HYPNOSIS *Leslie M. LeCron*	3.00
____ HOW TO USE AUTO-SUGGESTION EFFECTIVELY *John Duckworth*	3.00
____ HOW YOU CAN BOWL BETTER USING SELF-HYPNOSIS *Jack Heise*	3.00
____ HOW YOU CAN PLAY BETTER GOLF USING SELF-HYPNOSIS *Jack Heise*	3.00
____ HYPNOSIS AND SELF-HYPNOSIS *Bernard Hollander, M.D.*	3.00
____ HYPNOTISM *(Originally published in 1893) Carl Sextus*	5.00
____ HYPNOTISM & PSYCHIC PHENOMENA *Simeon Edmunds*	4.00
____ HYPNOTISM MADE EASY *Dr. Ralph Winn*	3.00
____ HYPNOTISM MADE PRACTICAL *Louis Orton*	3.00
____ HYPNOTISM REVEALED *Melvin Powers*	2.00
____ HYPNOTISM TODAY *Leslie LeCron and Jean Bordeaux, Ph.D.*	5.00
____ MODERN HYPNOSIS *Lesley Kuhn & Salvatore Russo, Ph.D.*	5.00
____ NEW CONCEPTS OF HYPNOSIS *Bernard C. Gindes, M.D.*	5.00
____ NEW SELF-HYPNOSIS *Paul Adams*	4.00
____ POST-HYPNOTIC INSTRUCTIONS—Suggestions for Therapy *Arnold Furst*	3.00
____ PRACTICAL GUIDE TO SELF-HYPNOSIS *Melvin Powers*	3.00
____ PRACTICAL HYPNOTISM *Philip Magonet, M.D.*	3.00
____ SECRETS OF HYPNOTISM *S. J. Van Pelt, M.D.*	5.00
____ SELF-HYPNOSIS A Conditioned-Response Technique *Laurence Sparks*	5.00
____ SELF-HYPNOSIS Its Theory, Technique & Application *Melvin Powers*	3.00
____ THERAPY THROUGH HYPNOSIS *edited by Raphael H. Rhodes*	4.00

JUDAICA

____ HOW TO LIVE A RICHER & FULLER LIFE *Rabbi Edgar F. Magnin*	2.00
____ MODERN ISRAEL *Lily Edelman*	2.00
____ SERVICE OF THE HEART *Evelyn Garfiel, Ph.D.*	4.00
____ STORY OF ISRAEL IN COINS *Jean & Maurice Gould*	2.00
____ STORY OF ISRAEL IN STAMPS *Maxim & Gabriel Shamir*	1.00
____ TONGUE OF THE PROPHETS *Robert St. John*	5.00

JUST FOR WOMEN

____ COSMOPOLITAN'S GUIDE TO MARVELOUS MEN Fwd. by *Helen Gurley Brown*	3.00
____ COSMOPOLITAN'S HANG-UP HANDBOOK Foreword by *Helen Gurley Brown*	4.00
____ COSMOPOLITAN'S LOVE BOOK—A Guide to Ecstasy in Bed	4.00
____ COSMOPOLITAN'S NEW ETIQUETTE GUIDE Fwd. by *Helen Gurley Brown*	4.00
____ I AM A COMPLEAT WOMAN *Doris Hagopian & Karen O'Connor Sweeney*	3.00
____ JUST FOR WOMEN—A Guide to the Female Body *Richard E. Sand, M.D.*	5.00
____ NEW APPROACHES TO SEX IN MARRIAGE *John E. Eichenlaub, M.D.*	3.00
____ SEXUALLY ADEQUATE FEMALE *Frank S. Caprio, M.D.*	3.00
____ SEXUALLY FULFILLED WOMAN *Dr. Rachel Copelan*	5.00
____ YOUR FIRST YEAR OF MARRIAGE *Dr. Tom McGinnis*	3.00

MARRIAGE, SEX & PARENTHOOD

____ ABILITY TO LOVE *Dr. Allan Fromme*	5.00
____ ENCYCLOPEDIA OF MODERN SEX & LOVE TECHNIQUES *Macandrew*	5.00
____ GUIDE TO SUCCESSFUL MARRIAGE *Drs. Albert Ellis & Robert Harper*	5.00
____ HOW TO RAISE AN EMOTIONALLY HEALTHY, HAPPY CHILD *A. Ellis*	4.00

____ SEX WITHOUT GUILT *Albert Ellis, Ph.D.*		5.00
____ SEXUALLY ADEQUATE MALE *Frank S. Caprio, M.D.*		3.00
____ SEXUALLY FULFILLED MAN *Dr. Rachel Copelan*		5.00

MELVIN POWERS' MAIL ORDER LIBRARY

____ HOW TO GET RICH IN MAIL ORDER *Melvin Powers*		10.00
____ HOW TO WRITE A GOOD ADVERTISEMENT *Victor O. Schwab*		15.00
____ MAIL ORDER MADE EASY *J. Frank Brumbaugh*		10.00
____ U.S. MAIL ORDER SHOPPER'S GUIDE *Susan Spitzer*		10.00

METAPHYSICS & OCCULT

____ BOOK OF TALISMANS, AMULETS & ZODIACAL GEMS *William Pavitt*		5.00
____ CONCENTRATION—A Guide to Mental Mastery *Mouni Sadhu*		4.00
____ CRITIQUES OF GOD *Edited by Peter Angeles*		7.00
____ EXTRA-TERRESTRIAL INTELLIGENCE—The First Encounter		6.00
____ FORTUNE TELLING WITH CARDS *P. Foli*		3.00
____ HANDWRITING ANALYSIS MADE EASY *John Marley*		4.00
____ HANDWRITING TELLS *Nadya Olyanova*		5.00
____ HOW TO INTERPRET DREAMS, OMENS & FORTUNE TELLING SIGNS *Gettings*		3.00
____ HOW TO UNDERSTAND YOUR DREAMS *Geoffrey A. Dudley*		3.00
____ ILLUSTRATED YOGA *William Zorn*		3.00
____ IN DAYS OF GREAT PEACE *Mouni Sadhu*		3.00
____ LSD—THE AGE OF MIND *Bernard Roseman*		2.00
____ MAGICIAN—His Training and Work *W. E. Butler*		3.00
____ MEDITATION *Mouni Sadhu*		5.00
____ MODERN NUMEROLOGY *Morris C. Goodman*		3.00
____ NUMEROLOGY—ITS FACTS AND SECRETS *Ariel Yvon Taylor*		3.00
____ NUMEROLOGY MADE EASY *W. Mykian*		3.00
____ PALMISTRY MADE EASY *Fred Gettings*		3.00
____ PALMISTRY MADE PRACTICAL *Elizabeth Daniels Squire*		4.00
____ PALMISTRY SECRETS REVEALED *Henry Frith*		3.00
____ PROPHECY IN OUR TIME *Martin Ebon*		2.50
____ PSYCHOLOGY OF HANDWRITING *Nadya Olyanova*		5.00
____ SUPERSTITION—Are You Superstitious? *Eric Maple*		2.00
____ TAROT *Mouni Sadhu*		6.00
____ TAROT OF THE BOHEMIANS *Papus*		5.00
____ WAYS TO SELF-REALIZATION *Mouni Sadhu*		3.00
____ WHAT YOUR HANDWRITING REVEALS *Albert E. Hughes*		3.00
____ WITCHCRAFT, MAGIC & OCCULTISM—A Fascinating History *W. B. Crow*		5.00
____ WITCHCRAFT—THE SIXTH SENSE *Justine Glass*		5.00
____ WORLD OF PSYCHIC RESEARCH *Hereward Carrington*		2.00

SELF-HELP & INSPIRATIONAL

____ DAILY POWER FOR JOYFUL LIVING *Dr. Donald Curtis*		5.00
____ DYNAMIC THINKING *Melvin Powers*		2.00
____ EXUBERANCE—Your Guide to Happiness & Fulfillment *Dr. Paul Kurtz*		3.00
____ GREATEST POWER IN THE UNIVERSE *U. S. Andersen*		5.00
____ GROW RICH WHILE YOU SLEEP *Ben Sweetland*		3.00
____ GROWTH THROUGH REASON *Albert Ellis, Ph.D.*		4.00
____ GUIDE TO DEVELOPING YOUR POTENTIAL *Herbert A. Otto, Ph.D.*		3.00
____ GUIDE TO LIVING IN BALANCE *Frank S. Caprio, M.D.*		2.00
____ GUIDE TO PERSONAL HAPPINESS *Albert Ellis, Ph.D. & Irving Becker, Ed. D.*		5.00
____ HELPING YOURSELF WITH APPLIED PSYCHOLOGY *R. Henderson*		2.00
____ HELPING YOURSELF WITH PSYCHIATRY *Frank S. Caprio, M.D.*		2.00
____ HOW TO ATTRACT GOOD LUCK *A. H. Z. Carr*		4.00
____ HOW TO CONTROL YOUR DESTINY *Norvell*		3.00
____ HOW TO DEVELOP A WINNING PERSONALITY *Martin Panzer*		5.00
____ HOW TO DEVELOP AN EXCEPTIONAL MEMORY *Young & Gibson*		4.00
____ HOW TO OVERCOME YOUR FEARS *M. P. Leahy, M.D.*		3.00
____ HOW YOU CAN HAVE CONFIDENCE AND POWER *Les Giblin*		3.00
____ HUMAN PROBLEMS & HOW TO SOLVE THEM *Dr. Donald Curtis*		4.00
____ I CAN *Ben Sweetland*		5.00
____ I WILL *Ben Sweetland*		3.00
____ LEFT-HANDED PEOPLE *Michael Barsley*		4.00
____ MAGIC IN YOUR MIND *U. S. Andersen*		5.00
____ MAGIC OF THINKING BIG *Dr. David J. Schwartz*		3.00

___ MAGIC POWER OF YOUR MIND *Walter M. Germain*		5.00
___ MENTAL POWER THROUGH SLEEP SUGGESTION *Melvin Powers*		3.00
___ NEW GUIDE TO RATIONAL LIVING *Albert Ellis, Ph.D. & R. Harper, Ph.D.*		3.00
___ OUR TROUBLED SELVES *Dr. Allan Fromme*		3.00
___ PSYCHO-CYBERNETICS *Maxwell Maltz, M.D.*		3.00
___ SCIENCE OF MIND IN DAILY LIVING *Dr. Donald Curtis*		5.00
___ SECRET OF SECRETS *U. S. Andersen*		5.00
___ SECRET POWER OF THE PYRAMIDS *U. S. Andersen*		5.00
___ STUTTERING AND WHAT YOU CAN DO ABOUT IT *W. Johnson, Ph.D.*		2.50
___ SUCCESS-CYBERNETICS *U. S. Andersen*		5.00
___ 10 DAYS TO A GREAT NEW LIFE *William E. Edwards*		3.00
___ THINK AND GROW RICH *Napoleon Hill*		3.00
___ THINK YOUR WAY TO SUCCESS *Dr. Lew Losoncy*		5.00
___ THREE MAGIC WORDS *U. S. Andersen*		5.00
___ TREASURY OF COMFORT *edited by Rabbi Sidney Greenberg*		5.00
___ TREASURY OF THE ART OF LIVING *Sidney S. Greenberg*		5.00
___ YOU ARE NOT THE TARGET *Laura Huxley*		4.00
___ YOUR SUBCONSCIOUS POWER *Charles M. Simmons*		5.00
___ YOUR THOUGHTS CAN CHANGE YOUR LIFE *Dr. Donald Curtis*		5.00

SPORTS

___ BICYCLING FOR FUN AND GOOD HEALTH *Kenneth E. Luther*		2.00
___ BILLIARDS—Pocket • Carom • Three Cushion *Clive Cottingham, Jr.*		3.00
___ CAMPING-OUT 101 Ideas & Activities *Bruno Knobel*		2.00
___ COMPLETE GUIDE TO FISHING *Vlad Evanoff*		2.00
___ HOW TO IMPROVE YOUR RACQUETBALL *Lubarsky Kaufman & Scagnetti*		3.00
___ HOW TO WIN AT POCKET BILLIARDS *Edward D. Knuchell*		4.00
___ JOY OF WALKING *Jack Scagnetti*		3.00
___ LEARNING & TEACHING SOCCER SKILLS *Eric Worthington*		3.00
___ MOTORCYCLING FOR BEGINNERS *I. G. Edmonds*		3.00
___ RACQUETBALL FOR WOMEN *Toni Hudson, Jack Scagnetti & Vince Rondone*		3.00
___ RACQUETBALL MADE EASY *Steve Lubarsky, Rod Delson & Jack Scagnetti*		3.00
___ SECRET OF BOWLING STRIKES *Dawson Taylor*		3.00
___ SECRET OF PERFECT PUTTING *Horton Smith & Dawson Taylor*		3.00
___ SOCCER—The Game & How to Play It *Gary Rosenthal*		3.00
___ STARTING SOCCER *Edward F. Dolan, Jr.*		3.00
___ TABLE TENNIS MADE EASY *Johnny Leach*		2.00

TENNIS LOVERS' LIBRARY

___ BEGINNER'S BUIDE TO WINNING TENNIS *Helen Hull Jacobs*		2.00
___ HOW TO BEAT BETTER TENNIS PLAYERS *Loring Fiske*		4.00
___ HOW TO IMPROVE YOUR TENNIS—Style, Strategy & Analysis *C. Wilson*		2.00
___ INSIDE TENNIS—Techniques of Winning *Jim Leighton*		3.00
___ PLAY TENNIS WITH ROSEWALL *Ken Rosewall*		2.00
___ PSYCH YOURSELF TO BETTER TENNIS *Dr. Walter A. Luszki*		2.00
___ SUCCESSFUL TENNIS *Neale Fraser*		2.00
___ TENNIS FOR BEGINNERS, *Dr. H. A. Murray*		2.00
___ TENNIS MADE EASY *Joel Brecheen*		3.00
___ WEEKEND TENNIS—How to Have Fun & Win at the Same Time *Bill Talbert*		3.00
___ WINNING WITH PERCENTAGE TENNIS—Smart Strategy *Jack Lowe*		2.00

WILSHIRE PET LIBRARY

___ DOG OBEDIENCE TRAINING *Gust Kessopulos*		4.00
___ DOG TRAINING MADE EASY & FUN *John W. Kellogg*		4.00
___ HOW TO BRING UP YOUR PET DOG *Kurt Unkelbach*		2.00
___ HOW TO RAISE & TRAIN YOUR PUPPY *Jeff Griffen*		3.00
___ PIGEONS: HOW TO RAISE & TRAIN THEM *William H. Allen, Jr.*		2.00

*The books listed above can be obtained from your book dealer or directly from
Melvin Powers. When ordering, please remit 50¢ per book postage & handling.
Send for our free illustrated catalog of self-improvement books.*

Melvin Powers
12015 Sherman Road, No. Hollywood, California 91605